Jerry Brown

IN A PLAIN BROWN WRAPPER

Jerry Brown

IN A PLAIN BROWN WRAPPER

John C. Bollens
and
G. Robert Williams

Palisades Publishers Pacific Palisades, CA 90272

Illustration Credits

Paul Conrad cartoons, copyright Los Angeles Times, reprinted with permission, 33, 67, 135, 211, 234, 244, 254. Dennis Renault cartoons, copyright, Renault/Sacramento Bee, reprinted with permission, 17, 96, 118. Los Angeles Community Colleges, 194 (bottom), 195. Los Angeles Times Photos, 196 (bottom), 198, 201 (bottom), 204. Office of Governor, 193. Sacramento Bee, 206 (top). United Press International, 197, 199, 200, 202 (top), 203, 205, 207, 208. Wide World Photos, 194 (top), 196 (top), 201 (top), 202 (bottom).

JERRY BROWN: In a Plain Brown Wrapper

Library of Congress Catalogue Card No. 78-53641
International Standard Book No. 0-913530-12-3

Printed in the United States of America

Preface

Jerry Brown is a highly significant and fascinating political figure who is the Governor of California with ambitions to be President of the United States. We have sought to write an important and interesting book about him, basically by each of us spending the past two years in intensive research and writing. But the collection of information through interviews, personal observations at public meetings and on the campaign trail, and wide reading of what others had reported about him, often in brief form, began long before this two-year period.

When young Brown, then just turning thirty-one, decided early in 1969 to seek his first elective office by running for a new and obscure seat on a local community college board, we sensed that he would be a man of upward political mobility, a probable rising political star. One of us had had the opportunity two years before, when Jerry's interest in politics was first maturing, to participate in a wide-ranging discussion in which Jerry and his father were the principals and to recognize the probing nature and incisiveness of young Brown's mind. With Jerry's electoral decision in 1969 came our decision to observe him closely from that day on and to start reconstructing his earlier years through interviews and the discovery and study of written records. (See Notes section in back of this book for details about sources.)

From the outset this became a study that simultaneously moved forward and backward in time—rebuilding the past and keeping up with the contemporary. There was no assurance as we progressed with the work into the 1970s, even after his election to another virtually unknown office, Secretary of State, that the information we were collecting and the analysis we were developing would ever justifiably constitute a book. Whether or not a written product would result really did not concern us, as we saw greater possibilities in the subject himself.

As we probed in both directions we came to realize that Jerry Brown was not merely another new political personality on the move. In the beginning we knew little more than that he was the son of a former two-term Governor of California with an identical name and that Jerry had dropped from the secular world for a time to prepare for the priesthood.

As our work proceeded in the first half of the 1970s, we concluded that this was an unusual person of uncommon political ideas and style, an individual whom it was difficult to fathom and understand. More interested than ever, we continued to try to comprehend fully this mysterious and enigmatic personality.

By late 1974, when elected Governor, Jerry was still largely known only as "the son of Pat" and a fighter against the political establishment. By this time, when a few people were beginning to express some curiosity about him, we already had an arsenal of background and current information and analysis to interpret his activities as Governor from 1974 on and his abortive effort in 1976 to gain the presidency of the United States.

During Brown's first months in the governorship, some others began to find him fascinating. Later several people commenced writing books about Brown, including a disgruntled former staff member who had been fired. Despite the richness of the material we had at hand, we continued to hold our literary fire, as we wanted to be able to diagnose his term as Governor into its final year.

Now we can present an analysis of Jerry Brown from his early years to the present.

This book seeks to be enlightening. We hope its readers will find it to be so.

J.C.B.
G.R.W.

Contents

Chapter One

A Political Alternative

Since the 1960s a kaleidoscope of shattered dreams, political discord, and governmental scandals has sent a series of shock waves through American society. From the resulting reverberations has come a strong public desire for the creation of a new mosaic of societal relationships and governmental responsibility. The disenchantment and the dismantling of many aspects of John Kennedy's New Frontier and Lyndon Johnson's Great Society have lead to much cynicism in the wake of unfulfilled dreams. The malfeasance of President Richard Nixon and many of his aides has left a dark hue of citizen doubt and distrust about government in the United States. This nation has become uncertain about its recent past and its immediate future.

The long-held belief that Americans are blessed with unlimited resources and governed by astute, candid, and honest officials has been shaken. So deep seated is this disillusionment that, like a woeful chorus in a Greek tragedy, many Americans speak in terms of alienation, aimlessness, and the possible impending doom of their society. Nevertheless, people in general are seeking answers to critical issues affecting basic political, economic, and interpersonal relationships. Unfortunately these answers are not easily found.

Several major political figures have come forth recently to address these concerns on a fundamental level. Edmund Gerald (Jerry) Brown Jr. of California ranks high (some say highest) on this select list. An enigmatic, charismatic, and complex individual, Brown is sensitive to the mood of the public in general and of many of the nation's restless, skeptical, and disadvantaged in particular. As he attempts to weave a lasting tapestry of renewed public faith, what he offers most clearly is a fresh political perspective that appeals to many people and deserves analysis.

If politics is an art as claimed by the ancient Greeks, then the images of governance that have emerged from Brown's composite philosophy, style, and actions are very uncommon. Politics, like most art forms, has both depth and texture that alternately serve to reflect the realities and absurdities of the universe, the fears and joys of living, and the beauty and torment of the world. Jerry Brown's perception of government and society mirrors the uncertainty felt by many Americans about the future of their nation. He recognizes this as a period of searching carefully and thoughtfully for answers and not of quickly jumping to "solutions" by pouring large amounts of money into new or existing governmental programs. Brown has fashioned what he calls a "new spirit" in government, a working philosophy that embraces prevailing contemporary concerns. He presents a different approach to politics and public decisionmaking—low-keyed contemplation and extensive questioning and inquiry made without ostentation or fanfare. It is truly government in a plain Brown wrapper.

But like all art, beauty is in the eyes of the beholder. Jerry Brown's political artistry has garnered him praise and criticism. Some have said that he exhibits well-reasoned judgment, while others charge him with being indecisive or ambivalent. In view of his perplexing nature, the conflicting mixture of public opinion is completely understandable—for if one thing can be said with certainty about Brown, it is that he is a political enigma who is very difficult to characterize and classify.

Many conflicting terms have been applied to describe this public figure: radical, reactionary, liberal, conservative, dynamic, introverted, compassionate, aloof, sexual, asexual, consummate politician, and idealist, for example. (*Cosmopolitan*, a leading American women's magazine, in its April 1977 issue, proclaimed Brown, along with Robert Redford, Paul Newman, Cary Grant, and others, to be "the world's sexiest men." Brown was termed as "enigmatic, tantalizingly aloof.") Obviously these dichotomies do not make for easy understanding of this man and his new spirit of government. Both the public and seasoned politicians find it highly difficult to appraise him precisely.

Some judge Jerry Brown incapable of providing or unwilling to furnish the necessary leadership. As a disgruntled Democratic leader snarled, "We need a Governor, not a guru." Such detractors believe that any politician who refuses to respond to political pressures immediately, don the hat of ceremonial chieftan, and cavort regularly with political functionaries and financial contributors cannot develop adequate programs. They see his approach of process instead of fast programmatic action to be irrational and something the American system of government can ill afford. This philosophic, meditative man, they say, cannot lead and govern.

Others see Brown as a kind of Moses come to lead his people out of the muck of corruption, out of bigness without meaning, and out of a technocracy that strangles and smothers humanity. These admirers approve of the Governor's refusal to accept the luxuries of fine housing and transportation available to him by virtue of his high office and view him as a man of the people. They hear him speak about new and mystical ways of looking at the world and believe new truths will come forth. They like his questioning mind that asks why many assumptions are accepted as facts without validation.

For various reasons these supporters feel a kinship to this individual who has never been poor or underprivileged, although at one time his family lived in modest circumstances. They know that by his choice he labored in the fields picking grapes, marched dusty roads with civil-rights leaders in Mississippi and farm workers in California, and joined some efforts to end the Vietnam war. He is also applauded by some simply for being the son of his now widely beloved father, former two-term California Governor Edmund G. "Pat" Brown Sr. who occupied a succession of significant public offices for many years. In sum, Jerry Brown is seen by some as the embodiment of the ideal leader.

Still other people regard Jerry Brown as something between these two extremes, which seems to be the truth of the matter. A person of considerable talent and varied background, Jerry Brown is not to them the prophet destined to lead the chosen people from the looming threats of a real or imagined modern-day Pharisee of government. Instead, to these people he is a human being with frailties who is attempting to leave whatever positive impact is possible. Thus, to portray him with a bevy of angels hovering over his haloed head would be as inappropriate as to sketch him as a creature of demonic ineptitude. He is a person of both greatness and imperfection.

If Jerry Brown ultimately becomes widely recognized nationally as an outstanding political architect, it will result from many influences that have served as his personal guild master. The new spirit of government has been formed in Brown's hands like the work of some medieval artisan. It is a hybrid of strong religious orthodoxy, the nature of the times, California's political environment of the inventive and the bizarre, and the wisdom gained as a child born into politics. A former Jesuit and a student of meditative and self-contemplative philosophy, the only son of a recent California governor, a supporter of civil libertarian causes, a fiscal miser, and a believer in citizen volunteerism in certain governmental activities, this is surely a politician struck from a different mold.

Brown reveals many sharply drawn contrasts. He is at once a person of real-world complexity and spiritual universality, of humaneness and depth, and of mystery and openness. Against the backdrop of brilliantly stark idealism emerges the personality of an individual of wisdom, a cynic, a grand inquisitor, a supporter of human rights, including increased participation in government by minorities—women, racial, and ethnic. Moreover, he is a low-keyed but attractive individual in many social situations, a man of strength and determination, and a hard worker expecting the same of his aides without generally extending credit to them publicly. And around Brown is an inner-circle staff that tends to be extremely loyal and devoted as they carry out a marathon schedule.

Defying precise definition, Brown early in his governorship, which began in January 1975, became one of the most popular public officials anywhere in recent American history. He gained such popularity quickly from the widely diverse citizenry in California—in both ideological and socio-economic terms. He has further exhibited an ability to retain in large part that popular appeal as his governorship continued. And he obtained a surprisingly positive response in six states where he entered presidential primaries in 1976. Jimmy Carter did not win in any of these six instances. In five of these races Brown, or an uncommitted slate with which he worked, defeated Carter. In the sixth—Oregon—Carter finished second to Frank Church and both of them had their names listed on the ballot. Brown had to conduct a write-in effort yet finished only a few percentage points behind Carter. All of these developments show the rapid rise of Brown to political prominence.

Some specifics about his popularity in California alone are startling indeed. In March 1976, after Brown had been Governor for almost fifteen months, the highly respected Field's California Poll reported that Californians' "love affair" with Brown was continuing unabated; six times as many people believed he was doing a "good job" as felt he was doing a "bad job." A poll released early in the next year, 1977, by the same firm showed that although Brown's popularity had dropped somewhat, his performance rating was still as high as that attained by his predecessor, the popular Ronald Reagan, at any time during his eight years in office. Later, as Jerry neared the end of his third year as Governor, these same pollsters revealed his high popularity standing remained virtually unchanged. Brown, only thirty-six when inaugurated as Governor, has accurately said, "I represent a new political generation and I have struck a chord here in California." However, the political beat that Brown plays and which many people hear affirmatively is inaudible to or not understood by many politicians.

Brown was elected to a position of great public power at a time when fundamental questions needed to be asked and answered. The Governor's relentless reliance on questioning all he surveys is central to his unusual political style. Preferring to seek the truth through the use of Socratic dialogue, where questioning helps in the development of analysis, Jerry does not produce quick or easy answers. In justifying his approach, he has explained that sometimes asking a question or exposing a contradiction is more valuable than a superficial program that purports to do more than it really can. He also has warned that the people must not expect all answers to come from government; the citizenry must find some of them not from public authority but from the private world.

Getting to the roots of Jerry Brown's popular appeal is not easy. For instance, many people feel he is considerably detached from the world about him. Some individuals who have been closely affiliated with him feel that he is often distant and cold. Other associates have used such terms as "rude," "non-supportive," "outrageous," and "Machiavellian" to characterize Brown's interpersonal relations. His father, former Governor Pat Brown, perceives his son as sometimes being harsh in his judgment of human beings. His humor, while evident and highly sophisticated, is frequently too intellectualized to reach much of his audience. In sum, Jerry's personality does not seem to match the image of a successful politician. Yet he has been remarkably well received by the public, principally because he is the antithesis of the hearty handshaking and promise-making politician so many Americans have grown to distrust. His "take me on my own terms" attitude has been refreshing to the public and consistent with the times.

Brown's entire life style contributes to this positive mystique and he skillfully employs symbolic expressions. For instance, many state-supported benefits are available to the Governor such as living in the $1.3 million executive mansion built at Ronald Reagan's request and located in a suburb. However, bachelor Brown has refused to live in the "Taj Mahal," as he has called it, deciding instead to rent apartment quarters at his own expense in downtown Sacramento near his office in the state capitol. In similar fashion, Brown has chosen to use a modest Plymouth car rather than a highly prestigious luxury automobile, fly on commercial airlines instead of a costly state-leased jet, and engage in other self-effacing actions. These decisions reflect his attitude that "those who serve should act as servants and not some kind of special favored people."

To his critics these actions are a new type of political ruse. Although their position may be justified by some inconsistency in life style—like his use at times of an expensive car as Secretary of State and his sudden austerity about transportation as Governor—much in Brown's background suggests that his present life style is compatible with his past. Whether or not these actions are political technique, the images they have portrayed have been highly effective in gaining popular support and in facing the funda-mental issue of political privilege.

Jerry Brown's relationship with the communication media has also added to his aura of the unusual. Politicians generally thrive when they have good relations with newspaper, television, and radio reporters and therefore exert themselves to obtain the best possible coverage. Brown has taken a very different approach; he speaks only to whom and about what he deems necessary or important. As a state capitol correspondent has observed, "It's impossible to control an interview with him." These challenges of gaining access to Brown and acquiring specific answers to particular questions have made him one of the most prized and sought interview subjects in the nation for the working press. Some news reporters have spent literally hours beside his office door in the hope of getting an interview. When finally a correspondent is so blessed, he or she may be inundated with Socratic questioning, Zen philosophy, and such facts as how the Governor engages in meditation. In interviews Brown at times seems to be addressing some cosmic force rather than the questioners. The story that was sought may not be obtained, but what Brown says usually makes good copy. Jerry realizes the potency of the mass media and uses them masterfully. Highly articulate, he knows how to gain wide communication exposure whenever he wishes.

Brown's orientation to the use of political power is also unusual. For many years Americans have accepted the premise that this is a nation where consumption of more and better material comforts is part of our national birthright. This belief in constantly increased consumption and ever-widening expansion has unfortunately resulted in heavy costs to both natural and human resources. Yet, until very recently, to challenge this quest for opulence was almost akin to attacking the national flag.

As recently as a few years ago it would have been inconceivable that a major political personality would be applauded for stating that he does not support materialism. But this is exactly what Brown has done. "Even a superficial reading of history indicates that there has rarely been a period of self-indulgence on such a mass scale as there is in America [now]," Brown has said in a tone that seems to admonish previous generations for ever aspiring to satisfy this dream. Interestingly, his attack has received much public support.

An expressed goal of Brown is to "reduce the sum of human misery a bit, give them [the people] an awareness of their own potential." Such a lofty objective cannot be faulted. However, it is one thing to have dreams and another to bring them to reality. But Brown believes this can be done. He feels that achievements can be brought about through reforming the processes of making public decisions rather than through adoption of an endless series of improvised governmental programs. The central foundation on which he governs has generally been the principle that meritorious programs emerge.

An early visual expression of Jerry Brown's era of limits philosophy.

The Brown approach is a synthesis of detachment, discipline, and thinking. He has told the public to learn that resources are not infinite and to adjust to this reality; the belief that everybody can get everything is preposterous. In American politics this is a rare view to propound, but here is a politician who advises the people that some of their desires are unattainable.

Brown has sent two very clear and closely related messages to the people since becoming governor. Underscoring his entire approach is the idea that this is an era of limits as manifested in several ways. One is financial; the fiscal resources of government are not unending and public demands must be considered in relation to fiscal capacity. This principle is exhibited by his stand against a general tax increase or the imposition of any new general taxes. A second limit is government itself; public authorities should not be expected to operate in all spheres of human activity, as some endeavors can be better performed by the private sector. The third is ecological; there are constraints on how much the environment can be changed without producing highly damaging effects but restraints must also be placed on environmental regulations so that economic well-being of a state or a nation is not lessened.

Brown has coupled this message regarding limitations with a pervasive optimism that this is also a period of possibilities. Brown believes that as government, private enterprise, and the people rethink and rework their critical interrelationships in view of dwindling resources, many new avenues exist for public explora-tion. His endorsement of research on and the development of space travel and space colonies ("My thought about space is it's part of the future, so let's get involved with it," Brown has said) and his advocacy of wide use of non-polluting energy resources like solar energy illustrate this message. Volunteerism—the duty of people to assume some responsibility for themselves by doing free work in such fields as health care, hospitals for the mentally ill, environment, criminal justice, education, and neighborhood development—is an extension of this philosophy of limitations and possibilities and is compatible with Brown's opposition to big government.

The public response to Brown's denial of unlimited material goods and his call for greater dedication has been as surprising and atypical as are Brown's pronouncements unique for a politician. Like some overindulged children who are seldom scolded, the people have generally reacted favorably to this warning. Brown's counseling and chiding have not substantially decreased his popular appeal over time. People continue to like his openness and candor; as a rule, they have decided to accept the message of the era of limits and possibilities as the truth.

Still many questions about Jerry Brown are not yet fully answered. Leadership accompanied by visions of a new order is not extraordinary in recent history. Many visionaries have assumed prominence during this century throughout the world. Unfortunately, such visions may be based on both good and evil. Hitler, for example, had a mission to create a great master race. Martin Luther King Jr. had a dream of a nation liberated from racism. Woodrow Wilson hoped for peace among all nations. Richard Nixon had a self-edifying view that by virtue of his presence and actions the world's major ills would be resolved. Mahatma Gandhi saw a world of universal love among all humankind.

Although these visions were all justified on the basis of advancing the cause of human dignity, obviously not all served that purpose. As with Hitler, some visionary efforts are merely perversions of humankind's most fundamental morality. In the case of Nixon, personal delusion and dishonesty effectively diminished his ability to make contributions. Society must constantly be on guard against possible abuses.

The mission thus far offered by Jerry Brown seems directed toward the same type of high-minded human goals as those found in the work of such people as King, Wilson, and Gandhi. Nevertheless history reveals the importance of monitoring the visions of any dreamer. Jerry Brown is no exception to this rule. Because Brown and other leaders have grand aspirations does not necessarily mean that the glitter they offer is gold. The Watergate events surrounding Nixon also demonstrate that public adoration cannot be regarded as a license for the unbridled use of power.

Brown's visions and actions must always be examined critically as is true of any person possessing considerable power.

Brown's extraordinary politics has found fertile soil in California, which has a long tradition of governmental innovation and idiosyncracies. This state has a history of both sound leadership and lackluster drifting and of well-conceived and eccentric ideas. It is here that numerous new political movements in various decades—some rational, others outlandish—have been born and prospered or died. Hiram Johnson led the Progressive era in California during the early twentieth century and from the gubernatorial office ushered in many political reforms. They included a comprehensive direct primary election system, crossfiling in the opposition party to seek its nomination, reinstitution of the true Australian (secret) ballot without party circle or column, nonpartisan local elections, and the initiative, referendum, and recall.

Some daring schemes relating to social and economic issues have had a brief time in the political sun. The Townsend and EPIC plans were two of them in the 1930s. Francis Townsend, a retired physician, proposed a monthly pension of $200 for everyone over sixty years old who had been a good citizen. A federal sales tax was to pay for these pensions. Even more drastic was the EPIC (End Poverty in California) plan, originated by novelist and political candidate Upton Sinclair, which called for the establishment of a self-sufficient system of land colonies and factories for the unemployed. Unlike these two propositions that were not adopted, pension promoter George McLain's initiative proposal was passed by the state voters in the late 1940s but was soon wiped out of existence. This initiative went to drastic lengths. It made the position of state welfare director elective and named the secretary of the promotional group to the top welfare post until the next election!

Governors such as Earl Warren, Goodwin Knight, and Edmund G. "Pat" Brown Sr. guided the state through rapid periods of growth. But this is also the state that elected a person primarily known as a song-and-dance man—George Murphy—to be United States Senator and that turned the governorship over to a surprisingly politically astute actor of declining stature who had converted to being the host of a television series—Ronald Reagan.

A state of vast territory and open space, the overwhelming proportion of its people live in crowded metropolitan areas and many of these residents look forward to repeated getaway weekends. It is a locale that accommodates every conceivable life style—from the most staid society to the drug culture—and a wide range of political philosophies—from radical and ultra liberal to highly conservative and arch reactionary, from ethereal to pragmatic. A land of highly mobile and ethnically diversified people (more people of Mexican descent live here than any place other than Mexico) and many suburban communities, California is also the nation's wealthiest, by many measures, and the most populous state with about a tenth of the national population within its borders. Given all this, its social impact and political influence are clearly immense. This is Brown's current domain.

Jerry Brown is a different type of political figure who is not easily understood. He is a person of contrast and yet an individual of almost complete consistency. In attempting to add a new dimension to the art of politics, Brown is trying to facilitate the development of an environment conducive to creativity in government. Whether considered a leader or a dreamer, he possesses a sense of mission that has been noted and approved by vast numbers of people.

Obviously many facets of the uncommon Mr. Brown deserve consideration. This we will now do, beginning with the activities and influences of his early years.

Chapter Two

In the Beginning

Jerry Brown is a study in change—the evolution of the life- and career-searching son of a longtime major public official into one of the nation's most extraordinary, interesting, and important political figures. This development is especially intriguing because of the exceptional nature of some of the principal influences, including individuals and ideas, on his life in its first three decades.

In examining the years before his first campaign for statewide office in 1970, in his early thirties, we are reminded of the agreement of most developmental psychologists that every person is a product of the sum of his or her experiences. Without engaging in a complete psychological profile, we are relying on these formative years as a foundation in this analysis. These years are portrayed here primarily as a basis for gaining greater insight into the roots of Jerry Brown's rapid rise to great political power.

Early developmental strains are traceable to the political ambition and perseverance of Jerry's father, Edmund G. "Pat" Brown Sr. An interesting personality in his own right, Pat Brown is in many ways a manifestation of the finest elements of the traditional American dream. In a long struggle that brought both rewards and difficulties, he achieved prominence on his own merit and effort. Pat Brown is a gregarious individual whose personal drive for success and service is seldom equaled.

Pat's progression through early life into the political fray differed greatly from that of his son Jerry. A native San Franciscan, as were his father and his mother, Pat, born in 1905, came from a family of fluctuating economic well-being. His Irish Catholic father operated a variety of enterprises—a cigar store, a photo arcade, a shooting gallery, and an illegal backroom gambling parlor (which some considered "quasi-legal" because it was at times tied to a charity organization). Pat's father, Edmund Joseph, was a lovable person who wore tailor-made suits and a derby and walked with a swagger. For a while Pat, his two brothers, and a sister were the richest kids on the block. However, this relative affluence did not last. Their father suffered gambling losses, much of the family financial resources evaporated, and the children had to work at different jobs most of their young lives. From his free-spirited father, Pat derived much of his love for interaction with all kinds of people.

Ida Schuckman Brown, Pat's mother, a woman of strong German Protestant heritage and beliefs, provided other elements of balance to the children. She was very bright, read a lot and introduced Pat and the other children to books, music, and plays. The mother was especially influential but the father, too, had an impact when he was home where he read poetry aloud. Both parents instilled in their children a love for education and endowed them with the riches of pride and ambition. All four earned professional or liberal-arts educations, an outstanding accomplishment for four children in a family of uncertain financial resources.

While in public grammar school Edmund G. Brown gained a nickname that was to stay with him permanently. In the midst of the 1917-18 Liberty Bond drive, he took part in a speech contest at school. Each room held an event to decide who made the best speech and, in turn, the winners made presentations before an assembly of all the students. The twelve-year-old Brown won the final runoff with a rousing piece of oratory in which he poignantly chose to incorporate Patrick Henry's defiant statement, "Give me liberty or give me death." Thus his nickname for a lifetime was born.

Pat's happy and vigorous youth continued at San Francisco's Lowell High School where he was a highly social person and a student leader. He participated on all the sports teams, usually ending up as captain; engaged in debates; and won a total of eleven student body offices, culminating often in the presidency. The United States was in a period of dynamic growth and extreme optimism; it was an age when educational objectives were directed toward handling the demands of a rapidly changing society. In many ways Pat was a perfect reflection of that time—bouyant, personable, aggressive, and full of faith in the future.

Upon completing high school, Pat devoted himself part-time to law studies and worked part-time in his father's business. He earned his law degree from the private San Francisco School of Law and set up a practice in 1927 at the age of twenty-two. That law practice was to extend for an unbroken string of sixteen years until his election to his first public office.

Three years after finishing law school Pat married his high school sweetheart Bernice Layne, the daughter of a San Francisco police captain. Several years younger than Pat, she graduated from high school when eleven and a half years old and from the University of California, Berkeley, at eighteen. When they decided to marry, she was holding a probationary teaching job which required that she remain single. As a consequence, they eloped to Reno and were married in an Episcopalian service. Upon returning home a local newspaper carried an item, "Police captain's daughter marries young lawyer." The result was that she lost her job.

Bernice's background was very different from Pat's. Raised as an Episcopalian of English and Irish parentage and the daughter of a law-enforcement officer who founded the San Francisco Police Academy, her parental influences were far removed from the free-wheeling high spirits of Pat Brown's father. Bernice and Pat even joked about the possibility of her father arresting his father for the latter's operation of a gambling enterprise. But love sometimes relegates differences to a position of minor importance, and such was the case with this couple.

As Pat's marital partner for life, Bernice has carried out vital roles as confidant, adviser, mother, and political asset. The type of person whose presence and beauty instill faith and tranquility, she nurtured the dreams and aspirations of her husband. Together they laughed and cried and built a life for themselves and their children. Bernice never wanted Pat to enter or to stay in politics, as she did not like the exposure of public life and the political attacks. Both then and now she preferred him to be a lawyer. Nevertheless, she provided stability for her husband's political drive and ambition and established an environment where small dreams could grow into large realities. Pat's rise to political prominence and the nature of this family unit are closely linked.

Pat's climb to political power did not come without initial setbacks. The name of Edmund G. (Pat) Brown first appeared on a public ballot in 1928 when as a Republican candidate for a state Assembly seat, then a part-time, low-paying job, he felt the harsh sting of electoral defeat. Six years later he re-registered as a Democrat. He did so because of talks with his friend Mathew Tobriner (whom Pat appointed many years later to the state Supreme Court), a change in political allegiance brought on by growing weariness over the pronouncements of former President Herbert Hoover, and increased approval of Franklin Roosevelt's developing programs.

It was 1939 before Pat would permit himself to be presented again as a candidate. In that year he campaigned for the nonpartisan position of San Francisco District Attorney, which possibly could be a stepping stone to higher political office. Here, too, he met rejection by the voters who returned a twenty-year incumbent to the post. For the next several years Pat's public life was largely confined to working on a state commission to codify many state laws and participating in various Democratic party activities.

While Pat's political aspirations went unrealized in the late 1930s, he was blessed with the arrival of a male heir. Edmund Gerald Brown Jr. was born on April 7, 1938. Named for his father, he was soon called "Jerry" because of his mother's dislike of the nickname Ed. Joined by three sisters, two older and one younger—Barbara, Cynthia, and Kathleen—young Jerry was pampered and loved throughout his infant years even though his sister Cynthia Kelly was to note later, "I'm not sure Jerry ever felt our father's love [when Jerry was little]. And dad was always a little disappointed that Jerry wasn't warmer." But as Pat's only boy child, he was assured a special place in the family. In 1939, with three children already born and baptized Catholic, Pat and Bernice remarried in a Catholic church.

The world Jerry entered that spring of 1938 was one of cautious optimism. Franklin Roosevelt's New Deal had provided not only new hope but also some solid programs to restore the economy and popular confidence in government. Although war clouds loomed in the near future, the environment in which Jerry took his first breath was relatively bright. It was a time when good and evil were clearly defined and the American way of life—filled with all its dreams for upward mobility—permeated the psyche of the citizenry. The ruling generation possessed an almost naive belief that the United States had unlimited resources and the highest-minded leadership. The America of Jerry's early years differed greatly from the nation he came to know later.

Jerry was only five years old when his father became San Francisco's District Attorney in 1943 in his second attempt for the office, thereby beginning an unbroken near quarter century of service in elective political posts. While Jerry was always important to Pat's life, the rigors of politics denied young Brown a close relationship with his father. "They were never pals," recalls his oldest sister Barbara Casey. "Father was a strong authoritarian personality, and it took me a long time to find my own identity. People didn't think of me as an individual, but as my father's daughter. I disliked it. Jerry, I'm sure, did too."

The Pat Brown family lived in modest financial circumstances in Jerry's early years, as Pat earned only an annual salary of $8,000 for seven years as district attorney. The family's limited finances at that time, Jerry has said, probably influenced his later thinking about limitations within which American society must operate.

Jerry and his sisters grew up in a strong political environment. Paraded around before friends, well-wishers, and political officeholders, aspirants, and hangers-on, subjected to picture taking on many occasions, and taken to political meetings, clambakes, and picnics by their gregarious father, the Brown children found it difficult to become their own persons in a manner made available to many other youngsters. Although Pat tried hard to include Jerry in his life, even trips to the Olympic Club gymnasium meant going to a place where politicians worked out (and where Jerry took some boxing lessons from a professional). As Pat has related, "Politics was our life at home. It was always around us, and I am sure Jerry rebelled against being dragged around."

Life in a political fishbowl forced Jerry to swim extra laps to achieve the solace of self-worth and recognition. The demands placed on young Brown were many; he was Pat's boy and had to act accordingly. A typical father-son relationship became impossible to establish under these conditions.

Jerry's early encounters with political life made lasting impressions on him and his attitudes toward politics. Many years later he said, "I was attracted and repelled by what I saw of politics in my father's house. The adventure. The opportunity. The grasping, the artificiality, the obvious manipulation and role-playing, the repetition of emotion without feeling, particularly that—the repetition of emotion. . . . I've always felt I could see the limitations [of politics] because I was brought up in it."

Bernice and Pat were mindful of the demands that a political career placed on their family. Bernice mightily and continuously sought to give her children balance, harmony, and love. Pat, using what little time his public officeholding permitted, concentrated mainly on trying to stimulate intellectual growth and creative thought. The dinner table, as the only common meeting place for parents and children, became the focus of family living. Here debate tempered with understanding was encouraged. Through such discourse, Pat and Bernice hoped to guide their youngsters through the extremely difficult problems associated with growing up in an adult world. As youngest sister Kathleen has remarked, "Debate was part of the game. Father was developing in all of his children a sense of critical thinking and we were encouraged to defend our ideas. . . . It developed our ability to think issues through, to defend them and to listen to other ideas."

Jerry often failed to recognize his parents' good intent. The discussions Pat found to be "rousing conversations" were frequently perceived by his young son as another means of squelching his personality. Consequently, Jerry used the dinner hour as a forum to express his resentment and to establish some self-esteem. His sister Cynthia recalls, "When Dad was District Attorney [1943-50] and surrounded by yes-men, he would come home and find himself confronted with a no-man in his own son." They would argue at the dinner table and Jerry would demand answers. His dad would at first be good natured about the questioning but would finally reach the point where he would say, "Do I have to go through all this again?" Pat did if Jerry thought he was wrong. Rebellion became a central feature of Jerry Brown's quest for self-recognition. Moreover, he developed a questioning manner that has been a hallmark of his ever since.

The early school years through the elementary grades, the first ones at a public school and the others at St. Brendan's in San Francisco, served a very useful function for young Jerry Brown. Miss Pons, his kindergarten teacher, found him a hyperactive person who had trouble sitting still for more than a minute and his mother called him "a super energetic kid who found it difficult to sit and be quiet." Nevertheless, in school Jerry could operate on his own terms apart from the domination of political life. The teachers provided him with the essential three Rs and other knowledge and gave his life a sense of order. In the classroom, too, he learned the value of logic and mental discipline, which helped him to develop proficiency in communication. Although he was not a particularly good student in these years, school furnished him the opportunity to raise questions and obtain scholastic skills for his future. Through Pat's two terms as San Francisco District Attorney, school often provided Jerry in his pre-teens with determination and comfort.

As a youngster, Jerry found himself in a number of predicaments as the result of mischief. One of his brothers-in-law relates that "[Jerry] was a hell-raiser as a kid, always in some sort of trouble at home or on the block." He adopted his father's relish for story-telling and also added some profanity, gained in part from his dad's political friends, to his vocabulary to enhance the stories. (Neither trait carried over to his adulthood.) He greatly enjoyed using his new words with the neighborhood children much to the dismay of their parents. This compulsion to share came directly from his father's example. In watching Pat amaze the local youngsters with the story of how the hole in the palm of his hand was caused when a gun accidentally discharged during a police raid, Jerry emulated his father's story-telling ability in an attempt to win the same type of recognition from his youthful friends. If profane words provided that kind of response, then so be it. Even then Jerry Brown had a good sense of how to capture and retain people's attention.

In another instance, Jerry and several boyhood chums decided to seek a touch of immortality by leaving their personal marks on cement freshly laid for a neighbor's driveway. Unlike his comrades, Jerry determined that to do the job right would require signing his full name for the world to behold. That proved to be a major mistake. In this case a little humility might have worked wonders. The deed done, it understandably did not take long for Pat to learn of his son's action. District Attorney Brown's response to his wayward offspring was as might be expected. Implementing the old adage that boys will be boys, he informed his son that the punishment would be to pay for repair of the driveway with the earnings he obtained from after-school jobs. Such a penalty for young Brown could scarcely be considered cruel or unusual. He has always shown a great affinity for hard work when he feels it is purposeful. The driveway was soon paid for by virtue of diligence and his increased respect for the consequences of his own action.

Pat Brown moved up the elective political ladder to state Attorney General, an accomplishment realized in 1950 when Jerry was twelve. By the time he entered St. Ignatius High School in the next year, Jerry's propensity toward rebelliousness seemingly had increased as his father's political career glittered more and more. The social demands of the political crowds and the need to perform in a fashion befitting the son of a major politician helped to produce Jerry's rejection of many things.

At St. Ignatius, where Jerry started an approximate decade of association with the Society of Jesus, the Jesuit Order, he became an accomplished debater. A fellow member of the forensics team says that regardless of the topic, Brown would always begin the debate with the same introduction. "What we need is a flexible plan for an ever-changing world." As a sophomore, Jerry was elected cheerleader, but he tended simply to stand in front of the crowds and look bored. He was different in other ways, too, as even then he seemed to walk to the cadence of a different drummer. His youngest sister Kathleen Brown Rice, for instance, remembers that "when everybody [else] was listening to American Bandstand [a television program of the popular musical hits of the day] and rock and roll, Jerry was into classical music."

Jerry was a different type of individual who insisted on following his own path. But in so doing, he tended to show little concern for the feelings of others, a characteristic some of his current and recent associates believe has carried over into the present. His mother, too, perceives her son at times as not being particularly sensitive. According to her, on such occasions as Christmas "he will not give presents every year just because everyone else is doing so." Other people's emotions seemed to have little meaning to him. From an early time he often had no place in his life for ceremonial events. Jerry was determined to go his own way and let others go theirs. Later, as a social reformer and then as a politician, he showed concern for humanity but often in a detached manner.

Jerry graduated from high school in the mid-1950s. It was a time of science-fiction movies, crew haircuts, bobbysocks, and "souped-up" automobiles. In between the Joe McCarthy red-baiting era and the heating-up of the cold war, the period was comfortable and carefree for most young people. But this was not so for Jerry Brown. With his drive for self-realization, coupled with his father's growing interest in running for governor three years hence, young Brown would not rest. In 1955, at age seventeen, he left his parents' home on the first leg of his personal quest. The Jesuit-run University of Santa Clara was his first stop. The then relatively sleepy city of Santa Clara, about forty miles south of San Francisco, put physical distance between his father's politics and Jerry's dislike for things political. For the first time he could have a real opportunity to be his own person.

At the University, Jerry was characterized as a "hang-loose" person who constantly made outrageous statements or posed absurd questions to provoke discussion. But university activity did not fulfill his total needs and after a year he decided to leave. He had perceived a higher calling for himself. Packing his bags and bidding farewell to the secular world much to the consternation of his parents, he entered the Sacred Heart Novitiate in August 1956 in nearby Los Gatos to become a Jesuit novice as the beginning step toward priesthood.

Looking over the rolling hills lined with rich foliage and acres of grape vines, one finds it is easy to understand why the early California Jesuits chose this site for one of their primary training centers and retreats. The mission's high location gives even a hurried visitor a feeling of inner calm and serenity. Its peaceful and unassuming beauty brings forth a feeling of oneness with the order of the universe and all living things.

31

Initially the Jesuit Order seemed an ideal situation for this restless and searching young man. Founded by Saint Ignatius Loyola during the sixteenth century as a counterreform agent of the Pope to return to first principles, the Order provided early Jesuits with a means of dedicating themselves to service free of personal avarice and ambition. The greater glory of God has been the focus of this activist group. As the Jesuit Order went through a series of reoganizations, it began to concentrate its efforts on several key realms of human concern, among them education. Today the Jesuits are among the world's premier educators, having established a number of fine schools and universities in many different countries. And in so doing, they have produced some of the world's great thinkers and contributed greatly to the growth of knowledge. This is the type of organization in which Jerry Brown desired to take part early in his eighteenth year as he began adulthood.

To his young and still impressionable mind, this environment must have seemed an ideal setting for Jerry who had for so long been the unwilling captive of politics. Here he would find solitude and eventually lose himself in thoughts and spiritual experience far greater than the superficiality and lack of meaningfulness of much of the secular world. He had found a new home.

The road to achieving the Order's ideal is not easy to travel. This was particularly true for young Brown. In his quest for acceptance, he would have to bow to many new demands. Above all, he would have to rid himself of any belief systems, insights, and attitudes that ran counter to those of the Order. No longer could he be a rebel who questioned all authority. Rather he would have to submit himself totally to the rigorous teaching of the *Spiritual Exercises of St. Ignatius.* There could be no room for compromise and no place for assertiveness. To succeed, he would have to make himself the instrument of his God. While stringent, these demands seemed reasonable to this novice in comparison to the alternative of the secular world.

This life style was exactly what young Brown craved. Put in his own words, "I wanted something I could really get into where you spend a lot of your time in silence . . . you pick grapes . . . you sweep floors . . . and the only books [you] have were the Bible, Thomas a Kempis [*Imitation of Christ*] and the lives of the Jesuit saints."

This regimen is precisely what he found. His days at Sacred Heart were spent chiefly in silence and contemplation. No communication was permitted with the outside world except for

"Brother Brown is in conference . . . can I help you?"

the sending and receiving of a letter once a week from a person's immediate family and a two-hour visit one Sunday a month from these close relatives.

Life was rigorously structured to help the novice understand what it truly meant to work toward the greater glory of God. A typical day began at five a.m. It started with meditation, mass in the chapel, and a meager breakfast, followed by an hour-long lecture by the master of novices on an aspect of spiritual life, and then work assignments. For work the novices replaced their long-flowing black cassocks and white collars with blue jeans, sweatshirts, and walking boots. After this labor, the seminarians did more meditation that involved the reading of Thomas a Kempis and each individual's examination of his conscience. Following lunch there would be organized recreation, usually carried out in complete silence, which led to a short period of rest or sleep, time in an academic class, recreation, further spiritual reading, another spiritual lecture, and then dinner. More recreation, another lecture and a third session of meditation rounded out the day before the final benediction and recitation of the Litany of the Saints in the chapel. Day in and day out, the novices engaged in the repetition of activity. Jerry and his fellow learners sought at all times to immerse themselves completely into this greater calling.

The annual grape harvest—a thirty-day work period beginning in mid-October and known as the "long retreat"—was a particularly grueling experience for young men unaccustomed to manual labor. The task of picking wine and dessert grapes found Brown and his associates spending long, often hot, days working the fields. Attired in juice-soaked clothes and at times caked with mud from the thick dust of the hillsides, the novices two-by-two and silent, sometimes kneeling and other times squatting, moved along the rows picking the grapes and then scrambled up and down the steep hills lugging boxes of them to trucks. From this activity they learned what it meant to be humble and to relate to

the earth on its own terms. This is an important lesson—
something that Jerry would not forget as he later fought for farm
workers' rights and ecological concerns.

Despite the hardships and restraints Brown relished this new
role. In many ways he manifested enthusiasm for the Jesuit life
but at times with some reservation. For example, a penitential
practice of the Order was the "taking of the discipline" (or
whipping oneself with a cord) and the employment of *catenellae*
(chicken wire-like chains wrapped around the legs and arms).
According to a fellow seminarian, "Jerry would wrap the chains
around his legs and arms so tightly that when he walked to the
chapel for morning mass, he would be limping and would look
like he was being tortured. On the other hand, he admitted in
sessions that called for self-confession that he had such a deadly
fear of whipping himself that he would beat his bed to make a
sound but could not bear to apply the stinging ropes to his bare
bottom."

While spending three and a half years behind the seminary's
cloistered walls, Jerry acquired much of value. The total
experience provided greater knowledge, inner strength, and the
kind of wisdom that can come only through the study and
contemplation of humankind's finest aspirations. "It's a life of
service, Brown recalls, that he "found very good. The idea that
the life of the mind or the spirit has purpose that transcends mere
financial or material considerations is still something I believe in.
In other words, I think some of the most important things in an
average person's life have nothing to do with government and
politics." This was a significant conclusion that was not forgotten.

But the monastic life also proved not to be Jerry Brown's
ultimate calling. The magnetism of secular life pulled on Jerry.
Having served a very important purpose, the Order did not
sustain his dedication. A different kind of service seemed to
demand his attention. As an affiliate of the novitiate has observed,
"The Jesuits were a phase in his life . . . what he decided to do in
the secular world is more Jerry Brown than was the Order."
Accordingly, Jerry Brown in the fourth year in this religious
locale and a year and a half after taking his first vows—vows of

poverty, chastity, and obedience—which made him a member of the religious order, reentered the outside world as a lay person.

Brown's explanation of his decision to leave shows his dissatisfaction and restlessness with ecclesiastical seclusion. "I began to consider: I sit here in poverty, but it isn't really poverty. I don't buy anything, I don't own anything, but I don't have to worry about it either. The mystical Three Degrees of Humility eluded me too. And chastity seemed like another form of detachment and separation. I decided I wanted to get into the real world." Echoing the thoughts of his father Pat earlier that "This [the seminary] is very nice, but is it real?", Jerry Brown reluctantly but firmly stepped out of the serenity of Los Gatos and back into the busy, polluted, and demanding secular world. So it was that Jerry Brown entered a new phase of his life.

The bustling activity of San Francisco was a welcome sight for young Brown as he spent his first day outside the confines of the novitiate. It was 1960 when this clean-cut twenty-two year-old man strolled along the North Beach section savoring all the visual delights of a rapidly changing world. "The book *Doctor Zhivago* had just come out [as a motion picture] and [Joseph] Pasternak has those great scenes in there about the winter turning into spring, and the whole natural cycle," Brown has said. "I could remember one of the lines, 'Man is born to live, not to prepare to live,' and I felt that kind of immediacy, of direct contact with life. Here I am, about to walk out on the streets, I don't have to meditate, I don't have any vows, I'm ready, here I am." He found himself in, a welcome new world, enjoying the sights, drinking a beer in a small bar, and listening to jazz and poetry. He was ready to embrace life to its fullest.

Soon Jerry Brown enrolled as an undergraduate student at the University of Califoria, Berkeley, where he took courses in English literature and Spanish, dabbled in psychology where his interest soon flagged, and then settled into the study of the classics, which had been the recent focus of his intellectual pursuits at Sacred Heart. His professors remember him only vaguely but as a bright, questioning, and responsive student. Outside the classroom he perennially engaged in debate and exchanged cultural nuances with residents of Berkeley's International House where he lived. To a degree he enjoyed his days as a Berkeley student although at times he found contacts with the faculty difficult to make or to sustain. Later Jerry would reminisce about his year at this public university. "There was a wasteland quality about experiencing the Berkeley campus in 1960—the thousands of people, the impersonal rules and bureaucracy, the lack of direction, the draft, the fragmentation, the void."

The Berkeley campus was not all scholarly endeavor and personal interaction while Brown was there. The seeds of student discontent brought about by the impersonal nature of the mega-university and the seeming aimlessness of the society were beginning to take root. A distance in thinking was already evident between the young, naive, and justice-minded students and a more cynical but possibly wiser older generation. It was a period of impending change and only superficial calm, as John Kennedy had become a nationally prominent political figure and then President. Brown sensed the transformation that was occurring and made it part of his concerns. As he left this campus with a bachelor of arts degree in 1961 and took up residence all the way across the country to attend Yale Law School, he heard the increasingly loud calls for social change. His response in helping to secure justice and to reduce alienation came in a prompt and active form.

The southern civil-rights movement gave Jerry his first opportunity to translate his beliefs into action. Joining thousands of others, he added his voice and person to the demands for an end to segregation and discriminatory practices. Temporarily leaving the safety of his Yale surroundings, Jerry entered directly into one of the highly popular liberal actions of the time by marching in 1962 through Mississippi with civil-rights leaders in protest against the rampant injustice of that region.

For Jerry this trip proved to be eventful. During this visit, Mississippi Governor Ross Barnett disclosed in a press dispatch that he had called his California counterpart Edmund Brown Sr. to inform him that Jerry "wasn't associating with the right kind of people" and that he would be arrested if he did not get out. The

California governor called his son and told him "Your mother is in a panic. Will you please get back to school?" And back to Yale Jerry went. While his involvement in the civil-rights movement did not actively continue after the march, mainly due to the pressure of law school, his personal commitment to the ideal of the movement has remained intact.

Returning to Yale Law School, he worked with his usual zeal. During his stay there he met a number of individuals who later became prominent in his administration as Governor. Somewhat socially inclined during those days, he took part in some traditional collegiate frivolities and enjoyed various friendships. As his roommate at Yale reported, "We had a lot of escapades at Yale, but I'm trying to think of some that are publishable." But above all, Jerry maintained a serious attitude toward his study. The need to succeed in this task was as great as his earlier desire to be a good Jesuit seminarian. He progressed through Yale and gained a law degree in three years. Now Jerry was ready to face the world as a professional.

After Yale, he visited a number of Latin American countries for a short while and then returned to California for the purpose of practicing law. In 1964 he took the state bar examination but failed to receive a passing grade. He had not studied diligently for the test. After a refresher course at the McGeorge School of Law in Sacramento, he passed his second attempt six months later. Jerry was then appointed to serve as a law clerk to Justice Mathew Tobriner of the state Supreme Court. (Governor Pat Brown had appointed Tobriner to this associate justiceship in 1962.) At the end of this year of service, Jerry joined a prestigious law firm, Tuttle and Taylor, in fashionable Century City in the Los Angeles area. (William Norris, a longtime friend of Pat Brown, was a member of the firm.) Not unexpectedly in view of his past behavior, Jerry worked tirelessly. An associate, in fact, characterized him as a "workaholic who liked to work his own hours [sometimes through the night]."

As with most activities up to this point in Jerry's life, the practice of law did not satisfy the needs of his eager mind. His next personal quest in worldly affairs placed him into a way of life he had sought to avoid for more than a decade. It was the Vietnam war that finally pulled Brown squarely back into the world of politics. The discontent and alienation of the university students at Berkeley had finally surfaced across the nation in the form of an anti-war movement. Brown's sense of justice did not permit him to remain silent very long. It "was 1967 and I was sitting there in my law office," Brown has said, "opposed to the war but not doing anything about it, and I decided this was wrong." Taking his anti-war sentiments in hand, he began to state his viewpoint before such groups as the liberal California Democratic Council, a volunteer party organization. For Jerry, this expression of protest "was my first taste of being in politics on my own."

Because of this interaction Brown assumed an activist role on speaking circuits and served as an organizer of the Eugene McCarthy for President effort in California in 1968. The war issue divided the Democratic party between the new politics of Eugene McCarthy and the Great Society and the pro-war policies of Lyndon Johnson and Hubert Humphrey. In accepting the post of McCarthy's Southern California campaign vice chairman and treasurer, Jerry could now test his skills and officially christen his own political rebirth. Notwithstanding the futility of his efforts for McCarthy, his political involvement separate from his father Pat was a big step for the former seminarian.

The events in Chicago in the summer of 1968 firmly cemented Jerry's commitment to political change. As an alternate delegate at the Democratic national convention, Jerry sat with many other dreamers and watched as the political dramas were played out on the convention floor and on the nearby streets. From the first banging of the gavel of the convention's chairman, there was little question about the outcome of the deliberations. The delegates at the Chicago conclave reaffirmed the established policies of the party while youthful protesters graphically illustrated their dissent outside.

As Jerry Brown observed the delegates vote to dismantle every anti-war plank from the party platform without consideration of the protests in the streets, he joined others in realizing the need for political parties and governments to be more broadly responsive to all the people. Jerry felt the convention was a "drag" and left early after a peace resolution failed to pass. This convention experience was remembered by Jerry and later drawn upon by him as a governmental official in carrying out the idea of increased participation by underrepresented elements of the public.

The defeat of Eugene McCarthy was not the end of Jerry's quest for social justice and of his political activism. Disillusioned and contemptuous of the established order, he returned to California and found another crusade. The cause of California's migrant workers became his next area of involvement. Under the leadership of Cesar Chavez the United Farm Workers had gained the support of many people by the late 1960s; Jerry Brown became one of their earliest and most adamant allies. Joining a dusty march through the Coachella Valley with Chavez and several thousand farm workers, Brown began a long and important political alliance. Since then the farm workers struggle has become a very significant part of his political career. He has been unyielding in his support.

Because of Brown's growing participation in the political arena, seeking elective office was a natural step for him to take. This was not an easy decision, however, for a man who had loathed politics as a child and a young adult. Like some timid creature initially unsure of the direction and swiftness of the current, Jerry was at first cautious about entering politics as a candidate. But once committed to the plunge, he was prepared to ride the full course of the political river.

Early into his initial elective campaign in 1969—for a seat on the Los Angeles Community College District Board—Jerry turned for reassurance to Joe Cerrell, a friend of his father and a veteran political adviser and campaign manager. Brown wanted an evaluation of his chances to be elected to this newly-created board whose membership of seven would be constituted for the first time through at-large elections. In disbelief of Jerry's innocence about the potency of his name, Cerrell told young Brown that "with your name on the ballot, you could sit in that chair from now until April and still win." Edmund Brown was a name that had been on statewide ballots when his father had run for Attorney General and for Governor, usually successfully, from 1950 through 1966 and was remembered by many voters.

In a field of 133 candidates (narrowed to fourteen in the runoff) in an officially nonpartisan election to a board with no incumbents and with no other highly visible candidate, name recognition was overwhelmingly responsible for Jerry gaining his first elective political victory. He ran as part of a slate—several of its members survived the primary but none of whom other than Brown won in the final election—but he often conducted an independent campaign and had separate funds. He ran far ahead of the person finishing second in both the primary and runoff elections. His margin in the final election was about 50,000 votes. Jerry wanted to "make a name for myself," but no doubt exists that Pat Brown indirectly gave this first electoral triumph to his son.

Jerry Brown's actions on the community college board were consistent with his liberal past but ran counter to prevailing thought on that body. As Pat Brown has pointed out, "He [Jerry] became very concerned about the supidity of the right-wing conservatives who were elected to the community college board at the same time." Steadily raising questions and assuming adversary positions, sometimes in an abrasive manner, young Brown increased the liveliness and heat at many board sessions. His positions were typically not the kind to gain much support from either the board's majority or various segments of the public, but he insisted on being true to his own conscience.

Brown voted to support the right of Students for a Democratic Society to meet at facilities of the college district, and he suggested the board convene in various communities at no cost to the college system. In promoting the farm workers' cause, he urged adoption of a policy requiring the district's campus cafeterias to boycott non-union lettuce. Brown attempted to protect from dismissal two teachers accused of reading "obscene" poetry in the classroom. In the wake of the United States' bombing of Cambodia, he joined local students in protesting the killing of some Kent State University students by the National Guard. And he vainly sought to have a campus of the system named after slain civil-rights leader Martin Luther King Jr. and to allow the football stadium to be used by the Congress of Mexican-American Unity. Most importantly, Brown constantly challenged the educational establishment to fulfill its primary responsibility of providing high-quality instruction to its students, and opposed expenditures that would increase taxes such as construction of a physical education building.

Practically all these efforts went down to defeat because a conservative majority controlled the board. Nevertheless, despite frustrations brought on by the conservatives and his short tenure of a year and a half on the board (resulting from his resignation when he was about to assume higher elective public office), Brown's effect was still significant in the college district because he caused it to undertake further thinking and reappraisals. At his farewell meeting, he stated that the central issue should be planning in the district. In addition, he felt that the board was not having sufficient impact on the district and that much board time had been devoted to matters and discussions not relevant to its functions. The scourge of the governing group, Brown demonstrated an uncommon perception and spirit and a strong student orientation.

From this unlikely elective educational position Jerry Brown was ready to launch forth on a fascinating political career. Emerging from the cloistered confines of a Jesuit seminary, institutions of higher education, and the quest to lessen social injustice, Edmund G. (Jerry) Brown Jr. came face to face with his destiny as a member of the Los Angeles Community College Board. Serving in public office would now occupy much of his life.

Chapter Three

First Step
Beyond Original Sin

Attainment and retention of power and position constitute the heart of politics, which is often an all consuming, driving force that possesses the lives of its disciples. Individual conversion to the adoration of things political is not always intended but is often the inevitable price for involvement. To a degree the transformation that takes place in a person seeking office can be likened to Eve's bout with original sin. Once yielding to the political serpent's promises of greatness, the often unsuspecting victims are suddenly cast from this ordinary human coil into another plane where they must stand naked before their own ambitions. The acquisition of power and position produce an opiated effect that dooms the once innocent to a life where craving of greater prizes becomes the center of all things. Those who might have once found pleasure in other activities and personal philosophies discover that their only gratification comes while on the prowl for bigger game in the form of higher public office.

This scenario seems to apply to the development of Jerry Brown as a public person. As a child born into an environment of political maneuvering, back-slapping, and ambition, he initially rejected this life. The rewards of political success, however, were too evident to ignore indefinitely. Upon savoring the sweetness of his election victory to the Los Angeles Community College board, he appeared destined to join the legions of other individuals in the partisan political arena. In 1969, soon after winning that public office, he had a discussion with Tom Quinn, a young newspaperman whom Brown had met recently at a political meeting and who soon became his chief political adviser. They talked about his desire to run for Secretary of State in the following year. Brown had decided, contrary to most people's view, that this office had extensive powers to regulate the reporting of political campaign contributions.

Jerry Brown discovered as a youth that survival in the political jungle is directly related to developing and keeping advantages over others similarly motivated. In the continuous battle for supremacy, the relative strength of opponents is usually measured in terms of their accessibility to resources, personal attributes, timing, and adaptability to changing environments. In Brown's case, his name provided a unique area of respectability and familiarity that has measurably helped his quests for victories. His easy election to the Los Angeles Community College board clearly demonstrated the full potency of his name and the advantage it provided. The positive popular image of the Brown name contributed to Jerry's electoral triumphs. In 1970, however, the amount of strength this neophyte politician could muster was not clear. But the answer was not long in coming. While retaining his seat on the college board, Brown embarked on his first major statewide test of political acceptance.

Unlike other figures roaming the ripe fields of California politics, Jerry Brown chose to avoid the ordinary well-traveled paths of ascent—through such politically volatile routes as district attorney, mayor, local or state legislator, and state Attorney

General. His opening decision to test his political attractiveness by running for a local college board seat is not the normal route to the office of Governor. The selection of the Secretary of State's post as his second venture was equally unique. This progression represents a distinctly unorthodox set of stepping stones for political promotion.

Since the inception of the post of Secretary of State in California in the nineteenth century, it had largely been of a clerical and custodial nature—overseeing and certifying elections held at all governmental levels in the state. Designed originally as a place of records, the activities of this sleepy office had been minimal at most. The position was a symbol of bureaucratic obscurity.

Understandably, this post had not been regarded as one of the state's major political prizes. In fact, it had so little appeal for ambitious politicians that for practically all of this century a single family had been able to pass the position from one member to a second (with only a two-year break caused by an appointment to fill the vacancy upon the father's death) without receiving any serious challenges. The father and the son had the same first and last names—Frank Jordan; only their middle initial differed on the ballot. The office of Secretary of State was among the least sought posts in California state government.

The dormancy but possibilities of the position made the office attractive to Brown. Possessing a shrewdness and a practical understanding of the office as the result of reading thoroughly about it, he sensed the extremely high potential of proceeding in a new direction. This officially partisan but traditionally politically neutral post could provide Jerry Brown with a forum for his ideas on political reform and for his ambitions without placing him squarely in the middle of normal political jousting where fatal wounds might be inflicted. The nature of the position offered him a buffer from which to make his statements and prepare for the gubernatorial race four years later. Maximum benefit with minimal risk was to be his goal as Secretary of State.

The death of the second Frank Jordan (his wife was unsuccessful in her bid to be appointed to the office) provided an opportunity for an enterprising political figure to revamp the organization and exercise its powers in a fashion to make political points. Jerry Brown alone saw this unique opportunity emerge as the almost moribund office fell vacant. Again, as in the case of the community college board race, Brown would not have an incumbent, who is usually considered to be a strong opponent, as a contender. Based upon name recognition alone, Brown seemed likely to be elected to the post even though the general political climate was far from calm. In this office he could test his political skills and develop prominence as a Democratic officeholder. If he were elected, his triumph would be heralded by the Democrats as possibly their only statewide victory for a state constitutional office in an election year dominated by popular Governor Reagan at the head of a ticket of Republican candidates for executive posts. As the new Secretary of State, if certain key Democrats were defeated, he might be within possible striking distance of being nominated for the governorship although he would probably have strong competition from other Democrats who had been biding their time.

Any path to political success obviously involves a certain degree of risk. In particular, to walk on the political road chosen by Brown entailed much potential difficulty. In a state as unpredictable as California and in a time of great uncertainty, nothing could be taken for granted. For over a decade California had been in flux. While Pat Brown served as Governor from 1959 to 1967, California was considered one of the nation's most liberal program-oriented states. Then with the election of Ronald Reagan, the state did an eight-year political turnaround to become a frontrunner in the conservative movement. These types of repeated reversals, where often the abnormal is regarded as the everyday, have come to be expected in this state. As has been suggested in comparing these changes with the relative consistency of eastern politics, it is as if "the country was tilted westward and all the loose nuts slide to the [west] coast." It is precisely this fluctuation that makes any political decision, including Jerry Brown's choice to enter the race for Secretary of State, full of potential surprises and hazards.

Other factors affecting the political environment of the times also left much room for uncertainty. Brown's first bid for statewide office was made in a highly volatile period. The nation's political power structure was colored by a decidedly conservative hue. In Washington, Richard Nixon was in the early part of his first term as President with much support for his stands on law and order and the conduct of the Vietnam war.

Activists on the other side of the political spectrum added much to the development of what became in part a generational social and political schism. Not surprisingly California was in the forefront. The Berkeley "free speech" movement of 1966 can be credited with originally fanning the flames of conservative reaction. After a long period of pride and unbridled support for the University of California system, the actions of rebellious Berkeley students in demanding a voice in the governance of the University were viewed by many people as a most ungrateful act. The "free speech" movement—sometimes labeled by the more conservative element as the "filthy speech" affront—signaled to many that a threat existed to the proper order of things in this society. Something very strange was happening to the nation. The eruption of the discontent suggested all was not perfect. A powerful period of reevaluation had begun.

The establishment was being rocked by its own children. No longer were protesters alien to the mainstream of the society; now they were the kids down the block or across the dinner table. What took place in Berkeley in 1966 and spread across the nation in various forms was a prelude to youthful disenchantment with the Vietnam war.

By early 1970, too, a cultural division between many young people and those of the older generation was in full bloom. The youthful demonstrations that had characterized the recreational activities of the nation's college-age students culminated in bloodshed on the Kent State University campus in Ohio in May of that year. With the bombing of Cambodia ordered by President

Nixon in the preceding month, widespread demonstrations were triggered throughout the nation as a manifestation of discontent. Even such traditionally conservative institutions as Nixon's own undergraduate alma mater, Whittier College in southern California, experienced student strikes. There was no doubt that millions of young men and women were encountering great difficulty relating to the actions of their government.

Beneath the anger and confusion there existed even more profound questions about this society and its government. Jerry Brown's first bid for statewide public office would have to be made in a time when no clear answers to many public questions were present.

Given the unstable times, one of Jerry Brown's first concerns understandably centered on the problem of how best to hedge against potential adversity while building a unique impression of his own public service assets. In weighing his possible options, he sensed that the day of the anti-politician—an image that well fits his disposition and personal philosophy—was at hand. Portraying himself as the anti-politician, his tasks were to convince voters that he was someone unique to the political world and to establish a well-directed campaign organization that would help him obtain a big win at the polls. To accomplish victory, he needed a team of politically astute individuals.

In recruiting a small support staff, Brown showed remarkable insight and skill. In fact, one of the most prominent accomplishments of this campaign was Jerry's ability to procure highly competent personnel. Brown, as a frequent student of the world's absurdities, needed political alter egos to help pull together the strategic and procedural aspects of his quest.

Tom Quinn and Richard Maullin emerged as the key campaign figures. Brown and Quinn had sought positions on different school boards in 1969. During their respective campaigns Brown had become extremely curious about Quinn's ability to get far more radio news air time for his campaign for the Los Angeles Board of Education (which he lost) than Jerry was obtaining in his race for the community college board. Jerry became determined to meet Quinn and did so after a political public gathering. Jerry and Maullin had become acquainted on a Latin American trip and became friends through their mutual interest in Latin American relations.

Quinn and Maullin provided insight into media use and analyzed campaign reactions and plans. The involvement of such well-versed tacticians to pull the necessary strings and make the required maneuvers in the background made it possible for Brown to play the well-conceived role of the anti-politician. Although young, Quinn (twenty six years old) and Maullin (twenty-nine) had a sense of the jugular of public responsiveness. Collectively this trio molded the public image that still envelops Jerry Brown today.

Tom Quinn is an affable, smooth, polished, and tough person whose choir-boy appearance is somewhat deceiving. He grew up in the shadow of his father Joe who is as much one type of California politician as Edmund G. (Pat) Brown Sr. is another. It was the older Quinn who as political adviser and deputy mayor helped steer the candidacies and administrations of Sam Yorty "through the deals and backstabbing of [Los Angeles] City Hall for twelve years and through political campaigns that were more memorable for their viciousness." Tom gleaned much about political techniques and tactics from his father's knowledge of politics based on the latter's long association with Yorty and his analyzing of local political news for many years. "We [His father and he] are different people," Tom has said. However, a man who lost a political fight to Tom Quinn says, "He is more his father's son than anyone thinks" and this man has for a long time wanted to caption a photograph of the smiling young Irishman: "Choirboy Commits Mayhem." Tom Quinn has also stated, "I suppose there are similarities between my father and me." If possessing a cold, analytical ability to get to the root of a problem and to turn it to his candidate's advantage is any indication, the similarities are indeed pronounced. Both father and son are remarkably gifted in this sophisticated art.

Beyond great political acumen Tom Quinn brought to the campaign an equally important asset in the form of a working knowledge of the printed and electronic media. His father owns

City News Service (CNS), which supplies more than 75 percent of the local news copy to the Los Angeles area. As a youth Tom worked as a CNS teletype operator and fledgling reporter. Upon completing his bachelor's degree in journalism and history at Northwestern University, he returned to Los Angeles to direct Radio News West, which specializes in pre-taped reports for radio stations throughout the state. With such qualifications, his involvement in the Brown campaign was highly relevant. Quinn's rich and impressive background made him an invaluable asset.

Quinn has been frequently thought to be the real power behind Brown. It is true that Jerry has turned to Tom for advice about the political practicality of Maullin's proposed strategies and that Quinn likes to act independently. It is also true that Quinn did a great deal of talking in Brown's campaigns for Secretary of State and Governor. However, Jerry makes the decisions; he is his own man.

Richard Maullin contributed the third side to the youthful campaign trioka. In an age of ever-increasing reliance on computer-based analysis of political trends Maullin offered considerable skills. A University of California, Los Angeles, doctor of philosophy (Ph.D.) in political science, Maullin had worked for six years at the Rand Corporation, a "think-tank" in Santa Monica, California, on analyzing Latin American affairs and carrying out other social science projects. Through Brown's friendship with Maullin, Jerry was able to enlist his aid in systematically seeking financial contributions and developing election strategies. Efficient, bright, and industrious, Maullin did his job with zeal. With his charts, demographics, and statistical studies the campaign took on a new dimension.

Described by a UCLA political science professor as "something less than a humanist," Maullin does not place much faith in the new politics of grass-roots movements. To him, people can be maneuvered in accordance with complex formulas and skillful analysis. Tom Hayden, Chicago Seven defendant later turned California politician, has noted that "if you ask him [Maullin] whether there isn't some value in the political experience for volunteers, or use phrases like 'citizen politics,' he stares in bemusement." According to Maullin, "There are no new politics, no old politics. There is only one politics, the competition for power over the allocation of goods and resources of the society. Politics is a business where you promote your product and the means are scientific."

The presence of Quinn and Maullin as campaign activists made one fact clear—Brown's entrance center stage as a candidate for Secretary of State would obviously not be a soliloquy. His sophisticated staff would play a major role in this election. Billed as the campaign of the "anti-politician," Jerry's race was guided by completely professional personnel. Jerry Brown as the son of a former governor, a student of practical politics, a veteran of several "people's" movements, and a scholar of legal and theological philosophy was a remarkably well seasoned figure at age thirty-two. Quinn, whose own birthright included knowledge of politics and communications, provided the necessary skills to get the word across. Finally, Maullin, the political systems analyst, served as production coordinator, seeking money and designing strategy. The drama they began to unfold in 1969 was continued in to Brown's campaign for Governor four years later.

Jerry Brown's campaign for Secretary of State might have had to be altered drastically because he did not let his father know of his plan to file as a candidate. While in Japan on a business trip, Pat Brown was telephoned by wealthy Democratic fund raiser Eugene Wyman who asked him to seek the Democratic nomination for Governor. The compulsively political Brown listened as his longtime friend and associate stated that many party regulars were prepared to kick off the campaign with a $400,000 event immediately upon Brown's return to the state. As icing on the cake, Wyman also reported the results of a recent poll. Pat was outdistancing his closest Democratic rivals, Jesse Unruh and Sam Yorty, by a two-to-one margin and was behind Reagan, who had defeated him four years earlier by over a million votes, by only four percentage points.

Pat Brown's first reaction was, "Play quarterback again? Why not?" If he had immediately followed through and announced his candidacy for Governor in this same election, the complexion of the race for Secretary of State would have undoubtedly been different. Win or lose, Jerry would have been directly linked to the politics of his father in the eyes of the vast majority of voters.

Fortunately for Jerry a telephone conversation between Pat and his wife Bernice prevented this from happening. It was not until the senior Brown excitedly called his spouse at their California home that he found out that his only son had entered the race for a statewide office. The reaction of California's former first lady to her typically overzealous husband's desire to reenter politics was, "Are you crazy?" Before giving him an opportunity to argue, she continued, "Well, there is something you ought to know. Jerry has just announced for Secretary of State. I don't think you ought to be doing anything to interfere in his career."

With a mixture of reluctance and father's pride, Pat stopped any efforts to make yet another run for governor. Edmund "Pat" Brown Sr. would henceforth act politically in the sole interest of his son. Pat's decision provided Jerry with the chance to strike a balance on his own terms—the use of the Brown name without direct association with his father's traditional liberal programs. Throughout the campaign, Pat Brown's shadow would serve only to protect his son from some degree of harsh scrutiny rather than smother his political identity.

The practical matter of campaigning now became central. Because of Jerry's strong desire for his own unique political identity, the establishment of an acceptable image became the focus of his campaign staff from that day forward. Employing Quinn's excellent media skills, the candidate sought to create a number of important impressions in the voters' minds. Honest, efficient, young, conscientious, and astute were among the attributes he hoped to implant. As an anti-politician, Brown saw himself as a man of the people who understood and could respond effectively to these troubled times. By divorcing himself from traditional political ties such as affiliation with the Democratic party's gubernatorial standard bearer Jesse Unruh,

Brown assured his image as an independent maverick. This candidate for Secretary of State established himself as an individual clearly distinct and separate from other politicians.

The issues employed in this effort were based on a shrewd set of campaign strategies. The campaign for Secretary of State was comprehensive and well conceived. In promising to "turn around" this sleepy "bureaucratic relic of another age," Brown hoped to create an image of importance and competence for himself and the office he sought. Much political mileage could be made by reorganizing even a small agency like that supervised by the Secretary of State and adding to its potency. His keen legal mind recognized that existing statutes provided the foundations necessary to build a powerful regulatory organization. Brown and his staff did their homework well before engineering their campaign. Vast powers had been vested long ago in that office to certify elections, oversee the conduct of all campaigns, and enforce related laws. When translated into hard-nosed political terms, this meant that the Secretary of State could place the spotlight on questionable campaign practices.

Eliminating the ineffectiveness and dormancy of the office of Secretary of State and thus bringing about more extensive honesty in government became Brown's main campaign issues. The honesty plank ultimately provided him with an unusual image among California politicians. In a sense, he suggested that other people in politics foresake their sinful ways and permit him to lead them down the path of electoral righteousness. Such an endorsement for integrity could not be faulted nor could it have been initially considered highly stimulating and inspirational. In this pre-Watergate period, this call for honesty had only marginal meaning when compared to the impact it would have after his election as Secretary of State. As certain corrupt actions in Washington and elsewhere began to be disclosed, this position served effectively to open fate's door on his future. Jerry Brown found himself with an instant and important identity, Mr. Clean Government.

Both the primary and general elections produced little public or media interest in the race for Secretary of State. Most attention centered on the contest for Governor that finally produced a one-sided showdown between incumbent Ronald Reagan and the former state legislative leader Jesse Unruh. Brown's primary opponents had little political strength, the chief one being Hugh Burns, once a conservative power in the state Senate from the Central Valley but now a person of declining years and stature. Neither of Brown's opponents conducted a campaign of specific issues. Brown decisively won the Democratic primary, garnering 68 percent of the votes in a contest with two opponents and running up a plurality of more than a million votes over Burns who finished second.

Meanwhile the Republicans were nominating James Flournoy, a Los Angeles attorney and the first black to be selected by a major party in California to be its standard bearer for a state executive office. Some politicians and political observers concluded that James Flournoy had decided to run for the office and had been nominated because he bore the same unusual last name as the incumbent State Controller Houston (Hugh) Flournoy. The Republican primary vote was much more dispersed, with winner Flournoy picking up about 30 percent of the tallies. Frank Jordan's widow ran a poor third in this contest, thus conclusively ending the family dynasty in this office. The Republican primary campaign was lackluster and not issue-oriented.

In the general election Brown hammered away at the themes of greater effectiveness in the office, more governmental honesty, and greater citizen participation in politics. He stressed that as Secretary of State he would attempt to reduce "the hidden influence of lobbyists" in political campaigns by requiring candidates to file more detailed reports on campaign expenditures, which could be done under existing state law. He also recommended that television stations give one minute to five minutes of free time to various candidates and the state grant a ten-dollar tax credit to persons giving that amount to a political party. He further urged extension of the mail franking privilege to candidates to send out literature and permitting persons to cast ballots on election day within a week or two after registering.

Occasionally Brown's utterances went far afield from his

campaign for Secretary of State. At one point he warned that radical students on three University of California campuses were planning major disruptions in the belief that by doing so they could undermine support for Democratic candidates and ultimately draw liberal Democrats into the radical camp. Brown said, "The vast majority of Democrats are sickened by violence" and he recommended the establishment of a campus strike force composed of specially trained law-enforcement officers who would be mobilized on command of the Governor. At another time Brown denounced his party's pro-abortion plan and criticized Republicans for depicting the issue as party-oriented.

Meanwhile James Flournoy centered his campaign on strengthening laws which govern corporations, stating that he was shocked to learn of underworld interests in such activities. "We need laws to guarantee that persons named are actually running the corporations," he said. He also asserted that one of the roles of his campaign was to help "bridge the polarization gap" because of his belief that the division between the races was wider than at any time since the Civil War.

In late August, slightly more than two months before the general contest, the respected California Poll conducted by the Mervin Field's organization showed Brown leading Flournoy by 42 percent to 33 percent, with the remainder undecided. In mid-October incumbent Controller Houston Flournoy revealed that a private poll he had taken disclosed that 65 percent of the electorate did not know the two Flournoys were unrelated. Houston Flournoy expressed considerable concern about this confusion and subsequently spent much of his time and campaign money on total name identification. Election officials in Sacramento County compounded the confusion by sending out 15,000 sample ballots that listed Houston Flournoy as the Republican candidate for both Controller and Secretary of State.

Soon thereafter James Flournoy claimed that race was the key factor in his trailing Brown—that if this Flournoy were not black he would be leading. Jerry Brown retorted, "Race is not *my* issue." Flournoy then said he wanted to "indicate the many moods of the Brown family . . . when father is saying one thing and son is doing another or when the son's saying one thing, and the father is doing another." To illustrate, he showed copies of what he said was a letter soliciting campaign funds on Jerry's behalf sent to lobbyists by Pat Brown during the time Jerry was criticizing them for their financial activities. Flournoy went on to term Jerry's call for minimizing the influence of the rich the "height of hypocrisy," as Brown, he said, had been born into an advantageous position. Jerry replied that all campaign contributions made to him would be made public knowledge. Furthermore, in a statement reminiscent of Franklin Roosevelt's famous speech about his dog Fala in defense of his family, Brown said, "his [opponent's] complaints are rather sorry if they were not so pathetic. . . . Now he's attacking my family, my father . . . he probably ought to attack my mother and three sisters. They probably raised more money than my father."

Despite the nature of Brown's campaign, the communications media gave only limited coverage to the contest for Secretary of State and tended to highlight the mundane nature of the office. Many of the news stories dealt with Jerry as the son of Pat and portrayed Jerry as an individual possibly capable of achieving innovation in the office. Some major newspapers and television and radio stations in the state endorsed no one for this position. However, the influential *Sacramento Bee* did endorse Brown, stating that he "has shown concern over the role financial contributors play in political concerns—by demanding detailed campaign expenditure reports from office seekers, [he] would be able to translate concern into action."

By the time of the November general election, it was clear that the Democrats were not going to fare well in gaining such state executive offices as Governor, Lieutenant Governor, Attorney General, State Controller, and State Treasurer. The Democrats' gubernatorial candidate Jesse Unruh was perceived by many people as a political boss. A robust man, he had a reputation among numerous Democratic officials and some of the general electorate as an opportunist who relished and vigorously exercised power. Trust of and respect for him were not high among either the public or many of the party faithful, and many of the party's big financial angels did not bring out their checkbooks to support him. His campaign was woefully under-financed, and his confrontation politics was a sad failure. Ronald Reagan, his opponent, was a trim, dashing incumbent with a strong party organization solidly behind him and a much more attractive image.

The other individuals seeking state executive office on the Democratic ticket also generally suffered defeat, and Democratic party hopes for executive officeholding was largely dashed for another four years. However, typical of the strange world of California politics, the Democratic party did maintain its control in both state legislative houses and picked up a U.S. Senate seat through the election of John Tunney, son of a former heavyweight boxing champion.

One exception did emerge to the Republican stronghold on state executive offices. Jerry Brown gained 50 percent of the votes for Secretary of State compared to James Flournoy's 46 percent with the remainder split between the nominees of two minor parties. Running better in southern California than in the northern part of the state, Brown rolled up a plurality of about 300,000 votes over Flournoy. This was a much smaller margin than the Brown forces had anticipated and seemingly could be traced to the overwhelming Republican victories for other state executive offices.

Jerry had accomplished the same feat his father Pat had registered exactly twenty years before when elected to the attorney generalship of the state: both were the only Democrats chosen by the statewide electorate to fill a state post. Like his father, too, Jerry's victory placed him in a prominent position in the state's Democratic party and made it likely that he would seek the governorship. He could now begin to groom himself for candidacy to that office, a bid he made four years later while his more cautious political father took twice that long to decide to make such a move.

The position of Secretary of State also offered Jerry Brown a means for developing his skills in government within the framework of his value system. As an executive, he would seek to mold this small bureaucratic agency into his own image and translate the office into the strong regulatory organization provided by statute but only marginally reflected in the Jordan regime. In addition, Brown hoped to send a message to those who would listen about the new societal mission available under his leadership. By being a hard-nosed bureaucratic chief, Jerry dreamed of contributing much to this office and to the people of California. Like most young people (Jerry was then thirty-two) in the political forest, Jerry sought to test the water to determine the fitness of his practical political capabilities.

From the moment the last ballot was counted for Secretary of State, Jerry Brown found himself where he wanted to be—thrust into the position of being a major future candidate for Governor. In the intervening time he had to nurture this obscure but potentially significant governmental office to prove himself capable of functioning in an even more important public post. As Secretary of State, Jerry Brown could further design his political destiny.

Chapter Four

The Anti-politician
Comes of Age

The inauguration of California's Secretary of State is typically about as exciting as watching a frog catch flies or listening to a convicted corrupt politician still profess his innocence. The traditionally innocuous and boring nature of this event is really not surprising, because for more than sixty years of the twentieth century this induction ceremony merely formalized an extension of another four years of bureaucratic record-keeping under one of the two Jordans.

The problem lay in the self-restrictive manner in which the Jordans chose to define their public responsibility. Through the terms of many governors the domain encompassed the recording and retention of certain legal documents including the licensing of notaries public, the filing of private and city incorporation papers, and the routine overseeing of elections. Under the

Jordans this somnolent office justified its existence by minimally performing a series of mandated functions that had very little meaning to the general public and even less political significance. Obviously, the Secretary of State's activities did not produce much popular excitement and attention.

This period of dormancy passed when death ended a dynasty and provided a golden opportunity for a remarkably astute neophyte mover of people and ideas. The end of one father-son dynasty marked the rise of another political family. With the final page of the Jordan history completed, Jerry Brown was now free to add another chapter to the legacy left by his father.

Jerry Brown was inaugurated into the office of Secretary of State on January 3, 1971. On the surface this event had an ordinary appearance. With a conspicuous lack of fanfare, there was little about this ceremony that separated it from any previous inauguration to this office. After former Chief Justice of the United States Earl Warren swore young Brown into office, the newly confirmed Secretary of State dutifully expressed gratitude to the approximately 150 well-wishers and media personnel who had assembled for the occasion. Turning to his obviously elated parents, he thanked his "mother for naming me after my father. I grew to like that name during the campaign" and committed himself to work in the same cooperative spirit of Pat Brown and Chief Justice Warren, both former California governors. Stepping out of his frequent role of a highly serious, detached person, young Brown revealed an unusual warmth seldom seen by the public. This was light-hearted interaction between the new Secretary of State and the crowd.

Beneath the exchange of pleasantries, a sense of expectancy ran through the proceedings. This feeling, as Brown would clearly demonstrate, was well founded. Before the occasion would end, the social niceties were put aside and replaced by a new message. The tone set by Jerry Brown that day suggested a radical change was in the making. The office of the Secretary of State, a dormant political power, was about to flex muscles few others seemed to realize it had or would use.

Secretary Brown's formal inaugural statement left no question about his intent. The audience realized through the message that this Secretary of State took his campaign promises seriously. Motivated by both noble desires to serve and personal ambition for political advancement, Brown put political hangers-on, party regulars, and the citizens of California on notice that he would invigorate this office. Unlike his unobtrusive predecessors, the new Secretary of State was eager to challenge the established order of politics. The point he made readily clear was that all those standing in Jerry Brown's way of carrying out his responsibilities were advised to beware.

The specific commitments Brown outlined were straightforward. Underscoring everything was a promise to make the Secretary of State's office a citadel of effectiveness and responsiveness. This he asserted would best be accomplished through the full exercise of all his authority. By vowing to employ powers that had been unused under the Jordans, Jerry set in motion a program so potent that the resultant rattling of political cages would cause much consternation throughout the state. Even the most basic goals sometimes unexpectedly took on special political significance. For example, few observers could have predicted that the noble objective of encouraging newly-franchised eighteen to twenty-one year old voters to exercise their privilege would culminate in a major political conflict. Yet within months of the inauguration Republican Attorney General Evelle Younger caused the issue to become Brown's first significant test of power.

Other inaugural commitments had even more far-reaching effects. Brown's call for enforcement of the election code "in a fair but vigorous way" eventually placed him at odds with many in the political establishment. He further promised to attempt to register the nearly 4 million people who were otherwise qualified to vote. But the most politically potent promise made by Brown to the inaugural assemblage was his support of full disclosure of campaign contributions. Insisting that "the people have a right to know the role money plays in politics," Jerry placed himself in the role of a crusading anti-politician. Largely because of actions arising from this commitment in January 1971, he would later emerge from the ashes of the Watergate affair as Mr. Clean Government and gain considerable public attention.

The political environment of 1971 differed greatly from that of a few years later. Trust in the government and its leaders was comparatively high. While the involvement of the United States in Vietnam had caused the estrangement from government of millions of young people, and many adults as well, faith in the honesty of most political figures was still relatively strong. Therefore Brown's decision to make clean government his primary goal might have well proven to be of slight importance to a voting public looking for identifiable, significant program accomplishments. The issues raised by Brown could have easily become nothing more than a set of unimportant promises were it not for his own determination and certain unexpected twists of fate.

Why so many cynical political observers caustically dismissed Brown's inaugural commitments as nothing more than political rhetoric is easy to understand. The temper of the times combined with an underestimate of the skills of the new Secretary of State suggested that his administration would offer little of consequence. But through Brown's purposeful design and the accident of timing, these skeptics were proven incorrect. Within days of the inauguration, the political promises perceived by many to be simply tired, hackneyed phrases were transformed into action with form and substance.

Brown sprang onto the Sacramento scene like a modern Prometheus who had come to bring light to the masses. Through the darkness of political divisiveness and malfeasance, he dared to offer new illumination. As Secretary of State, he fought the illegal political activities of major corporations, helped bring the second term of a corrupt President to an early end, and turned an obscure bureaucratic office into a powerful regulatory agency. In addition, he expanded public awareness of various aspects of the elective process, revealed the incomplete campaign financial reporting of many candidates, and worked successfully for a comprehensive campaign reform measure. By the end of a four-year term as Secretary of State, Brown would be viewed by millions of Californians as the conveyer of a new political faith and the provider of insights in a most perplexing time.

From his Olympian heights as Secretary, he proceeded to gain favorable responses by mixing abstract and retrospective statements with dramatic action. Despite comments from some Republican leaders and others that "Brown has unilaterally redefined and exceeded the legal limits of his authority," his use of executive power placed the office of Secretary of State in its rightful position. Stated simply, the crusading Brown opened a Pandora's box that the political and private establishments could not contain.

The central people around Brown during his statewide political grand opening were again Tom Quinn and Richard Maullin, both of whom were appointed deputy secretaries of state. This trio, fresh from an election victory, joined together to achieve two equally important goals. The first objective was to serve the public interest. Because concern over responsiveness to the public and effectiveness are so deeply rooted in the Brown concept of governance, the task of remolding this agency was naturally of paramount interest. Second, the desire for progress up the political ladder underscored this noble cause. In serving the people, the Brown-Quinn-Maullin trioka remained mindful of the need to make political mileage whenever possible. Consequently many of the Secretary's decisions presumably were calculated in terms of their potential implications for the 1974 gubernatorial race. Much like a master merchandiser, Brown and his top aides sought to maximize current production of goods and services to the people while skillfully promoting his wares for even greater political profits for the future.

In this quest to develop an electoral product that voters would be willing to purchase later with their gubernatorial votes, this team left very few stones unturned. Throughout these four years, Brown's office continually issued news releases designed to produce and retain a positive image of Secretary of State Brown. Latching onto the "anti-politician" image, the team portrayed Jerry as a man whose public objective was to bring a non-traditional approach to government. Each action undertaken by the Secretary of State was followed by a deluge of media data. Tom Quinn was constantly on top of all potentially newsworthy events. Releasing a constant flood of press communications, Quinn and his associates were determined to have Brown's achievements strongly articulated. As a state capitol reporter has observed, "[Brown] and Quinn [during the time Brown was Secretary of State] knew those deadlines. The morning paper deadlines, the evening paper deadlines, the wire deadlines. They couldn't get much TV in the early days but they got play [in the newspapers and on radio] with those releases."

An early major altercation pitted Secretary Brown against Attorney General Evelle Younger, a Republican, on a voting rights question. At issue was the legal place of voting of college students between the ages of eighteen and twenty-one. With the adoption of the twenty-sixth amendment to the national Constitution in 1971 granting those who had reached the age of eighteen the right to vote, some politicians feared that important shifts in the state's voting would occur. Many conservatives were alarmed at the thought of particular young college elements— anti-war protesters, rock music enthusiasts, drug experimenters, and other "radicals"—through bloc voting tipping the election results in certain state legislative and congressional districts.

Evelle Younger took steps to dilute the impact of this youth vote. The tactic he utilized to try to reduce the concentration and the size of this vote was based on his authority as Attorney General to render a formal opinion on the voting residency requirements. Younger proceeded to define the voting precincts of college students to be the same as their parents. This ruling would mean that thousands of college students residing in dormitories and nearby campus housing would be required to return to their parents' precincts to vote. Obviously, many students living a considerable distance from such designated polling places would have to forfeit their newly given right. The effect of this interpretation would have been to lessen substantially the potential voting strength of that element of the younger population—many college and university students—of which the conservatives were highly suspicious.

The Attorney General's opinion did not go over well with many liberal politicians who would conceivably benefit most from the college vote. They saw this vote as a decided advantage that they were unwilling to see diminished without a struggle. To new generation political figures like Brown the possible loss of these votes was even more important. In attempting to keep his campaign commitment to register the maximum number of young voters, Brown unabashedly used the power of his position to achieve this end.

The Secretary of State, as the legal guardian of electoral policies and as one who had much to gain from the youth vote, took out after Attorney General Younger. To set the proper stage, Brown made a series of public attacks on the Republican administrator's opinion. After raising the public consciousness about Younger's "politically motivated actions," Secretary Brown proceeded to take the matter to court for final resolution. The case he presented reasoned that the Attorney General had denied a segment of the population the vote based chiefly on its role as students. According to Brown, the residency question was an empty justification. The college student, he argued, should be treated in the same manner as an apartment dweller whose life style might necessitate as frequent residency shifts as the student. After short deliberation, the state Supreme Court found in favor of the Secretary by granting him through local election officials the right to register students at their college communities if that was their preference.

The court victory provided Brown with more than a favorable judicial decision. It also signaled the elevation of his office from the status of document pushers to a viable politically active power. Such a turn of events would have been inconceivable under the long Jordan reign but with Brown all this had changed. The new

Secretary of State was not to be ignored. With the added strength and confidence gained from this victory, Brown was ready to do battle with others and further establish his office as something worthy of public attention.

Through a press release Brown called for an accounting by 134 candidates for public office who had not filed campaign reports. In a dramatic press conference where state legislators were condemned, he produced campaign contribution reports by lobbyists which carefully blacked out the names of the politicians. He brought suits against three major oil companies that had made illegal campaign contributions against a measure to divert certain gas-tax money for highway construction to rapid transit development.

Brown resurrected a campaign-fund law of 1893, which his father Pat, when Attorney General, had interpreted narrowly. Under Pat's ruling campaign contributions were identified only by an initial and a surname. The names were not listed on the official forms in alphabetical order or, for that matter, in any logical order at all. Nor were the amounts contributed listed alongside the shortened names. Jerry declared that "If you read my father's opinion allowing this, you will find it absurd. . . . I think I have pretty well convinced him it is absurd." He went on, "The law in 1893 was taken out of the English disclosure act. If you go back and trace the English law, you find the California version is almost verbatim. The original idea was crystal clear. The only thing we didn't borrow was the English form, which contained precise instructions on how to file."

Disregarding his father's advisory opinion (which did not have the force of law), Jerry prepared new regulations that required the complete listing of names and addresses of contributors and the amounts of the contributions. He then compiled his rules into a booklet of sixty-four pages that included ten pages of detailed instructions. He took the galley proof of the booklet to leaders in the state legislature to show them what he was doing. They were shocked and told him that if he did not reconsider there would be dire consequences. Brown went ahead and issued his booklet, saying that its guidelines would "serve notice to all men and women who seek public office that from this day on they must open their books to full public view." Jerry also pointed out that these rules would eliminate the use of dinner committees through which candidates had been able to hide the sources of their campaign money, as "the dinner committee evasion is illegal and will no longer be allowed."

The legislators proved that they meant what they had said when Brown proceeded. They withdrew funds, forcing him to vacate

The quick fox Brown jumped over the lazy dog.

quarters in Century City as his branch office in Los Angeles. In addition, they reduced his budget, which made him abolish one of the deputy secretary of state posts and several other jobs.

Another assault made by Brown worked indirectly toward the demise of President Richard Nixon. As noted earlier, the Secretary of State in California is responsible for administering the certification of notaries public. While conducting an investigation of one notary, attorney Frank DeMarco Jr., the staff discovered information that suggested the President of the United States had engaged in willful tax evasion. DeMarco, Nixon's tax lawyer, was found guilty in court of backdating the deed accompanying Nixon's gift of his vice-presidential papers to the National Archives that resulted in Nixon's being able to claim a half million dollar tax deduction. So strong were the suspicions of the President's guilt of tax fraud, that one of the five impeachment articles considered by the House of Representatives in the summer of 1974 was based directly on the evidence brought to public attention by Jerry Brown.

Brown ran a very large risk by attacking Nixon, a fact that is difficult to understand today. In early 1974 when the full Watergate story was beginning to unfold, the vast majority of the nation's people were still clinging to a belief that their President was incapable of such dishonesty. In point of fact, because of the almost irrational faith many people placed in this presidency, anyone who dared to attack the integrity of the nation's chief executive ran the risk of facing a backlash by the electorate. DeMarco therefore took to the media to brand Brown's action as "an obvious ploy" to gain votes. Never presenting evidence of his innocence on the charge brought against him by Brown except for a general denial of guilt, the tax lawyer's denunciation of Jerry fell largely on deaf ears.

Brown revoked DeMarco's notary powers because DeMarco had not reported the notarization of the deed correctly to Brown's office, and the state bar stripped DeMarco of his right to practice law. DeMarco, like so many others, miscalculated the strength of his opponent and misread the mood of the times. Jerry Brown as Mr. Clean Government emerged with another victory, and the

President of the United States moved a step closer to his political end.

In the meantime other events were working to change the political climate. During the four years (1971-75) that Brown undertook his one-man crusade against private and public malfeasance the public witnessed a string of events unparalleled in American history. A Vice President of the United States would be convicted of income tax evasion. The President would become embroiled in other activities that threatened the public operations of the Republic. The contrast between the affairs in Washington and the actions of the Sacramento "kid" could only serve to endear Brown more and more to the public. Against the darkness of corruption, the image of purity represented by this former Jesuit seminarian turned governmental guardian could not miss being noted by the public. Jerry Brown was a new breed politician whose time had come.

Brown was among the early political figures to speak out forcefully for the impeachment of Richard Nixon. At an impeachment rally in early December 1973, Jerry remarked, "I don't think this country can hang together, can stand together, as long as Richard Nixon stays in the White House. I really don't believe we can ask the people at the bottom of the economic ladder to obey the law when people at the top violate it with impunity." Later in charging that Nixon had spoken untruthfully about the conduct of the war in southeast Asia, Brown showed his utter contempt for liars and lying, "I don't like lying under any circumstances. If we go back to our natural law, that's got to be one of the easy ones. You don't lie. Once you lie, you break the trust, you break the connection. Then there is no trust, there is no security, and how can you operate? It breaks down the whole basis of relationship."

The electoral process in California also greatly contributed to Brown's image as Mr. Clean Government. His involvement in attacking some ballot measures and supporting another provided

Brown with his greatest public exposure. The initiative process, which is widely used in California, allows direct public participation in the creation of laws. The process represents an important avenue by which legislation can be enacted that might otherwise not be passed by the Legislature. However, problems exist with regard to such populist lawmaking. A constant hazard is demagoguery. Misrepresentation has become a major possibility in any initiative election. Often Californians muse at election time about the fact that they do not always know precisely how to vote because sometimes a Yes vote means No to the proposition or the other way around. As Secretary of State, Brown sought to minimize this type of misrepresentation and confusion.

Previous secretaries of state paid scant attention to such fundamental electoral issues as the proper procurement of legitimate petition signatures on measures seeking qualification for the ballot or the submission of fraudulent ballot arguments. This fact made Jerry Brown's actions take on special significance. When he laid down the law demanding honesty in these realms, it understandably came as a major surprise. In fact, the zealousness with which Brown pursued this end caught the advocates of two different propositions so off guard that they were forced to watch their measures go down to defeat because of the Secretary's action.

Proposition 8 on the November 1972 ballot was a measure written with the help of a major oil company and was designed to produce a substantial tax break for that firm. Obviously a proposal that would shift a greater proportion of the tax burden onto the general public would gain very little voter support. Therefore proponents of the proposition were charged with clouding its true effects. Ordinarily this type of deception is restricted to media campaigns, but the Proposition 8 people took their cause a fateful step further by attempting to employ an official state election publication as a vehicle for promotion.

When measures are submitted to the Secretary of State for inclusion on the ballot, favorable and unfavorable arguments written by opposing forces are also delivered. These arguments are printed before each election and forwarded to every registered voter along with a sample ballot. It was this publication that the promoters of Proposition 8 attempted to employ for their own purposes, thus depriving the public of an opportunity to determine rationally its voting preference.

Fortunately for the people of California this tactic failed. In routinely performing the task of preparing the ballot summary publication, the Brown staff unearthed evidence seemingly indicating that the arguments written both in support of and against Proposition 8 had been authored by the same source. Noting that both statements had been typed on the same machine, Brown took swift action. On August 20, 1972 the Secretary of State officially withdrew the negative argument that he termed "phony" and said he would have two Democratic assemblymen draw up a true one. Invoking powers never before used, Brown ordered the removal of the questionable statement with a comment that "we have a group of people who were trying to put something over on the people by writing a phony argument to get a tax break." The Secretary angrily continued that "all I can do is to reject the phony argument and bring the fact out to the public." The louder those responsible for the "phony" argument shouted that the Secretary of State had no business taking such action, the more public sentiment turned toward the Brown position. Jerry's public pronouncements contributed importantly to the crushing defeat of the measure, and Mr. Clean Government gained additional political mileage.

The second issue on the November 1972 general election ballot to be criticized by the uncompromising Secretary of State was Proposition 22. This was an initiative sponsored by the state's strong agribusiness interests and supported by the Republican leadership. The measure was designed to dilute the unionization efforts by Cesar Chavez and the United Farm Workers by forcing open-shop conditions to prevail throughout the state's rich agricultural sections. Although Brown philosophically opposed the intent of this measure, his official intercession into the fray was grounded on matters relating to electoral mechanics rather than moral substance. In this case signature procurement in qualifying the initiative for the ballot served as the crux of the ensuing battle.

Less than two months before the general election of 1972, Brown called a news conference to make a characteristically unexpected announcement. Speaking to a conclave of capitol correspondents the Secretary stated that he had taken action to disqualify Proposition 22 because many signatures on the initiative petition were "unlawfully obtained by means of fraud unprecedented in the history of California." Jerry said that more than 63,000 signatures, enough to disqualify the ballot proposition, were "obtained as a result of fraudulent and misleading presentations made to the signers." In talking with the reporters, a Brown aide spelled out the specific charges, "We have uncovered evidence that supporters of Proposition 22 misrepresented the initiative while circulating petitions to place it on the ballot [by stating it would protect the farm workers' right to organize unions], concealed the Attorney General's official summary of the measure and even forged signatures on the petitions."

On September 14, Brown officially set the wheels in motion to remove the initiative from the November ballot. A pioneering action of this type for any California Secretary of State, the resulting publicity surrounding Brown's court actions served to destroy effectively any hope of the measure's electoral success.

In a state where agribusiness interests play a strong role in politics, this issue might have gone either way before Brown's actions. The agricultural interests, however, underestimated Jerry's effect. As the Secretary aired his accusations, the agriculturists were convinced they could still pull off a victory if they could stall legal action to remove the measure until after the general election. Ted Hohn, the manager of the Central California Farmers Association, and others were successful in gaining the necessary support to halt judicial action temporarily.

The Attorney General and the Governor, both sympathetic to the proposal, worked to delay court adjudication. Despite the legitimacy of Brown's action, they both purposefully ignored requests for state-sponsored litigation against Proposition 22. Refusing to conduct even an investigation "without more specific evidence," the Secretary of State's motions were rejected out of hand. However, due to Brown's well-engineered appeals to the public, thousands of voters victimized by the illicit signature scheme began to turn against the behavior of the Attorney General and the Governor.

Governor Reagan attempted to hold back the tide of public rejection of this measure. At one of his weekly capitol news conferences, he blasted away at Brown in an effort to leave the impression that the Secretary of State's only concern was for his own aspirations. Reagan told reporters that "it seems to me that the whole fuss smacks very much of politics." When asked by reporters specifically if the entire issue were politically motivated, Reagan whimsically stated, "I don't know whether I should get into that or not. All I can say is that when you walk down the hall any more you really have to be careful not to bump into a candidate."

In addition to labeling Brown a political opportunist, Reagan took the occasion to criticize Jerry on the grounds of incompetence. The Governor contended that the job of Secretary of State entailed the checking of signatures before certifying them. "Suddenly now after validating all of these and approving them he discovered what he claims are evidences of fraud." To Reagan's mind, this simply was not logical.

Brown was not one to let such an accusation rest without a challenge. He responded that Reagan "obviously misunderstands that law regarding initiatives. . . . the governor's claim that my current investigation is an effort to influence voters is ridiculous." While it is easy to dispute the latter part of Jerry's reply, he was correct in contending that his actions followed the letter of the law. The Secretary's exercise of his powers in first accepting the petitions and then moving to decertify was correct and proper.

As the November election neared, neither Brown nor the agribusiness interests knew who would win. After months of public discussion, the negative publicity surrounding the signature procurement issue was obviously eroding much of the measure's early support. At the same time Brown could not force Reagan and Younger to pursue efforts to remove Proposition 22 from the ballot. On election day the voters defeated the proposition by a wide margin. Again, clean politics won largely because of one man—Jerry Brown.

Amid Brown's battles over Propisitions 8 and 22 and the

accompanying widespread publicity he gained, Bob Moretti, the Assembly speaker who would contest Jerry for the Democratic gubernatorial nomination in less than two years, made a sage observation about the Secretary of State. He commented, "Brown has taken the Secretary of State's office and made elections at least a visible issue. But he escapes negative publicity because he does not have to respond to issues on an across-the-board basis. He's got the best of both worlds. If the press asks him about school finance, he can say that's not in the scope of my responsibility and dodge the issue. It's a pretty nice place to be sitting."

Propositions 8 and 22 did not end Jerry Brown's crusade. While continuing to exert pressure on those responsible for wrong-doing, he also began an aggressive push toward fundamental campaign reform. Much of his remaining time as Secretary of State centered on the establishment of initiative legislation forcing such changes as requiring full funding disclosures. This position would add many California politicians to his list of adversaries.

Changing campaign disclosure regulations was perceived as an unforgivable sin by seasoned politicians and lobbyists. Liberals and conservatives alike shuddered as the crusading Jerry Brown attempted to fulfill this promise made to the voters—to strive for tighter regulation and public revelation of money flowing into the political coffers of candidates for elective office. Despite the outcries of many governmental officials throughout the state and the threats of some of them to resign if such a law passed, the time for this type of change had come.

While formulating a plan for attack on behalf of campaign reform legislation, Brown became acquainted with a new grass-roots citizens' group whose objectives closely paralleled his own. Ed and Joyce Koupel, founders of People's Lobby, a small organization of forthright nontraditional political zealots, originally had sent a copy of a proposed initiative to many political leaders including Brown. Upon receiving a copy of this document that eventually served as the basis for Proposition 9 on the 1974 ballot, the Secretary of State telephoned the Koupels, saying, "This is what I've been thinking about." After this initial contact was made, a number of meetings were arranged to draft a ballot proposal and plan the subsequent campaign. "We decided to work together," recalled Ed Koupel, "because Brown's people knew we could do it." An alliance born, Brown and the People's Lobby joined with the California branch of Common Cause, another citizens' organization, in an effort that would serve the objectives of cleaner government while adding to the Secretary's political fortunes.

Jerry Brown recognized that People's Lobby would play a fundamental role in assuring the passage of this initiative. The group represented the type of force that seems to emerge mainly during periods of great uncertainty or injustice in this nation. As a people's action organization working to force change in the society, its basis for power is not much different from that manifested earlier by the Grange and the Suffragettes. Reflecting beliefs held by a segment of the population, such populist movements serve as giant societal release valves—their actions relieve pressures by instituting change before major explosions occur. Coming on the heels of the Watergate affair, People's Lobby aimed at attaining more responsive and honest government.

Brown's alliance with People's Lobby unquestionably benefited the organization's cause as much as it provided the Secretary with more political attention. People's organizations generally rise outside the mainstream and seldom become blessed with strong supporters within government until their cause has virtually been won. Most politicians avoid populist movements that do not conform to the standards of normality in the body politic. Thus Brown's willingness not only to support the People's Lobby but also to work with it on developing this reform initiative legislation, which later was referred to as "largely a brainchild of [Jerry] Brown," served to create a formidable force.

The proposal that emerged sent shock waves throughout the state because of its many restrictions. First, the measure demanded identification of all contributions in excess of fifty dollars. Concealment of large donations under this law would become impossible. A second provision prohibited lobbyists from making contributions to persons running for elective offices. In addition, lobbyists and their employers would have to file with the Secretary of State detailed financial reports, which would be available to the public. Understandably this aspect of the measure received much flak from lobbyists attempting to influence decisions and from those elective officials reaping the benefits of the influence-brokering. Rather than permitting lobbyists opportunities to wine and dine elected legislators, purchase expensive presents for their relatives, or pay for travel junkets, the proposed initiative would force the amount of money to be spent by lobbyists on legislators to be lowered to the inconsequential level of ten dollars a month for each person. Brown often contended that "enough money for two hamburgers and a coke" should be sufficient if a lobbyist feels compelled to show gratitude to an official who listened to him.

Other provisions of Proposition 9 would require candidates for all state elective offices who spent more than two hundred dollars to file financial reports of all contributions and expenditures, plus a complete listing of all contributors and individuals to whom payments were made in excess of fifty dollars. The proposition would also create a fair political practices commission for monitoring, interpreting, and enforcement, and would require rotation of names on the ballot in various precincts. (Still another provision of Proposition 9 would place specific campaign expenditure limits—so many cents per voters—for candidates for statewide office. It ran afoul of a United States Supreme Court decision on protecting freedom of political expression and association.) These provisions would definitely alter the basic relations of elected officials and contributors, lobbyists, and the people.

As the primary election of 1974 approached, it often became difficult to separate Brown's bid for the Democratic nomination for Governor and his support for Proposition 9. While this intertwining forged some internal strife between Jerry and People's Lobby, it served to promote both causes. In asking the voters to "send a message to Sacramento that we are sick and tired of secrecy and millions of dollars" used to influence elected officials, Brown was able to force his major primary opponents into a showdown on a substantive issue. San Francisco's Mayor Joseph Alioto, despite the specter of malfeasance which lingered over his head after a major newsweekly published inflammatory articles suggesting corruption (he later won a suit against this publication), resolutely refused to endorse the measure. Bob Moretti, then Speaker of the Assembly, was too closely tied to the capitol political establishment to support actively the provisions of the initiative for fear of losing valuable contributions. Although he privately expressed agreement with its intent, he could not openly endorse this measure. As a result, the Speaker became a "silent fighter for it." Among the major candidates, only Jerry Brown publicly stood as the white knight come to slay the evil manifestations of corrupt practices and bloated corporate influences in political matters. Riding the crest of a Watergate backlash, the wave would push both Brown and Proposition 9, which Jerry called "the culmination of my four years as Secretary of State," to victory.

The June 1974 primary election marked the passage of Proposition 9, the nation's strongest political reform act. The overwhelming victory of a more than two-to-one margin gave Brown further credibility as a major political power. It also furnished the state with a statutory hedge against corruption, provided citizens with a feeling of strength, and gave some powerful groups a sinking feeling that their influence may have been sharply curtailed.

So it was that Jerry Brown ended his term as Secretary of State. There can be little question that Brown accomplished all that he promised the people. He was singularly responsible for turning a sleepy bureaucracy around and creating a strong regulatory agency. His resourcefulness gave him the necessary strength to fight corruptive forces as powerful as the President of the United States and to provide the people with a degree of added faith in their government. A new campaign practices and lobbying regulation law, defeat of those seeking to distort the initiative electoral process, and insuring the right to vote for college students within their own academic communities were among his achievements. When compared to the activities of his immediate predecessors, Brown could justifiably look back on these four years with much pride.

But the story of Jerry Brown's four-year tenure cannot end with an assessment of his accomplishments in that office. His actions were also undeniably linked to personal political aspirations as well as to service to the people. We next examine his pursuit of the governorship in the closing period of his time as Secretary of State.

Chapter Five

The Anti-politician Wins the Governorship

From the day Jerry Brown took office as Secretary of State speculation was common about his gubernatorial aspirations. The son of a well-liked former governor and the only Democratic candidate to win his statewide bid for a state office in 1970, Jerry Brown was in an enviable position. A respected name combined with a political platform, he was viewed as the Democratic frontrunner in a California Poll conducted by the Mervin Field's organization more than a half year before the primary election of June 1974. With change in the political environment emanating from the Watergate revelations and with the establishment of a strong reputation as a corruption fighter, the Secretary of State's political fortunes grew increasingly more substantial. Through his numerous actions Jerry Brown had become a popular champion to many people.

An early question asked about Brown's candidacy for Governor was whether he could avoid making a serious campaign mistake and see his lead disintegrate. Some of his opponents felt his lack of widespread political experience would do him in. Up to the time of this race Jerry Brown had benefited greatly from his father's name and popularity. Now as a political figure in his own right, Jerry was obliged to stand or fall—to a greater extent—on his own strength. In so doing, he had to enter into a gubernatorial contest in which political adversaries outnumbered friends. Democrats and Republicans were both generally united in their dislike for the crusading Brown. In enforcing election procedures Brown had understandably alienated many politicians. Therefore, he faced a determined opposition party and an indifferent Democratic organization. For all his positive assets his lack of a strong political alliance with the political establishment seemed to dilute his perceived strength as a gubernatorial candidate. Actually he turned his stance of independence into an advantage.

Jerry Brown's general inexperience and somewhat aloof personality further conspired in the eyes of some observers to countermand his accomplishments. These cynics thought he had flaws in his personal makeup and that his unorthodox behavior also would weaken him politically. They felt that he did not have the personal attributes necessary to be a successful politician in a major political fight. In essence, many seasoned politicians grossly underestimated Brown's real capabilities.

Brown's announcement of his candidacy for Governor, despite four years of accomplishments and increased visibility, was also tempered with reservation and concern. His political popularity still largely untested, Brown would have to prove himself by jumping to the top elective state position in California. But he was ready for the challenge. Characteristically unconventional, his approach was dramatic and surprisingly effective. We will examine in this chapter how an anti-politician—in terms of his opposition to making many political promises and his attack on the existing political order—became Governor.

In addition to Brown's positive image as an anti-politician, the race for Governor also proved him to be a keenly astute politician, a master of the art of politics. As embodied in Brown, these phrases anti-politician and politician are not conflicting. Because of his unorthodox and uncompromising style, he is regarded as a different kind of public personality. Yet he is also a seeker of upward political mobility and thus is willing to employ certain conventional political methods such as rallies and hand shaking to achieve his goals. He strives for moral ends while sometimes employing tough methods. He is able to play political hard ball.

In the gubernatorial race Brown's campaign efforts were dominated by two strategies. The first was a continuation of his advocacy of cleaning up the state's political process. This could be accomplished in part by the passage of Proposition 9 at the same election when the Democratic and Republican nominees for Governor would be chosen. Some of Brown's opposition contended that this was a straw-man issue, an empty proposal much in the manner of a figure fashioned from straw standing in an open field to scare birds because of their fear of the seemingly threatening specter.

But this issue was not a straw man. Artie Samish, state lobbyist extraordinaire, had openly boasted of his control of the Legislature to a magazine writer in the 1950s and thereafter more and more money was poured into the campaigns of candidates and initiative measures with only a modicum of required reporting. On the other hand, on a comparative basis, the government of this state had been ranked in recent years among the best (sometimes first), and no major scandals had erupted at the state level of government. However, the possible transgression of one state politician—a Republican gubernatorial candidate— became formalized two months before the primary when he was charged with perjury.

Notwithstanding these differing appraisals, Jerry Brown was able to turn public attention to the subject of corruption. Many voters thus decided there was a need for sweeping reorganization, including a new face in the Governor's office, one not belonging to a veteran politician. Brown created the impression of possible vast public malfeasance in California at a time when the American public in general was becoming increasingly agitated by the revelations surrounding the presidency. Jerry sensed Californians' unrest over Watergate and made various broad intimations about political corruption in the state without substantial proof.

Bob Moretti, who was a candidate against Brown for the Democratic nomination for Governor, was painfully aware of the effectiveness of this tactic. At the end of the primary race he said, "I don't know that I could have done what Jerry did and felt honest about it. What he did to some extent was to build a straw man that didn't exist. The state of California is not corrupt." Of course, this type of protestation by Moretti was written off by some voters because he was part of the political establishment that Brown felt needed to be changed.

The second tactic Brown commonly employed was to use abstractions skillfully so as to avoid being pinned down to specifics on particular issues. Grand phrases and little substance became his method of campaign operations. Contending that he was "not part of the old locker room crowd in Sacramento," he promised a new spirit in government. Speaking from his Olympian heights, the former Jesuit seminarian interwove political philosophy with the absurdities of the universe and produced a vaguely-worded campaign. He consistently did not articulate clearly defined alternative programs and refused to make any promises he might not be able to fulfill. Stated simply, specific plans and programs had no place in his campaign. Brown took stands on some issues but did not talk about development of programs.

Jerry's elusiveness was most difficult for bare-knuckled politicians like his major Democratic foes Bob Moretti and Joseph Alioto to confront. Brown's great popularity in the primary seemed to be inconsistent with the state's political history of the twentieth century. This has not usually been a state where strictly philosophical campaigns could match the power of programmatic commitments. California has generally been a program-oriented government in which the people have placed considerable trust in their elected officials. However, suddenly this environment began to deteriorate. Veteran public officeholders Moretti and Joseph Alioto obviously marched to a different beat than Brown. As they soon discovered, only Jerry's cadence was in time with that of the necessary number of voters.

In addition to misreading the political environment, Brown's Democratic challengers joined the ranks of those who have greatly underestimated the capacity and political acumen of their young opponent. "They thought he'd fade as soon as he's out in public," Pat Brown has concluded. "I think they thought he was some kind of gimmick boy, but they were wrong. He amazes me. His knowledge . . . is superb." Pat was not alone in this assessment of Jerry's full potential. Among others Charles Manatt, chairman of the Democratic State Central Committee, judged the Secretary of State as "very smart politically. He has a real sense for the jugular." Jerry had learned many lessons about the strengths and weaknesses of the traditional political game while living in his father's house. Early exposure to the giant gaming table of power provided Jerry Brown with the insights necessary to pass go and to win political victories. Grabbing political properties like Monopoly players might bid on Boardwalk or the B&O Railroad, the Secretary of State far outdistanced his primary election opponents in the public opinion polls with every throw of the dice. The old-boy politicians were no match for the "governor's son" and his able staff.

The primary saw Jerry Brown pitted against two well-seasoned and politically-wise public officials—Bob Moretti and Joseph Alioto. Unlike Brown, each had a significant power base, although of limited geographical area, that included union, party, and minority group organizations. Bob Moretti, the hardhitting Speaker of the state Assembly, the larger of the two state legislative houses, was initially judged to be the Secretary's primary rival. Energetic and forthright, Moretti was believed by many early political observers to be the odds-on favorite if Brown should falter. San Francisco Mayor Joseph Alioto, who was also a prominent attorney, emerged from the pack of other candidates as the second major contender in the primary. Charismatic, wealthy, erudite, and stylish, Alioto's strong cosmopolitan outlook provided the people with a third alternative as the campaign moved on. In spite of Brown's frontrunning status in the opinion polls throughout the primary campaign, these two men proved to be formidable opponents.

The approach Bob Moretti took was fairly typical. He sought to portray Brown as lacking the same high qualities Moretti embodied. Citing experience, maturity, and ability to work with the Legislature as the basic criteria for selecting a good governor, the Speaker hoped to enhance his own appeal while causing people to appraise Brown as a person unworthy of their support.

In this quest the generally astute Moretti realized that his task would not be simple. He is a very capable politician though somewhat dogmatic and abrasive in his manner. His many qualifications to be the state's chief executive were impressive. However, notwithstanding his record and knowledge of numerous issues, the Speaker could not shake the yoke of being in a position of high and long standing in the governmental establishment and being an important member of the old politics.

In Moretti's own campaign platform, he focused on items like welfare, education, and governmental spending. Unfortunately for him these issues proved to be out of touch with the perceived needs of the times. His campaign was based on programs in a year when fundamental assumptions about the role of government at all levels were being questioned. As the leader in the passage of major liberal Democratic-sponsored laws during the conservative Reagan administration, Moretti's preoccupation with the practical precluded consideration of such vagaries as philosophies of government. The Speaker had a proven record of competence as a legislative power and possessed great promise as a governor, but he was not attuned to the contemporary mood of the voters.

Some of the Assembly Speaker's personal attributes also reduced much of his potential electoral appeal. In an age when electronic media serve well those with photogenic features,

Moretti sometimes looked on television and in news pictures like a "tough guy" movie character. His image of toughness was reenforced by his aggressive methods as the leader of the legislative house over which he presided. There he had been hard driving and concerned with party discipline to gain approval of important legislation. In the era of the anti-politician, Moretti was viewed by many as an old-style, hard-line political figure.

In comparison to the resilient pragmatism of Moretti and the generalities and abstractions of Brown, Joseph Alioto appeared as an urbane, bright, and witty elder statesman. A symbol of the cosmopolitism of San Francisco, he was equally at ease at formal dinner parties or at union negotiating tables. Immensely popular in his home city, Alioto was plagued with problems ranging from discord with his wife Angelica, who made a number of biting statements and moved from the family home, to unproven charges of corruption—principally in *Look* magazine. These factors weakened his political potency by casting him into the role of a traditional politician with a set of tired alliances. In view of the growing revelations about Watergate, such difficulties became definite handicaps.

These disadvantages did not curtail Alioto's efforts to run an aggressive campaign. Calling attention to his strength while casting aspersions on Brown's campaigning, he made his service as a strong and able local executive serve as the focal point of his appeal for votes. In many ways his efforts paralleled Moretti's. As a public official friendly to labor's cause, Alioto attempted to gain his greatest support from the "ordinary working man," a group many thought was beyond the electoral reach of the intellectual Brown. Alioto, like Moretti, was strongly oriented to advocacy of public programs, particularly law and order, in a time of considerable distrust of government.

Brown, Moretti, and Alioto, the three main Democratic gubernatorial contenders, fought the June primary contest with the respective images of Mr. Clean Government, Mr. Legislator, and Mr. Cosmopolitan Working Man's Friend. Regardless of the potential for controversy and loud clamor, the sounds coming from this campaign were strangely muffled. The race simply did not capture the imagination of the public, in part because of many people's contemporary revulsion of "Watergate-type" revelations. The political wrangling was so lackluster in tone that only a handful of events emerged to cause even mild excitement. The Brown-Moretti debates ranked first on this list.

Direct face-to-face oral argumentation is sometimes part of political discourse in America. Such was the case in the 1974 gubernatorial race in California when Brown and Moretti squared off (without Alioto) in two debates. The first Moretti-Brown confrontation was predominantly an ordinary affair that more clearly demonstrated the difference in their styles than disagreement on substantive issues. In late May at a California State University, Fresno, meeting of the two candidates, students and faculty were given the opportunity to observe the very distinct political styles of these two opponents. Anti-politician Brown was stiff and ill at ease while "Sacramento locker room" member Moretti moved casually with simple grace.

The differences in style and policy emphasis were wide. Moretti, with coat off and shirt sleeves rolled up, informally addressed the crowd, using simple, earthy language to articulate liberal policy positions in their traditional framework. On the other hand, the former seminarian, formal in speech and dress, discussed the issues in a somewhat stodgy manner. Brown looked more like an insurance agent or a stock broker in his pin-stripped suit than a counter-cultural political figure. Wearing suits—which is Brown's usual public attire—tones down his youthful appearance. He was only thirty-six at this point on the campaign trail for the governorship but looked younger.

The substantive content of the debate was thin. Brown lambasted the Legislature as inactive and called for a "new spirit in Sacramento." Telling a fairly responsive crowd that the "public spirit and public confidence must be revitalized," he explained that this "is why I have laid such a heavy emphasis on cleaning up the political process." In addressing such vague issues, Brown suggested that he alone would be able to breathe new life into the inefficiency of executive branch bureaucracies. As to qualifications, he cited his record as Secretary of State and his support of a long list of liberal causes such as support of minorities and farm workers.

Moretti similarly referred to himself as a paragon of honesty, a defender of liberalism, and an able public servant. As an individual skilled in the legislative process, his goal as a chief executive did not rest with changing the character of the governorship but with creating a positive governmental environment where laws highly beneficial to the people of the state could be enacted. Moretti stressed the need for cooperation between the Governor and the Legislature, for instance, and condemned Brown's propensity to work unilaterally.

Two days later a second and much different set of polemics ensued that provided an extensive audience with a different kind of visual perception of candidates Brown and Moretti. In an effort to force the frontrunner to face the people directly on the issues rather than to deal in generalities and abstractions, the Speaker inflicted a major wound on his own effort. Moretti, appearing at a scheduled Brown news conference in Sacramento to try to force an impromptu debate, succeeded in his objective with an assist from the press corps. "Have a debate now," the reporters yelled. "Talk out your differences. Where do you differ? Talk on the issues. Let's have your debate." Trapped by the circumstances, Brown agreed to the debate before 100 news correspondents and many rolling cameras. For once in this campaign, newspaper reporters set the agenda and Brown was in a situation that he did not control.

Stomping his foot and acting more like a child than a gubernatorial candidate, Moretti accused Brown of being naive and inexperienced in terms of human suffering. "The amount of information you know about things around here could be written on the head of a needle," stated the Speaker in a curt tone that projected the "tough guy" image he had tried to escape. In a tirade unbecoming a person of power, the irritated Moretti continued by saying that "I just think that the real difference between us is that I have lived in the real world and Jerry has lived in a very protective kind of world. He doesn't know what it is like to try to support a family, to be flat broke, to try to pay medical bills from week to week, from check to check." In responding to these charges, Brown showed considerable maturity and poise and a real sensitivity to the issues being presented. "I identify with those people whose struggles are greater than yours or mine." Recalling his days of "marching along dusty highways" with the farm workers, Brown turned to Moretti and stated, "I didn't see you there."

Slightly shaken by Brown's skillful and insightful retort, Moretti continued his wrangling. After the personal attack failed to place Brown clearly on the defensive, the Speaker turned to the Secretary's position on Proposition 9 that, among other things, limited the amount of money a lobbyist could spend in influencing a governmental official. "Jerry, you must be a man of very little security if you think that because someone buys you dinner he owns you. You must not have much confidence in your own strengths and your ability and your honesty," Moretti snapped. Here, too, Brown met a strong accusation with simple candor. "Maybe we do have a difference here. I think a system that permits millions of dollas a year to be spent on wining and dining elected officials is wrong. . . . It is a form of political payola." Like a skilled swordsman, Brown managed to turn the attacks around by again relying on his oft-repeated message that "those who serve should act as servants and not as some kind of special, favored people."

Brown artistically defended himself and placed Moretti in the role of advocate of the "wicked" status quo. The Speaker not only lost points on important issues but also had his personal image damaged. A Brown staff member later said that Moretti's actions were a blessing in disguise for Brown because "that confrontation showed Moretti for what he is—a bully." Brown obviously came out the victor in a session he had not anticipated, and Moretti suffered in the eyes of the electorate for allowing his emotions to prevail.

Meanwhile Joseph Alioto was no doubt delighted by the turn of events. He hoped to embarrass Brown into a formal debate where Alioto felt he would hold the upper hand. Calling the Brown-Moretti news conference debate "unseemingly adolescent behavior," Alioto formally challenged the Secretary of State to a debate that would dignify the high office of Governor. Alioto attempted to paint Brown's portrait as a child afraid to meet face-to-face "because I would ask tough questions." In making such charges, the Mayor expected to gain political advantage. In the event that Brown would accept the invitation, Alioto was convinced he would outdazzle Brown. On the other hand, if Jerry refused, Alioto would claim that the Secretary had been preaching open government while practicing the opposite.

The answer Alioto received produced neither result. Tom Quinn of Brown's staff announced that the Secretary of State not only refused to debate on Alioto's terms, but also would cancel the tentatively planned television debate scheduled for immediately before the primary election. Brown's reason for making such a move was that any such activity in light of the Moretti news conference intrusion would be "unseemingly unproductive." Speaking for the Secretary, Quinn stated that "Bob Moretti conducted himself like a child . . . I think it's demeaning to everyone who particpates in a table-pounding screaming confrontation like that. It's demeaning to us all." During the course of this same news briefing, Quinn also contended that a debate with Alioto was out of the question because of the San Francisco Mayor's unpredictable and volatile nature. In the name of party unity, as well as because of Brown's apparent lead for the nomination, the debate was cancelled.

The position taken by the Brown campaign team was not without considerable risk. Indeed, this stance might well have been regarded as a lack of openness. However, the refusal to debate had two important advantages. First, these attacks helped to implant an impression that his two opponents were weak. Second, it served to shield Brown from public scrutiny that could erode his lead in the polls. The decision to take a calculated risk by refusing to debate was made after serious consideration of alternatives.

Naturally neither of Brown's principal challengers greeted this decision with delight. Alioto in particular reacted strongly to Brown's decision. Piqued by Jerry's move, Alioto told news reporters that "I think it shows who is running an open campaign and who isn't. . . . and I think that Mr. Brown wants to continue his campaign out of a closet." "Closet" is a common term used to describe any homosexual who conceals his or her sexual preference, and many people took Alioto's statement to imply that Jerry Brown had such a sexual preference. Despite Alioto's worldly sophistication, he later vehemently denied that he knew the term "closet" had this connotation.

The subject of homosexuality has come up time and again in relation to Brown; it is one of the most frequent questions asked of politicians and political writers and reporters about him. The topic therefore deserves consideration at this point. Brown's ascetic and private life style, plus his bachelorhood in his mid-thirties when running for Governor (and still his status today), make him a target for this kind of rumor. No proof has ever been offered that the accusation is true, and none of his opponents ever goes beyond the stage of innuendo to make a direct charge.

Connie Chung, an anchorperson for Los Angeles television station KNXT, has reported that Jerry has told her that he is not a homosexual. "It titilates people," Brown said to her, "to talk about sex and public officials. The subject is not relevant to me." To another interviewer, Brown responded, "Homosexual innuendo is a cheap shot that could be used against any politician. It's like Red-baiting in the fifties. Now I'm accused of running around the state with too many women. You're damned if you do and damned if you don't". And in a further instance, in commenting about the demands a political career makes on a person, Jerry remarked, "I think the job's breakneck pace is incompatible with marriage. For two people to be together constantly takes a lot of consideration and attention. I don't have the time right now."

Jerry Brown has dated numerous women, including show business personalities Candice Bergen, Natalie Wood (before her remarriage to Robert Wagner), Liv Ullman, and Linda Ronstadt (still a current interest), journal columnist Shana Alexander, and various people not in the limelight. He stays clear of political women, noting "I like women who are intelligent and sensitive and not taken up with all the technical distractions [like precinct lists and poll findings]. The more you are able to cope with your own reality, your own life, the more you're able to share with somebody else. Then love is more accessible and available." Brown naturally dislikes discussing the topic of homosexuality. As a magazine writer has well said, "It's a vicious little non-issue."

A whispering campaign about Brown's alleged homosexuality— a frequent technique employed against bachelor candidates—was already under way before Alioto's "closet" statement was issued. As a protection to Brown, two of his political strategists did thorough research into the backgrounds of his two principal primary opponents Alioto and Moretti. According to political writer Richard Reeves, a strong eastern-based critic of Brown, Tom Quinn, Jerry's campaign manager, told Reeves that after the compilation had been completed, "I informed Moretti and Alioto that if they tried anything we'd let this stuff go." Moretti's campaign manager confirmed to Reeves that he had received telephone calls from Quinn telling him to be careful because "Quinn claimed he had stuff that could destroy Bob's life."

According to Tom Quinn, Pat Brown did not play a major part in his son's campaign for Governor but functioned chiefly as a good-will ambassador. Pat helped by raising some campaign money although he has never relished doing this. Jerry was at the point where he wished to exercise considerable independence from his father. Early in the contest for Governor, Jerry said, "I am running on my own record. I am running on what I've done and what I've been. . . . The fact that my father was Governor, I don't think makes any more difference than the fact that Teddy Kennedy was running for Senator when his brother was President. . . . What difference does that make? I'm the one that is going to have to make the decisions."

Pat Brown's good name throughout the country was partially responsible for the race gaining so much national media attention. However, like a number of local commentators, some of these observers tended also to ignore or downplay the considerable strengths of Jerry Brown on his own. Nationally-syndicated columnists Rowland Evans and Robert Novak wrote a typical appraisal only a few days before the primary election. "The reason for the largely unspoken Democratic self-doubt is that young Brown scarcely seems the ideal candidate to cash in on those Republican weaknesses [of Watergate and the economy]. What's more, this self-styled 'reformist's' campaign may be a basic misreading of the public mood. Indeed, California is a warning beacon that Democrats have forgotten the lessons of the 1972 McGovern debacle and are drawing the wrong conclusions on Watergate." Contrary to this assessment, the warning beacon was telling the opposite story—Brown had read the public's mood correctly and would be the winner in both the gubernatorial race and the California presidential primary two years hence. Numerous commentators and political leaders did not accurately read the voters' sentiments. The conclusions they drew were unrealistic. The people through their ballots would prove this point to be true.

The opinion polls consistently showed that Brown had statewide voter strength, while Alioto's was chiefly confined to northern California and Moretti's was limited mainly to southern California. Despite the fact that Moretti had successfully fought on a statewide basis Governor Ronald Reagan's recent tax-limit initiative, Moretti's longtime base of electoral support was confined to one of eighty Assembly districts. Similarly, Alioto was primarily known as the Mayor of San Francisco, California's third most populous city but occupying only a small portion of the state's total territory. In contrast, Brown had been elected by the statewide voters to an office from which he had derived considerable and geographically widespread publicity.

June 5 marked the end of the 1974 primary election. Despite a low voter turnout Jerry Brown was projected to be the clear winner soon after the official balloting ended. When all the votes were tallied, Brown's victory was of considerable proportions. The Democratic nominee received more votes (38 percent) than the combined totals of Joseph Alioto (19 percent) and Bob Moretti (17 percent). The meaning of the election was summarized by Moretti, "Jerry just had the issues that people wanted to hear about this year, this business about changing government. Nixon and the Watergate thing made people suspicious of government." Obviously Brown had been the only Democratic candidate astute enough to recognize the depths of public discontent. The first hurdle to the governorship had been overcome. The victorious Mr. Clean Government was ready to test his skills against a Republican foe.

The political environment faced by Jerry Brown as he prepared for the general election ran parallel in many ways to that in which his father had operated in 1958 in his first bid to be Governor. In both cases, the Republican party was in the midst of struggles that weakened its organizational effectiveness and unity. In 1958 the aspirations of then United States Senator William Knowland to become Governor without regard for the wishes of the incumbent Republican officeholder Goodwin Knight to seek reelection caused a bitter split in the party. It opened the door for Pat Brown to be the first Democrat elected Governor in twenty years. At the time of the 1974 general election the Grand Old Party was again deeply divided and decidedly shaken by the events surrounding the Nixon resignation.

Other similarities existed in the two elections. Neither Pat nor Jerry was received with great enthusiasm immediately upon nomination by many leaders and campaign workers within their own party. However, while these people did not regard them as the ideal candidates, both father and son did obtain strong party and labor support as the general election campaign gained momentum. Also, both men had solid liberal records. Finally, the 1974 election for Governor was the first since that of 1958 in which no incumbent of either major party was in the contest.

On the Republican side, Houston (Hugh) Flournoy, the State Controller and former state legislator and professor of political science, also had won his party's nomination by an overwhelming margin. He acquired 63 percent to 30 percent for Ed Reinecke, his nearest opponent. However, Flournoy, an articulate, easy-going and handsome man, suffered from the same lack of party support initially felt by Brown. Flournoy simply was not the first choice among party regulars, yet he was their nominee. In fact, his emergence at the top of the Republican ticket came as a result of political default rather than from the type of aggressive campaigning witnessed in the Democratic race.

Two of Flournoy's major competitors were victimized by the malfeasance of the Nixon administration. Robert Finch who had been elected Lieutenant Governor in 1968 had resigned from this position to become Secretary of Health, Education and Welfare under Nixon. While not personally involved in any aspect of the Watergate scandals, Finch nevertheless became "tainted" by his association with that corrupt administration and dropped out of the race for Governor. Ed Reinecke, appointed to replace Finch as Lieutenant Governor and the personal choice of Ronald Reagan to be his successor, permitted party loyalty to outweigh his better judgment. Reinecke literally committed political suicide even though he continued his candidacy. He was indicted for perjury in an investigation relating to an International Telephone and Telegraph (ITT) contribution to the national Republican party. (Although later found guilty, Reinecke's conviction was then overturned on a legal technicality). Attorney General Evelle Younger talked about running but decided to wait for another time. That time proved to be 1978.

As a consequence of these events, Hugh Flournoy became the only viable Republican candidate, thereby winning the party nomination virtually by the abdication and defection of others. Flournoy, only eight years older than Brown, then proceeded to wage a campaign that almost ended with a surprise victory in November.

Flournoy's style was much different than those manifested by Brown's major opponents in the Democratic primary. A courteous individual, he struck from his speeches words that might offend. He was well respected by the press corps as a knowledgeable, warm, and friendly human being. He portrayed himself as a family man, with an attractive wife and three children, as a contrast to bachelor Brown and said he knew more about state government and would run it more rationally. He spoke of himself as a person of superior character—with the precise meaning of the phrase never explained—in an apparent effort to show that it was a politician's character, as in the case of Nixon, and not his ideas about which the electorate should be concerned. But he did have problems. A compulsive intellectual, he would sometimes complicate answers to simple questions with complex scholarly reasoning. This propensity, plus his unexciting speeches, lessened his appeal with some voters. He also lacked the instant name recognition of Brown.

Jerry's own inability to come across as a warm human being helped to counterbalance Flournoy's weaknesses. A chronic problem faced by Brown throughout his term as Secretary of State and well into this campaign was an image of aloofness, detachment, and lack of humor. Both media and political detractors tended to latch on to this apparent inability to function easily in the secular world. In suggesting the depth of this perceived "coldness," a fellow Democrat commented that "it makes me wonder how Jerry will react in terms of welfare mothers, of prison reform, of issues when it's not just theories but people that count." This stiffness, as much a function of Brown's cloistered existence as a probable reaction to his father's natural gregariousness, did not endear him to the electorate on a personal level.

As much as Brown's personality defied easy comprehension, so too did his positions on major issues often evade understanding by many people. To many voters the positions taken by young Brown appeared inconsistent. It became very difficult for the public to relate calls for fiscal responsibility with traditional Democratic big-spending programs. Throughout the campaign Brown sided with fiscal conservatives in holding the line on spending while still maintaining strong liberal positions on some others. Voters more inclined to rely on party labels than specific programs presented by individual candidates unquestionably associated Brown with big-government spending programs despite his statements to the contrary.

The image of inconsistency by Brown was due to the voting public's inability to perceive correctly the full extent of his message. The voters failed to recognize that the Secretary of State had both liberal and conservative sides. He was liberal on issues such as collective bargaining for public employees, the decriminal-

The flying young man on the daring trapeze.

ization of marijuana, abolition of capital punishment, and laws regulating sexual behavior between consenting adults. On the other hand, his positions on crime and public finance were in the conservative mold.

Brown's visionary thrusts also did not help define him better as a political figure. He talked often about the need for new societal missions and yet busily ran a bureaucracy with strong administrative control. As an executive, he had shown much competence as well as flare and flamboyance. However, as an individual his personality invoked images of shyness, reserve, and cool detachment. In large part, it was then (and still is) difficult to assess this man on a human level. Is he a conservative or a liberal, a gentle or an arrogant human being? These were the type of questions that produced lingering doubts in the minds of many voters as the election neared.

The general-election campaign was lackluster. According to political reporter Richard Reeves, an uninteresting campaign is exactly what the Brown forces wanted. Reeves points out that Quinn, Brown's campaign manager, said, "We were ahead so we wanted a dull, dull, dull campaign. We wanted to avoid any discussion of substance. We found obscure, boring issues and talked about them. Jerry's real ideas were dangerous, but we were generally successful in avoiding them."

The critical factor in this election came not from these contenders themselves but from the political environment. Flournoy had the difficult task of coping with certain unprecedented events in Washington. The Nixon resignation near the beginning of the campaign coupled with his subsequent pardon by President Ford near the time of the November election placed Flournoy in the impossible position of condemning the actions of party leaders Nixon and Ford while attempting to maintain strong party ties. In a state with an overwhelmingly large proportion of voters registered as Democrats (although many are independent in their voting), Flournoy recognized that he could not afford to incur disassociation from many Republicans. Somehow, too, he needed to convert a large number of Democrats. The Republican nominee faced a very difficult situation.

On the other hand Brown was still enjoying the Promethian image of the giver of light in a period darkened by corruption. Riding a wave created by the Watergate affair and an economy in a depressed condition, the political environment seemed ready made for his easy ascendancy to the governorship. With his "new spirit" representing something different to many voters, apparently the only person capable of destroying Brown's dreams was the candidate himself. Jerry Brown did make the mistake of coasting too much on his lead; in addition, some voters continued to have doubts about him.

Brown was the aggressor, the governmental philosopher; Flournoy was the defender, the rebuilder of shattered Republican political bridges, and the teacher of government. The new spirit versus the old rationalism underscored the campaign between these two nontraditional candidates.

The best example of the pedestrian quality of this campaign is the televised debates that took place between these candidates near election time. They signed an agreement to limit their campaign spending to not more than $900,000 each; to engage in six debates or joint appearances, three to be televised on only one local station, one to be aired on the state educational network and the two others to be before a press club and on a campus; and to submit disagreements about these matters to arbitration. This provision was inserted in the agreement, "No other television or radio use of all or any part of the program may be made by any person, including a candidate or the station except for regular news coverage."

The debates were so well orchestrated that they gave the appearance of being rehearsed. A forensics instructor from University of California, Davis, described the first encounter in this manner: "Brown can punch. Flournoy can, and does, jab. Neither is a slugger. . . . Both are using an approach that is not only appropriate to their political situation but to their own personalities and communication styles." When translated in terms of Brown's natural aloofness and Flournoy's often academic and complex approach, the debates provided neither candidate with a clear victory nor the public much motivation to watch. The debates, like the campaign itself, were dull. Nevertheless, despite the lack of inspiration in the debates, they did articulate some of the major issues before the people of California.

The debates and other pronouncements by the two contenders revealed that they agreed on a number of substantive issues. President Ford's unconditional pardon of Richard Nixon met with instant condemnation from both of them. Their view on fiscal conservatism, crime in the streets, and various social welfare issues were practically identical. Philosophically, they both called for renewed faith in government and the need for society to reassess its basic value system.

Some issues did emerge in the debates and elsewhere on which the candidates differed. The use of marijuana provided such a distinction. Called the killer weed in the previous generation, the widescale use of marijuana had become a standard part of the youth culture. By the time of the 1974 election, its usage had spread from the university and college campuses into the homes of families in every geographical region and of every economic class. Notwithstanding its widespread employment, much resistance still existed in terms of efforts to legalize it. Flournoy assumed the long-held stance against the reduction of penalities for this "drug." Conversely, Brown, the younger of the two candidates, took the opposite stand. Without directly endorsing this product, Brown took a strong position for individuals to have the right to smoke marijuana without fear of suffering strong legal penalities. He said that marijuana laws that prescribed a sentence of "10 years for the possession of one marijuana cigarette to be ridiculous." Even a few years earlier such a position would have meant political death to its supporters, but in 1974 Brown's action added to his liberal credentials, especially among young people. Speaking primarily for a new generation of voters, Brown's support of limited decriminalization of marijuana helped to differentiate the two major finalists for the governorship.

The issue of capital punishment also provided a distinction. Jerry proclaimed, "I'm against it. I've been against it all my life. I'll be against it the rest of my life." Wisely understanding that the Governor cannot take unilateral action on such a matter, however,

Brown also promised to "review each case with a great sense of compassion and whenever possible, I will exercise the power of [executive] clemency. But to commit myself in advance on each and every case, I won't do that."

Flournoy took the contrary position. The State Controller advocated the death penalty as a rational deterrent to crime. To his mind, the morality of state executions was secondary to the expediency of crime prevention. He believed in restoration of the most severe punishment possible.

Attitudes about national economic policies furnished a further indication of the candidates' political differences. Running under the Democratic banner, Brown criticized the economic policies and programs of Presidents Nixon and Ford. Brown openly attempted to feed the fires of doubt regarding his opponent by linking him to the Nixon-Ford policies, thereby employing the tactic of guilt by association. Utilizing circular logic, Brown stated that the Republicans created the economic situation, Hugh Flournoy was a Republican, and therefore the depressed economy was at least partly caused by the policies and programs advocated by his opponent. Reagan and Nixon were the specters Brown brought forth to tie Flournoy to economic programs judged by Jerry to be ill conceived. This technique so irritated Flournoy that on one occasion, he informed an audience, "My name is Houston Flournoy. Houston Flournoy. I repeat my name because Jerry Brown seems to be running against Ronald Reagan and Richard Nixon." And indeed Brown was running against them.

Unfortunately for Flournoy, Brown was also running against Gerald Ford, the first person to become President by appointment. Not suspecting that the President might pardon the malfeasant Nixon, Flournoy had initially given Ford his unabashed support. Stating that Brown's approach was a "shoot-from-the-hips, headline-seeking style of campaign which put him out of step with the rest of the country," Flournoy reprimanded the Secretary of State for not rallying to the support of the nation's new President. "Democrats and Republicans are answering the President's call to an economic summit meeting. They are putting aside past differences in a common fight against inflation.

While Democratic leaders were working with the President, my opponent was busy criticizing what he called the Ford-Flournoy economic policy. He is condemning the President before he's even had a chance to make a mistake."

Within a short time Gerald Ford made what many people regarded as a big mistake by granting Nixon an unconditional pardon, thereby weakening the vote-getting ability of Flournoy and other Republican candidates. Hugh Flournoy's image had been tarnished by an event beyond his control, which made Brown's coat of integrity and clean government shine even brighter.

A political strategist of exceptional cunning, Brown kept associating Flournoy with the state and national administrations. He called Flournoy a "yes man" whose support for the Reagan-Nixon-Ford program was "disastrous." Another time Brown referred to Flournoy as a "passive, weak-kneed, sleepy administrator, a private Santa Claus for the special interests of this state." And Brown specified what he considered to be the central issue of the campaign, "This election is going to determine whether we put a new team in Sacramento or whether the disastrous fiscal and monetary policies that are creating hardships that are unparalleled since the depression will be allowed to continue."

The most important commitment Brown made in the general-election campaign was a promise of a "new spirit" in government. Many Californians obviously were dissatisfied with the old-line political standards, the malfeasance of certain officials, and the instability of the economy. As Secretary of State, Brown had accomplished all that he had promised and instilled faith that new directions could be taken by persons holding governmental power. By making the Secretary of State's office a viable agency, establishing increased credibility to the electoral process, and challenging political giants, more people gained greater confidence in his ability. While detractors were horrified by his actions as Secretary of State, these steps did indicate to many voters in the gubernatorial election that the promises of a new mission that had been made by Brown might be realized. With the turbulence of Watergate still very much an influence on the reasoning of many voters, Jerry's proven ability as Secretary of State to fight successfully against great odds and to attain cleaner government represented a decided asset for him.

Hugh Flournoy also gave the public a degree of reassurance. His attitude provided an aura of likeability unaccompanied by much emotional appeal. He was candid in his condemnation of Nixon and his disapproval of several Reagan decisions such as the veto of an important housing bill. Yet he maintained sincere loyalty to most Republican positions.

Some observers felt that Brown's approach might cost him this important victory. Youthful and often distant, Brown was occasionally depicted as a kid desiring another new toy. Although he had served in the executive branch for four years, Flournoy had been there for eight years plus six more in the Legislature. Brown's critics still accused him of being inexperienced and politically naive. Because of his repeated criticism of the existing political order and its way of playing the political game, some party regulars were unenthusiastic about and even hostile to Brown.

November 5, 1974 was the fateful day for Brown and Flournoy. Jerry had led the opinion polls throughout the general campaign, being ahead by as much as fourteen percentage points at one time, and the final pre-election results of the Field California Poll showed him to be eight percentage points in the lead. Brown had his own polls taken regularly.

After the first two hours of official tally counting in the lowest voter turnout in thirty years, Brown edged into the lead and won the governorship. He was the victor by a scant margin of 176,805 votes of a total of about 6 million ballots cast throughout the state. Brown won because of strong support in the state's most heavily populated county, Los Angeles, where he received 53 percent of the vote. The Democratic candidates for four of the other five statewide constitutional offices ran decidedly ahead of Brown, including state Senator Mervyn Dymally, a black who became Lieutenant Governor. Also, in the state vote totals, Democratic contenders for Congress, state Senate, and state Assembly far outdistanced Brown.

Jerry Brown became the third Democrat in the last thirty-six years and only the third in the twentieth century to be elected California's chief executive. His father had been the second of the three. (Moreover, Jerry and his father constituted only the second such combination—George Docking, the father, and Robert, the son, in Kansas were the first—to materialize in the present century.) It was the closest race for the governorship in California since 1920. Despite the narrowness of his victory, the Governor-elect recognized that the true test would come after assuming office. In electing Jerry Brown Governor, the people of California had indeed ushered in a new and unique era for state government.

Chapter Six

The Philosopher
Governor

The immediate aftermath of the gubernatorial election of 1974 was traditional. The victor expressed appreciation to supporters and breathed sighs of relief that his efforts had not been in vain. Meanwhile the loser gathered strength to soothe bruised egos and ruptured dreams. But it was the ritualistic wish of good luck and congratulations by the incumbent to his successor that signaled the end of one era and the beginning of another.

Ordinarily these meetings are marked by much verbiage and little substance. The exchange between Governor Ronald Reagan and the victorious Jerry Brown at a morning session was typical and good humored. Reagan offered his congratulations to which Brown replied that the "last eight years seemed to have served you [Reagan] well." However, as the two men posed for a barrage of flashing cameras and a few polite questions from only moderately inquisitive news personnel, what was superficially reported as political trivia actually revealed a basic part of Brown's political philosophy. With a touch of banter the outgoing governor asked, "I've been wondering what you are going to substitute for jelly beans," referring to his widely-known compulsion for eating these simple treats intermittently in the office. The Governor-elect smilingly retorted, "I've been trying to avoid hasty commitments. That decision will have to wait a few days." As flippant as this comment may have seemed, it actually reflected the basic character of the "new spirit" administration.

A close analysis of Brown's response provides real insight into the nature of this individual's personal view of power. The Governor-elect was not a person inclined to make decisions without first carefully thinking through the subjects. This fact was made abundantly clear before this November day had ended. After the social niceties were over, reporters pressed Brown about the nature of the specific programs he planned to initiate. The newly-elected chief executive simply answered, "I don't know. . . . They'll emerge." This was a phrase that would be repeated often during the early months of his administration.

This was generally a period nationally of a multitude of public programs, often labeled with catchy titles or slogans and aimed at dealing with every problem facing humankind from ending crime in the streets to destroying exotic insects. As a consequence, the lack of responsiveness of young Brown assuredly caught the general public and most seasoned correspondents off guard and brought forth many hours of speculation about the competence of the new governor. Was this a man ill prepared to make decisions? Or was he somehow profoundly in touch with the best roles of government and society? Was Brown a conservative, a liberal, or something yet undefined? Was he an eccentric, an old-style politician in fancy and well-tailored clothes, the incarnation of a political savior, or something else? Over time none of these questions has been easily answered.

To be sure, Jerry Brown was then and is still largely considered an enigma, a most unique creature in the political jungle. He has risen to prominence by means of using vague imagery to gain the support of the people of California. His only real commitment early in his administration was to let programs emerge—a promise so vague as to defy normal description but meaningful enough to bind millions into a mesmerizing adoration of his approach.

Jerry Brown is both an anti-politician and a consummate politician. He is an anti-politician in his rejection of the old political ways of doing things and of the sham, hypocrisy, and ritualism of the existing political establishment. But he is also a consummate politician in his ability to sense the wishes and attitudes of the people and to communicate with and influence them through his masterful use of the mass media.

Although Brown is a consummate politician of this time, he is somehow separate from it. He seems to be at once in touch with the real essence of the living body politic but intellectually and spiritually apart from it. Because of these dichotomies it seems appropriate to take a few steps back in time and look more closely at certain things that have served to create this aura. It is important to understand more about his philosophic background, as only through such analysis may the enigma be better understood. Not every philosophic base will be touched upon in this analysis nor will our interpretations of these philosophies be voluminous. However, greater insight about Brown may be derived through this presentation.

Why does Jerry Brown stand out as such a different type of chief executive when most governors perform the same official functions? In attempting to explain Brown's appeal, a common contention is that this is a man who accurately reflects the mood of a time of uncertainty; but then so do some other individuals who have yet to achieve even a fraction of the Governor's stature. Evidently this explanation does not satisfactorily answer the question at hand. It must be concluded, therefore, that other factors within the man himself have produced the differences. We believe philosophical influences have helped to mold his character and shape his thoughts.

The philosophic base on which Brown governs is so intrinsically part of his words, actions, and style that it is difficult to talk about one without the other. Part of the reason Jerry has been considered such an enigma is that he has not been afraid to expound those sometimes paradoxical philosophical strains that consciously and subliminally guide his actions. In so doing, he offers a fresh perspective to the people of California and the nation. His experiences as a child, a young man, and an inquisitive intellectual have all served to affect his personal means of operation. Brown, as a product of these experiences, reflects a type of high-minded wisdom not commonly seen in the political arena. Few political persons have been schooled in the art of governance from their early years; and far fewer have then ventured into a monastic world and returned to synthesize the practical with the transcendental. Specifically, we will concentrate on Brown as the rebel, the orthodox thinker, the mystic, and the practicalist.

When Brown speaks about the need for a "new spirit" or a "new mission" he is addressing the conscious concern of the rebel within him whose basic philosophic foundations are firmly grounded on change to improve a less than perfect present. His view of humanity as a brutish conglomeration of original sinners in need of salvation may be traced partly to strong orthodox Jesuit influences of his late teens and early twenties. The renunciation of basic Western assumptions and material motivations as a means of becoming more at one with the earth, the universe, and the essence of living stems most directly from his later interest in Zen and American counter-culturalism. (Zen is a school of thought that suggests enlightenment comes from self-contemplation and meditation, tied to specific physical practices.) Finally, his administrative theories spring from the childhood training as his father's son in the political arena's special schoolhouse where graduates are guaranteed knowledge not ordinarily given to the general citizenry. In analytically pursuing each of these major influences, we have sought to match together a sufficient number of pieces so that the puzzle of California's enigmatic governor may be better comprehended.

In both Jerry Brown's personal and political life he is a rebel. How can the Governor of the nation's largest state be considered in any way a rebel, one bent on the major change of what he oversees? The answer rests on how one defines what is revolutionary. For example, if the rebel is thought to be a force of destruction, then such a label is indeed inconsistent with what Brown has addressed. A rebellious soul, however, can also be an instrument of good. Much like the world's great architects, this kind of rebel has the ability to overcome obstacles placed in his path and build on an old foundation a new structure hopefully better constructed for human needs. This nation has had a long history of such political architects and spiritual leaders. California's Governor seems to be in this long line of individuals willing to place their careers on the line for needed change.

In light of Brown's personal view that this is a society in need of reevaluation, he must be regarded as a rebel. Individuals who question the basic assumptions of their society and actively seek to disengage it from the things they consider ugly, immoral, or merely inappropriate to the better interests of humankind generally place themselves outside the mainstream of the political arena.

On becoming such a rebel, they reach an almost metaphysical oneness with humankind by identifying with causes larger than themselves. In listening to Jerry's rhetorical pronouncements and observing his actions, one senses the kinship he feels with the universal. In repeated statements, the Governor has suggested that "I identify with those people whose struggles are greater than mine." His is a vision not based upon the utopian-type Camelot stimulated by many liberals preceeding him. Rather he is attempting to realign himself and those he serves with a life style that permits a closer association with the essence of being, the process of living.

Brown's new spirit of government is a reaffirmation of those things he perceives as basic to a living organic society. Whether Brown's efforts will have a long-lasting or profound effect cannot yet be determined, but his rebelliousness has at least temporarily bound many thousands of people to a common, yet largely undefined, vision. As California's political maestro continues to wave his baton, there is much to suggest that a deep rooted chord has been struck.

The great symphony conductor will venture beyond established musical paths and breathe new life into rousing choruses and converging and harmonious tones. To a large extent, the rebel must perform the same task by rejecting the norm and accepting the vibrations of a larger vision. Albert Camus, a modern political philosopher who has had an impact on Brown, defines such a rebellious spirit as being embodied by a "man who says no, but whose refusal does not imply a renunciation. He is also a man who says yes, from the moment he makes his first gesture of rebellion." Like the embattled servant whose thirst for freedom is quenched only when that last command is met with a negative response, does freedom then become real. In so doing, he strikes a blow not only for his own dignity as a human being but for all persons held in physical or psychological bondage. Just as Prometheus answered negatively to the oppressive edicts of Zeus by bringing fires to earth for the huddled masses, so too did he respond affirmatively to greater callings of a never quiet world. There is much of this rejector-accepter in Jerry Brown.

Brown's entire life has been a constant struggle of spurning and embracing. As a youth he entered the priesthood in a profound denial of the secular world of politics. In accepting what virtue he was able to absorb through the monastic life, Jerry reentered the world as student and later as lawyer and politician. Due largely to these roles, many critics have characterized the Governor as a child continuously looking for new and bigger playthings. However, this view is an oversimplification. In Jerry's seeming renunciation of every phase of his life, he is not childishly casting away the toys of life, but rather he is advancing to newer heights and accepting greater challenges.

The rebel who never stops striving for more knowledge cannot be considered a real danger, as one who is of this mind and spirit can only help to inspire others to follow suit. His is an acceptance of the fundamental premises that society can be made better, that certain cosmic forces bind all humanity together, and only through grander visions shared by the multitudes can the human race hope to achieve its full potential.

Not afraid to offer new and often radical ideas, as exemplified by his positions on the era of limits, the death penalty, farm worker rights, solar energy, space colonies, and other issues, California's enigmatic governor is providing an alternative. Whether his ideas will have a profound and lasting effect on the psyche of the people is important. So is the fact that he is undaunted in his effort to break new ground. Even a few years ago a politician willing to engage in such a public discourse would have surely had a short-lived career. This is a time, however, when many people are in search of a new image of governance. The vision painted by Brown provides something refreshing and potentially meaningful. Like Jerry, many have come to reject the promises of the Great Society of the 1960s and have in turn begun to seek a new awakening at least partially separate from government. The popularity of this governor suggests that he has developed a harmony with many citizens.

One of the major reasons for Brown's strength seems to rest on the manner in which his rebellious spirit emerges. This insurrection is void of bloodshed and tears, as it is a revolution of the mind. His new spirit is composed chiefly of ideas, questions, and process. Jerry Brown has not made the serious mistake of many other political personalities by assuming that humankind lives by bread alone and that government can only respond on this level. To the contrary, he believes that society should be structured in such a fashion as to permit the nourishing of the mind as well as of the body. Hunger and poverty are symptomatic of a society which refuses to address the whole person. Countless programs can be established to feed the less fortunate but without also nurturing the mind the vicious circle will remain unbroken. As the Governor of the nation's most populous state, Brown has attempted to employ his power and influence to address these fundamental concerns.

The development of a political will among the people—arriving at a public consensus—to cope with instability and even chaos is the ultimate goal of Brown's leadership. It is not surprising that among his heroes is Gandhi who also questioned the basic assumptions of his society and in so doing brought about the creation of a political will and a common mission among the people. He was able to build an idea into a force that could transform an entire society into something vital and dynamic. Brown is profoundly aware that "sometimes even the powerless has a power of its own. Who is it who took India? Some guy in his underwear. Gandhi seemed a pretty powerless character. And yet because of the idea and the moment he was able to galvanize millions of people. Power may be an idea, style, things we haven't thought of before."

This orientation toward a process is predicated not on the avoidance of conflict so much as it is in the evasion of programs designed without people in mind. "You don't have to do things. Maybe by avoiding doing things you accomplish quite a lot," Brown has said. Confrontation is not always necessary. Simple avoidance is sometimes a more adequate solution. The message to the people is clear. Reliance must come from within—the support one really needs to survive in this world cannot come from government alone but also is derived from a person's unity with self and all humankind—that is, one's ability to embrace life properly and to take responsibility for his or her own destiny. The major role of government rests on helping the individual find inner strength and permit all members of the society to co-exist optimally. "The answer in government always seems to be to add more. . . . I think that's wrong," Brown has suggested on numerous occasions.

For Brown government's role is to synthesize rather than to create, to slow down rather than to expand. Unlike many of his contemporaries, Brown does not see leadership as just passing laws. Leadership must come from other sources. While it is true that political powers that are granted can bind humankind by physical means, such legalistic muscles have little meaning in relation to the intellect or the soul. Unfortunately, this fact is too often forgotten. Basic questions are seldom asked and synthesis rarely achieved. In the busy day-to-day lives of elected officials, the easiest avenue has been the passage of yet another law to regulate this problem or create that program before needs are fully understood. Programs and legislative enactments mean nothing if the public will is not in agreement.

"The fascination with legislation as the big solution to everything is overplayed," Brown has frequently reminded other public officials in the state capitol. In taking a position not widely held by them, Brown suggests another alternative, "A person in a significant position of power can lead by the questions he raises and the example he sets. Much political energy comes from a certain vision, a faith that communicates itself to other people. People who stand for an idea that has energy connected with it have real power." In most ways Brown has been a perfect example of his own model. His accomplishments have come as a result of seeking answers.

As much as a constant stream of legislation is not the remedy, the same is true of many other revered ideas that are not carefully thought through. Education for one has come under extreme and largely justified criticism by the general public and by Brown. Closely associated with the American dream of success, education has fallen from its place of reverence. The problem as Brown sees it is that the teacher, as theoretically the transmitter of the cultural values of this society, has failed to impart these most important tools. In addition to dealing with advanced problems in calculus, the student also needs the intellectual capacity to cope competently with a sometimes hostile world.

Brown believes that the educational system has unfortunately not provided even the rudimentary instruments. The school has become a giant holding tank where baby sitting is more important than the conduct of learning. Likening the teacher's role to the Tower of Babel, Brown sees the present-day classroom as a lot of discussion with each person expressing his own perception, which conflicts with many others, and so what happens to the children? Education in any society—whether highly technological, agricultural, underdeveoped, or tribal— must prepare the young to enter into the world of adulthood with a degree of common wisdom and faith. A reawakening of proper acculturation is but one more revolutionary concept held by California's Governor.

Money, called by many the root of all evil, is traditionally also seen by most politicians as another important cure-all. Not surprisingly, Brown firmly rejects simplistic monetary solutions. Can simply spending millions of dollars have a real effect on problems rooted deeply in the psyche of the people? Jerry answers in the negative. The billions of dollars spent annually to prevent crime in the streets, cure alcoholism, assume warlike postures on poverty, and a host of other serious matters will be without avail if the political will is not first developed to attack the problem.

At best these "remedies" only serve to cover up the maladies until such time as the poisonous antibodies resurface in new and possibly more pronounced forms. It is much like using makeup to disguise a skin cancer. While the visible effects of the disease are covered from public view and the victim is somehow psychologically reassured that the strange growth will not damage the cosmetic facade, the cancer continues to take its toll until more radical measures become necessary. If only the basic question had been asked regarding the nature of the skin elision instead of superficially masking the symptoms, much pain and resources could have been spared.

Brown does not object to the use of large resources to address the ills of this state and the nation, but he wants to make sure that the fundamental diagnosis is made before the treatment is applied. Accordingly when the Governor suggests that his programs will emerge and will not be forced, he is speaking directly to the need for analytical investigation to determine the political will in approaching decisionmaking. For too long this nation has jumped erratically from one big spending program to another, often without measurable positive results. The war on poverty, the war in Vietnam, and the war on governmental malfeasance have all come from the perceived need to cure a malady and all have lead to less than successful conclusions because the essential questions of why and how were not first considered.

In 1977 after the Legislature failed to pass property tax reform legislation before adjourning, some people urged the Governor to convene a special legislative session immediately to take up this problem. Brown refused to do so, noting that sufficient interest had not yet shaped up among the voters, and as Gray Davis, Brown's executive secretary and chief of staff, went on to say, "We have had our ear to the ground for the soothing sound of a two-thirds consensus of the Legislature." In other words, the political will on this issue had not yet developed.

Jerry Brown is indeed a rebel. He is addressing causes larger than himself in a world of politics that often precludes such efforts. In rejecting basic assumptions about the role of government, leadership, education, and the use of material resources, he is reaffirming a stronger faith in the society. The American dream must be tempered with a spiritual and intellectual awakening. Conservative progressivism that emanates from the process of thinking is the key to this revolution, a tripartite merging of the mind, soul, and body—the bringing together of all aspects of human existence. Programmatic change of itself and for itself means nothing. Only that which develops the political will of the citizenry and responds to its collective needs has any real power. This is the essence of the modern revolution being advanced by California's Governor. The rebel within Jerry Brown will not be silenced.

To be orthodox is to incorporate numerous values and beliefs of society into words, thoughts, and actions. Jerry Brown is definitely in touch with such orthodoxy. But how can an individual simultaneously be a rebel and a traditionalist? It would ordinarily be presumed that a contradiction in terms inherently exists in calling a rebellious spirit a follower of orthodox principles. Yet Brown is the embodiment of this seeming paradox. On the one hand, there is the revolutionary whose dreams of change in the temporal order underscore what he says and does. On the other hand, there stands a man of enormous reliance on a host of personal values and beliefs. He is a revolutionary person who has as his foundations a conforming faith in the grander order—a universal force that gives rhyme to the temporal and reason to the eternal.

This is a man of many seasons whose rebellious and orthodox strains flow cyclically as surely as leaves fall from trees only to be regenerated. As summer must give way to fall and then to winter, so also does the individual pass from periods of growth into times of dormancy when reflection must preceed the sprouting of new gardens of thought. There is a faith that despite whatever disaster falls in a given year the earth will continue to nurture the process of living, whether it be a tree or the society of humans. It is to this fundamental faith that Brown addresses himself when he poignantly questions, "Do you really think anything we do will make any real difference?" He is speaking not of life's futility but about the glory of a force that provides continuity to humankind's lot to enjoy and to endure. For him there is no inconsistency in being an orthodox rebel. What emerges is a vision of positive faith in the order of the universe coupled with a profound distrust that all things of the moment may not be as they seem.

As a child Jerry Brown had to participate in a political life style he found most uncomfortable. The Church offered an avenue of escape, a sanctuary for the establishment of self worth and personal growth. The lesson the nuns impressed upon the young minds at the parochial elementary school required the students to look inwardly to find their own guiding force so that they might venture into the world as effective instruments of the Almighty. These early inculcations, developmental psychologists say, are not divorced from the individual any more easily than breathing can be separated from the vital life processes. Many lessons learned by Brown during these formative years are clearly echoed in his calls for discipline, order, hard work, assessment of values, and distrust of the contemporary.

Jerry's personal and political styles speak to the traditionalism that runs deeply within his psyche. The pin-stripped suits and the quiet eloquence of his gait suggest the nature of his upbringing. His speech mannerisms, which inspire but do not arouse emotions, demonstrate a kind of internal calm. His styling leaves the impression of stability, an ongoing love affair with those things of the past which still have a place in the living present. One need not shout from roof tops to be rebellious. To the contrary adopting the refinements of the orthodox shows that a person is neither afraid of the present nor irrationally abhorrent of the past.

This approach to contradictions suggests a Jesuit imprint on the Governor. The Jesuit seminary is a place where the novice and the master are made to feel as though they are central characters in humankind's struggle between heaven and hell. Any person so touched with this feeling of non-worldly importance cannot help but be affected whether deeply or cursorily. At seventeen, Jerry Brown was such a person whose mind was geared to do something of worth. When he left the seminary several years later to pursue a secular career that lead in time to great political heights, he took this spiritualism with him. Obviously many of his current actions engage original sinners in this most monumental of struggles. Government is not to be trusted to move on uncontrolled nor is the individual to function unrestrained.

Brown's distrust of temporal programs and public enterprise might well be linked to this spiritualistic embodiment. The struggle between the worldly and the spiritual is as old as society. "Give unto Caesar what is Caesar's" is a maxim that has as much applicability today as it did many centuries ago. Public enterprises have a place in human society but their ultimate authority is limited. Government simply does not have a legitimate part to play in some human activities, and should have a restricted role in others. Human welfare is basically the responsibility of a society in touch with the omnipresent, and no amount of governmental patchwork assistance can solve the problems of hunger and poverty unless the public will dictates the change intelligently.

Order imposed by an all-powerful cosmic force is the ultimate universal truth. Government, the church, the community, and the individual have places in the master scheme. It is often difficult to understand clearly the exact role any one of these components should play at any particular moment. But Brown maintains a faith that directions eventually emerge as a natural outgrowth of the living process.

Here is a man who believes that for all things there is a place, a time, and a reason. People must not constrain themselves with a lust for that which they are not destined to achieve. Limitations must be realized and priorities reassessed. In the omnipresence of the universe every action has a reaction, every program has an effect. There are fundamental truths that act as the guidelines for any revolution of the intellect, spirit, and life style. This is the essence of Jerry Brown's orthodoxy.

On numerous occasions, Brown had denounced some of the assumptions of the American dream—the proclivity toward opulence, the largeness of government, and the insensitivity of public bureaucracies. In stating that "American values need reassertion in terms of fundamental roots," he is contending that this society is out of step with the grander scheme. The constant American quest for more material comforts is merely a mask for deeper needs. Americans have collectively come to this impasse because of the inherent weakness in the human society. "I think the notion that human nature changes is a complete absurdity refuted by every chapter of history."

Invoking the ever-present belief in original sin, the Governor feels that humankind is essentially "weak, [and] it needs a type of government that recognizes that mankind is really brought down by its own instincts." Far from advocating totalitarianism, he calls for the people, not institutions, to take greater personal responsibility for the human condition. "We have to take the darker side into account in all that we do" by focusing on the obligations all should shoulder as intelligent creatures sharing the same space.

Jerry has greatly internalized these perceptions into his personal life. Discipline is surely a characteristic Brown has assumed as a means of overcoming that "darker side." Often called a "workaholic," he has proceeded to spread this habit to his staff. Working sixteen-hour days, he demands from all his aides the same devotion to duty as he himself gives. Despite his perception that humankind is essentially brutish and that nothing fundamentally can be done to alter its basic nature, he is zealously dedicated to the ultimate objective of relieving "the sum total of human suffering a little." Incorporating a Jesuit strain of disciplined service with a large dose of the Puritan work ethic,

Brown has steadfastly become immersed in this grandest of goals.

With regard to Brown's Jesuit training, various parallels exist between his approach to the governorship and the *Spiritual Exercises* of St. Ignatius Loyola, the founder of the Jesuit order. The *Exercises* are a renewing procedure that takes place annually and involves a month of silent devotion. The first week of this

The Sacramento Bee

"Ask not what your state can do for you; ask what you can do for your state."

yearly ritual of silence has at its core *deformata reformare*, the reformation of that which has been deformed. What has been spoken of the soul, it can be argued, should also be applied to the society of humans. Brown's first objective in the governorship was reform. His insistence about placing government in a proper perspective is indeed an effort to reform the deformed.

The second phase of the *Exercises* continues to place internalized demands on the novice, as he is made responsible for assuring that the reformed is in harmony with the ultimate goals, *reformata conformare*. Brown has entered this stage of administration. Programs have emerged that possibly will slow down government, be more people-centered, and remove programs that do not address fundamental human needs from the spectrum of government. The *reformata conformare* is the consolidation of ideas and conceptions that can be understood by the greatest number of people. On the basis of this governor's extraordinary popularity, some aspects of this transformation have already begun to take place. Appointment of large numbers of women and racial and ethnic minorities to high offices is an example of this reforming spirit.

The last two steps of the *Exercises* are the *conformata confirmare* and the *confirmata transformare*, to add support and to transform the goals that have been predetermined into a new and lasting order. These are monumental objectives, and their achievement can only be measured after the winds of time have blown open these new pages of history. Regardless of Brown's eventual impact on history, at the very least he has articulated clearly-defined goals; that is, the transformation of this society into a more perfect order underscores this administration. At this point, the rebel and the orthodox merge into one. The high-minded objectives of this rebellious person are nothing more than the purification of the oldest dreams of humankind for peace, happiness, love, and spiritual and intellectual fulfillment. The rebel and the Jesuit share a common bond in their dedicated desire to serve and make more perfect. This is the bond Brown embodies.

Jerry Brown is a man of principles, of deep-seated beliefs in the fallibility of humankind and in the perfection of the universe. His perceptions of government cannot be separated from this belief system. As he continues to reform the deformed these influences will probably become more pronounced. As a rebel and a traditionalist, Brown is paradoxical only in the sense that he has been able to incorporate apparent extremes so well when so many other political figures have even failed to recognize their existence. In a period of public searching this mixture of rebellion and the unmoving has found an apt home.

A third philosophic strain exists that underscores Brown's approach to the state, its people, and its power structure. This dimension, unlike the other two that are engendered in Brown's character and unique background, springs directly from an entire generation's anguish over a world racked with the carnage of abusive inhumanity. This generational mind set can best be described as a counter-cultural movement. In speaking of counter-culturalism we are generally not alluding to the phenomenon portrayed in the 1960s on television news by war protesters, dope smokers, and hedonists, although some of these manifestations seemingly had varying degrees of influence on Brown.

Instead we refer to the persisting fundamental shift in attitudes and morals that call into question the basic foundations of Western thought. This is a seldom articulated ideological transposition that places Eastern mysticism and aesthetics face to face with Westernized technology and aggressiveness. As a result, Westerners have come to incorporate almost unknowingly the principles of such philosophic ways as Zen as surely as people of the Eastern world have flung themselves into the pursuit of technological accomplishment. As cultures meet and ideas grow, many understandable changes occur.

In many ways the meeting of Eastern and Western schools of thought is an undefined movement without clear boundaries, recognized leaders, and organized goals. It is a dynamic emergence of thought that was generated after the Second World

War and has since grown geometrically in proportion to the problems facing this society. Germinated by small clusters of people as the winds of dissent in the 1960s blew with greater furor, the seeds have now been successfully sown for a perceived better way. The resulting cross-pollination of thought has profoundly affected the postwar generation in America. As this group reaches maturity, this world view is beginning to assume form. Already politicians are emerging who are alumni of this generation school. Jerry Brown, for one, has not only been touched by cross-culturalism, but he has also become one of its most outspoken proponents.

As the antithesis of Westernized detachment and aggressiveness, the internalized mysticism of Eastern theology and thought has offered another path to follow. In making available this alternative the Eastern philosophies such as Zen do not threaten to destroy Western life but merely to supplement it. Zen is an approach that embraces but does not smother. It is a method of addressing this mortal coil within the context of something larger than one's self.

On at least several levels there is much compatability about Zen and the Christianity espoused by the Jesuits. The perception of the universal that binds all humanity together, the rejection of worldly materialism as a primary motivator, and the desire to live in the physical world while maintaining intimacy with the universal are mutual characteristics. It was easy for Jerry Brown to step from the seminary and accept many of the precepts of this counter-culturalism into his personal framework of life.

Many concepts articulated by Brown flow from the ancient Zen. For example, he warns that government has a limited capacity to respond to human needs and that government should not be burdened with programs but they should emerge from the natural course of things. One can hear in these words echoes of such Zen teaching as Tilopa's six precepts, "No thought, no reflection, no analysis, no cultivation, no intention: Let it settle itself." Underlying all human affairs, a force exists that binds all things together and that responds to the human condition in due course. One cannot seek but only accept these gifts. The Zen master provides the same message as California's political chief—let it emerge.

Brown's philosophy of government is not much different from the Zenrin poem that suggests

> Sitting quietly doing nothing,
> Spring comes,
> And the grass grows by itself.

It is assumed that government has a role as do all creations of nature. But an overabundance of government can cripple a society and remove the humanity from the people as surely as too much water, sun, or other natural gifts can stifle growth. Government must not overshadow nor must it be neglectful. It must be one with the people and the people one with the government. The "political will" so often discussed by Brown is nothing more than this oneness of the people with their institutions. Unfortunately, this unity does not exist sufficiently in contemporary America. "When problems don't go away, we escalate the attack until someone gives up." Jerry tells us that he is "rethinking some of that escalatory social intervention. Inaction may be the highest form of action."

This is not to suggest that passivity to unjust human conditions is the Zen way. To the contrary, political will can only emerge in a system predicated upon open exchange. Only through open discourse can a true union exist between object and subject, the rules and the ruling. As Zenri Kushu poetically wrote,

> To receive trouble is to receive good fortune;
> To receive agreement is to receive opposition.

All things being equal, an open administration is the sole means of permitting people of all political persuasions to approach the chief executive without fear of party or other prejudicial entanglements and to develop a viable political will of the people. This is Brown's "creative inertia."

The obvious question then is, What can this creative inertia mean to a highly mechanistic society such as ours? The answer is unfortunately undefinable at this period of time for clear reasons. America is a nation of high compartmentalization where human worth is measured in terms of product quotas. The machines of its industrial complexes have, to the minds of many including Brown, robbed Americans of their ability to relate to their own emotions and fundamental needs. Technology has quickly become the be-all and end-all of this society's life blood. In such a world every step is toward specialization and materialism. An individual's feelings toward his or her work, family, and daily way of life are sublimated in the quest for a new automobile or other comforts. Even social planning has been assumed by "think tank" brainstorming conglomerations.

The mega-machine that keeps the factories operating and more material comforts coming has produced the highest standard of material living in recorded history, but it also has resulted in one of the most psychologically strained living environments. Many Americans have simply forgotten how to react as human beings. This is a society that will passively stay indoors and hear the cries of a young girl while she is being raped or while an elderly citizen is getting mugged and shrug its collective shoulders and say something about not wanting to get involved. It is a nation that relishes its own freedoms yet spends millions to support facism elsewhere. Americans are a people who will give John Dean, H. R. Haldeman, Spiro Agnew, and others of similar ilk lengthy ovations on talk shows and buy their books of "revelations" long after their crimes against the people have been revealed. This is also a people who have made violence a major money maker in television and movies. The preoccupation of many Americans with material goods has sidetracked them from higher goals. A society that fails to ensure the maintenance of human values is in need of much self-evaluation.

The counter-cultural movement—which has been manifested through Zen to anti-war protests and then to new citizen groups— has attempted at least to slow down this mega-machine that has ground away at the very essence of living. Jerry Brown has assumed a significant role in this fight. His administration represents the first test of the movement's ability to govern and also may provide the people of this nation a critical choice.

Whether this war is won or lost will probably be determined on the battlefields of education and economics. Both of them are inseparably important to the life blood of this society. A technocracy depends totally on the educational system to train the needed experts to staff the economic system that is geared to expansion, whether such growth creates human or resource waste. If the negative outcomes of a technocratic existence are to be neutralized, close attention needs to be paid to these basic areas. Because of their crucial nature Brown has given extensive amounts of time to the discussion of the legitimate role of these enterprises. "I am committed to the learning process, but not to pouring more money down this pipeline in a formula I don't understand." The justification for education must rest on the concept that it "gives you the intellectual tools to think clearly. It may or may not have anything to do with getting a job." Education is fundamental to both the welfare of the industrial complex and the individual. This simple principle must be reestablished as paramount. How this will be done, the Governor is the first to admit that "I don't know."

Economics also plays a major part in the new spirit of Brown counter-culturalism. He believes that the economic system must be responsive to the individual and not the other way around. As a result, Brown has acquired an image of "Mr. Small is Beautiful." Of all Brown's stances, his approach to business through this philosophy is possibly his most vulnerable political position. (However, recently he has sought to promote business through trips to Japanese automobile manufacturers and New York financiers and visits to high Canadian and Mexican officials to discuss the transmission of fuel to California).

Not an original perception with Brown, California's chief executive has borrowed heavily from the late British economist E. F. Schumacher, author of *Small is Beautiful: Economics as if People Mattered*. As the title suggests, this book calls for economics to be based on something besides production schedules and gross national products. Using a blend of classic economic theory and Zen philosophy, Schumacher questions the fundamental assumptions underlying such traditional givens as property rights, unlimited consumption, and constant expansion, "Ownership and consumption of goods is a means to an end, and Buddhist economics is the systematic study of how to attain given ends with the minimum of means."

This position is something that goes against the Westernized propensity to rush headlong into exploiting every material and human resource necessary to maintain and surpass rationally-undefined objectives. According to the British economist, "There is the immediate question of whether 'modernization,' as currently practiced without regard to religious and spiritual values, is actually producing agreeable results. As far as the masses are concerned, the results appear to be disastrous—a collapse of rural economy, a rising tide of unemployment in town and country, and the growth of a city proletariat without nourishment for either body or soul."

In an economy gone wild the society becomes nothing more than an uncontrollable social reactor. A fusion of spirit, intellect, and body occurs as millions of individuals collide without order and meaning in a chain reaction that continues its bombardment until the societal mega-machine explodes. The energy lost in such an economic fusion can never be regained. In this giant social reactor known as government, Brown is attempting to control the mega-machine's mindless division of human resources and is struggling to accomplish the conceivably impossible task of reversing the process. His objective is to infuse human energies into systems that flow with natural grace from the body, soul, and intellect of each individual. To him, "Grace is the energy that allows you to do things."

The counter-cultural movement has sought to bring the American way of life needed symmetry. A society that fails to maintain the balance provided by intellectual, spiritual, and material symmetry is surely destined to roll at an accelerated rate down the path to an eventual crash. Brown seems to perceive that, despite all the positive dynamism of this society, this nation has at least temporarily lost its balance. Deeply moved by the messages of the generation growing up in the 1960s and the generations of Eastern philosophers of long ago, Brown has attempted to articulate a new way. This is a time of reevaluation, limits, possibilities, and spiritual awakening. To these objectives Brown has verbally committed his energies.

Most directors of large organizations regard themselves as the coordinator of all affairs. The feeling one gets while observing Brown is that this type of power brokering is alien to his makeup. Instead of unilaterally making decisions that affect the welfare of the people, he consults and ponders, questions and dissects, often meeting with many aides simultaneously for long stretches of time in brain-storming sessions. Socratic questioning is the basic cornerstone of this unique approach. Yet he maintains all power centrally within the group. There is never a question about who is the boss. Brown pulls all the administrative strings.

Jerry questions his own actions and insists on constantly inquiring about those of all public servants. As a legislative leader has noted, "Brown really rattles those cages to see what will come out." Nothing is taken at face value. Decisions are made only after extensive thought and a determination that such action will be in consort with the political will of the people. While possibly naive, this approach suggests an underlying faith that by engaging in such dialogues a greater good will be achieved. Time and other considerations of expediency should ideally take a secondary position to the quest for the correct solution.

Some modern administrative theorists have been shocked by Brown's methods. They feel organized chaos can lead only to organizational disaster. They contend that Brown's "folly" will become increasingly known. Here we emphasize simply that it is important to recognize that Brown's typical independence has lead him to a highly unorthodox approach to governance.

As Brown's rebellious nature provides him with motivation for change, the orthodox underpinning a sense of direction, and cross-culturalism color, depth, and variety, practical politics gives substance to his administration of government. All political leaders must develop a style of governance that in and of itself reflects a personal philosophy. As with any political personality, Jerry's success will be largely determined by his ability to cope with practical matters effectively. The tapestry of administrative theory Brown has woven plays as much a part in method of operation in office as do the strains of rebelliousness, orthodoxy, and counter-culturalism.

The principle Brown presents of the paramount position of process over action differs substantially from that of many other governmental officials. His concern does not rest with increasing productivity or attaining better public employee benefits, but instead he questions the existence of governmental organizations themselves. Do they respond to the real needs of society? If so, should they be operated by the bureaucratic systems that currently manage them?

Brown's approach to administration can best be described as eclectic or, as one staff member has called it, "organized chaos." It is predicated on the flow of information upward but not necessarily through normal scalar channels. Jerry operates the organization both laterally and horizontally; he may confer with a junior staff member instead of a department chief. Orders are maintained not by threats but by mutual understanding.

Jerry Brown is an individual whose strengths and weaknesses emanate from various influences. He is first a rebel who quests for a more perfect world. In this search the miasma of orthodoxy has pointed a direction of service to the human spirit, intellect, and body. The counter-culture has given his fight the dynamism of a young and growing movement. Finally, the philosophy that grows out of practical administrative and political concerns has provided him with the tools for his personal brand of substantive decisionmaking. In total, the personal and professional life of Jerry Brown flows along the same political current as other Americans examining their roles in this society. Whether these pure waters will remain so or will be diluted by the mucky turbulence of political reality remains to be seen. The perceptions he has revealed to the people have by themselves been a considerable contribution.

In conclusion, it seems appropriate to speculate about what the Western world's first political philosopher might have thought of this most unique chief executive. In the *Republic*, Plato described what some contemporary people still consider the ideal leader— the philosopher king (or head). In the course of a lifetime of special training, Plato believed that an individual would emerge with the proper mixture of wisdom and administrative skill to rule with grace, honor, and facility. As Plato said, "He who at every age, as a boy and youth and in mature life, has come out of the trial victorious and pure shall be appointed a ruler and guardian of the state."

In looking at Jerry Brown, Plato might have taken kindly to California's philosopher governor. Born into politics, cloistered in the study of the profound and the absurd, schooled in law, and nurtured in the movements of the 1960s, Brown has taken on the mantle of power with credentials Plato might have well accepted with pride. In professing this strange mixture of the real world, Socratic logic, the teaching of Thomas Aquinas, ethical thought focusing on the uniqueness and isolation of individual experience in an indifferent or hostile universe (existentialism), Judeo-Christian-Zen theology, and legalistic rationality, Brown has provided the people with what few other politicians, in or out of public office, have been able to incorporate in their personal lives. If training and rhetoric are effective measures, Jerry Brown is possibly the closest embodiment of Plato's classic view of the ideal public guardian. Because of these parallels, the Brown administration may be providing a testing ground for the wisdom of the Western world's most important early political theorist. Can a philosopher ruler actually function effectively in the real world of politics?

Chapter Seven

Brown's Activities
as Governor

When Jerry Brown took office as Governor, after winning by a razor-thin edge, the general public knew little about him. He had conducted a low-profile campaign and had spoken largely in generalities while promising to bring a "new spirit" to state government, whatever that might mean. Some people re-membered he had been a reforming Secretary of State but found it difficult to project the significance of that experience to the governorship. Most individuals who tried to make a prediction about Jerry felt that, in view of his earlier support of social causes and his father's liberal record as Governor, young Brown would be liberal and probably a big spender. Few people apparently had heard his fiscally conservative pronouncements during the campaign.

The new Governor, who is a master of the unexpected with great ability to capture and sustain the interest of the media, soon began to surprise and delight many people and quickly developed a high level of public popularity which has continued. From a narrow win at the polls to broad popular appeal in a short time is one of the most amazing developments in Brown's life.

A major way in which Jerry brought about this transformation was through a series of actions that demonstrated his personal frugality and unpretentiousness. He refused to live in the newly-completed $1.3 million executive mansion, a cavernous eight-bedroom river-bluff villa of 12,000 square feet stretching over 11.5 acres in suburban Sacramento, a considerable distance from the state capitol. Bachelor Brown called the mansion, among other things, an appropriate location for "a halfway house for lobbyists." Instead he chose as his residence a state-owned two-bedroom apartment of 1,500 square feet across from the state capitol. The apartment is furnished with state-provided used furnishings and with simple eating utensils, the latter brought over from the Reagan's executive residence. Brown pays the monthly rent from his own funds; it was at first $250 and later raised twenty-five dollars. By declining to live in the new executive mansion, Jerry saved the state an estimated $1 million in housing upkeep in four years' time. After the executive mansion stood vacant for almost three years, Brown signed a bill authorizing its use for state seminars and conferences and two couples were hired as housekeepers and caretakers, thus reducing a large expense for security.

Another early step of thriftiness and avoidance of ostentation by Brown was the sale at his request of the Cadillac limousine that had been chauffeured for Governor Ronald Reagan. For this low-mileage automobile, Jerry substituted a new-model but more economical Plymouth Satellite from the state car pool. Although the change produced only minor money savings, the public also liked this example of economy and unpretentiousness. Brown's preference emanated in part from an early experience. In an interview with magazine reporters, the Governor recalled, "I can remember a time when I was going to a [San Francisco] Giants' [baseball] game in my father's [official] limousine driven by a highway patrolman. At one point as we drove through the crowd, people started pounding on the windows. It made me disinclined to have a limousine, let alone drive around in one."

In like fashion Brown gave up the state-chartered jet airplane for travel on regular commercial airlines. On some trips such as those to Japan to talk with business tycoons and to Colorado to solicit the 1984 Olympics for Los Angeles, Jerry paid his own air fare; and on a trip to England for a memorial service and to talk with British businessmen, he not only used his own money for the flight but also went economy class. As further illustrations of economy, he cut salaries of his chief aides 7 percent and made it clear that his salary was adequate. (Almost three years later when top officials in the state received sizable increases, Brown refused to have the Governor included in the raises, even threatening at one point to veto the bill if he were not exempted.)

From an early time Brown also sought to convey openness. For one thing, in the second month of his term he ordered his staff to dispose of three paper shredders used by the Reagan administration. "They simply have no place in an open government," he said. In the same week Jerry announced that he was returning more than 150 gifts, passes, and memberships that had been received since his election. They had been given by oil corporations, race tracks, a pharmaceutical firm, a real estate association, a construction company, public officials, and industrial associations and firms. The same rule was applied to members of the Governor's staff. Regarding the return of these gifts, Brown remarked, "A government job is an occasion for public service, not special privilege. The undivided loyalty to the public interest required of the governorship makes it inappropriate to keep the profusion of gifts that arrive each day at this office. We are sent to Sacramento for a single purpose—to serve all the people. That includes those who declined to vote as well as those who did. It includes those who have no lobbyist to represent them in Sacramento as well as those who do. It includes those who can't afford to send gifts as well as those who can."

In fighting ostentation, Brown has also eliminated the opulence of the governorship. From the start he shunned hosting lavish banquets and cocktail parties. There was no inaugural ball nor any big official galas; in contrast, Reagan had been inaugurated at midnight amid much pomp and ceremony. Jerry has only occasional luncheons and infrequent small office dinners. Although he has a yearly allotment of $17,500 for official entertaining, he spent only $750 in his first nine months in office. For instance, when Jerry hosted Britain's Prince Charles at a luncheon in October 1977, cold roast beef, cheeses, tossed green salad, and ginger ale were served.

From the start of Brown's governorship, the communications media did a turnabout concerning him. Previously they had judged him a dull campaigner worthy of scant attention, thus fitting Jerry's choice to be a nearly invisible candidate. Upon his becoming Governor and taking unexpected personal steps and showing governmental restraint, the media became entranced with him and gave him extensive coverage (and still does). Jerry Brown, with his rise to a position of much political power and his attention-getting actions, had become interesting copy for audio, visual, and written communications—a development that numerous observers believe demonstrates Brown's genius in manipulating the media.

In all these illustrations of personal thrift, unpretentiousness, openness, and avoidance of luxury, the Governor succeeded in enveloping himself in a plain Brown wrapper. In an age of great cynicism, distrust, and apathy about government, an overwhelming proportion of Californians were greatly pleased by these actions. Jerry's only exception has been the expensive and well-tailored look of the suits, blazer jackets and trousers, and the shirts and ties he almost always wears in public. This is a calculated risk in order to look older, for although Jerry turned forty in early April 1978, his appearance is more youthful.

Brown also astonished and satisfied many people, including his predecessor Ronald Reagan, by proposing in his first state budget a total figure only slightly higher than that of the last Reagan year. The increases were largely due to inflation factors such as cost of living adjustments. In commenting on fiscal and other matters, Jerry spoke about the need for the general public to lower its expectations and to recognize it was living in an era of limits. In a time of generally increasing taxes at all levels of government, many people were happy to hear Brown preaching conservative finance.

Jerry Brown's popularity skyrocketed quickly after his close gubernatorial election because of personal actions and widespread public belief in his desire to restrain governmental spending. His popularity has remained exceptionally high and these same factors have continued to be important to his popular appeal.

Notwithstanding the attempts by some of Brown's opponents to depict him as a virtual do-nothing Governor, a person of symbols instead of action, he has indeed been active in many important fields. In this chapter, we look at a number of these areas, but of course not all. They are agricultural labor relations, the death penalty and criminal justice, public schools and higher education, environmental protection and business growth, and state governmental finance. As shown in the pages that follow, these are often perplexing and very controversial subjects that require difficult decisions.

The passage of an agricultural labor relations act in 1975 represented one of Jerry Brown's major legislative successes and demonstrated his considerable skill as a negotiator. In Brown's inaugural address he had recommended the enactment of such a law, but there was little expectation in state governmental and private circles that a bill of this type would be approved. A struggle over unionization and collective-bargaining rights had gone on for many years between farm workers (chiefly harvest-season, migratory laborers who were geographically scattered and of foreign extraction) and farm owners and growers (most of them operating on large amounts of land).

For several years before the start of the Brown administration, legislative bills concerned with farm labor relations had been introduced but had failed. The delicate balance of power existing among Cesar Chavez's United Farm Workers of America, the Teamsters, and the growers seemed to make a compromise impossible. The Teamsters had entered into the quest for representation of farm workers primarily to safeguard other people they already represented, such as those in canneries, packing sheds, and trucks, rather than to pick up new members. They sought to represent farm laborers to reduce the possibility of harvest-season strikes which would cause unemployment among workers they already represented.

While possible legislation remained stalemated at the state level in California, a farm bloc in Congress showed its strength. It prevented farm workers from being brought within the unionization and collective-bargaining rights of the National Labor Relations Act, which had been passed for their urban counterparts in the 1930s. The more enlightened agricultural interests sought to establish such a board in the national Department of Agriculture, an agency with stronger sympathies toward growers; but progress was slow on this proposal and did not particularly please farm-worker organizations.

In 1972 the California Farm Bureau Federation packaged many anti-union proposals into an initiative, which was vigorously opposed by the United Farm Workers and Teamsters and was defeated. Cesar Chavez, the Chicano leader of the UFW and a folk hero, realized that the entrance of the Teamsters as a bargaining agent in negotiations with lettuce and grape growers had severely diluted the potency of his nationwide effort to boycott their products. He sensed that a counterattack was urgently needed. A strong supporter of Brown in his campaign for Governor, Chavez now turned to the sympathetic chief executive for assistance. Many people thought the supportive effort would be futile.

Rose Bird, then Secretary of Agriculture and Services and one of the brightest talents in the Brown administration, sought to find out if a common legal ground could be established to which all the relevant parties might agree. She discovered that the most serious difficulty was to get the contending forces to put aside the rhetoric and to focus on the specific details of a piece of legislation. Once this transition was made, she reported to Jerry that a compromise might be attainable.

Brown brought all the parties together in his suite of offices in the state capitol and proceeded with his aides to engage in shuttle diplomacy. Placing the various participants in different rooms in the suite, Jerry and his assistants scurried around the connecting

"My name is Juan Garcia and I could use your help here in California!"

maze, engaging in discussions, relaying messages, and reaching points of consensus. Brown demonstrated a great aptitude for mediation and, after a lengthy session, a compromise was hammered out for presentation to the Legislature. A cooperative relationship between farm laborer and agricultural grower had been developed to replace boycotts, long marches, fasts, and violence. All the problems, as it turned out, were not at an end, however.

The Legislature, highly pleased with Brown's accomplishment which seemed to eliminate a continuing difficulty it had been unable to solve, promptly passed the Agricultural Labor Relations Act of 1975. The legislation incorporated the elements worked out by Brown and the contending forces. The law set up the Agricultural Labor Relations Board (ALRB), composed of five members appointed for five-year terms by the Governor with state Senate approval. The ALRB was authorized to conduct secret-ballot elections among farm workers to determine which, if any, union would represent them in collective bargaining. This board was also given the power to take action against employers and unions participating in unfair labor practices, order offending parties to pay the injured for particular losses, settle disputes arising from union elections, and set up rules and regulations to implement the act. The level at which the annual salaries of the board members was fixed—$42,000—was added evidence of the importance given to this new law.

The ALRB was allotted a budget of $6.8 million for the first year of its work, and under the new law Chavez's organization won most of the elections. It soon became evident, however, that the amount of money needed by the agency had unintentionally been greatly underestimated. By the end of the first six months its funds had practically run out and it sought an emergency appropriation of $3.8 million, which required a two-thirds vote in both legislative houses.

Growers and rural-area legislators balked at further funding, arguing that the ALRB had been extravagant in its spending by holding unnecessary hearings on alleged unfair labor practices and by paying large staff salaries. They also contended that the board was pro-labor and thus not impartial, and had passed a highly controversial access rule which gave union organizations permission to enter farms and ranches to talk with workers at certain specified times. The grower interests and legislators representing them opposed giving more money to the agency until changes were first made.

Brown and key legislators refused to alter the law, saying that compromises had been worked out when the legislation had passed in the previous year. The ALRB shut down in early February 1976 due to lack of funds, thus bringing to a halt the voting by farm workers on the question of whether or not to unionize. Stung by the demise of the ALRB in less than a year, which Jerry blamed on the lack of good faith by the growers, Brown changed from mediator to advocate.

Shortly after the shutdown Brown spoke out strongly about this issue. "There have been 400 elections across the dusty fields of this state. They gave people a right to an election who never had that right before, and the unions won 95 percent of the elections. The poorest and most oppressed people in the state or this nation [won]. That's something we have to keep in mind when people start talking compromise, rewriting the law, saying that something is wrong with it. I'll tell you what's wrong with it—a group of people who never had any power, and some people think that's wrong." An aide to Brown further pointed out that the ALRB performed a quasi-judicial role and cutting off its money would be equivalent to reducing the budget of the national Supreme Court just because of disagreement with a few of its decisions. The growers, he said, made a commitment and then used the worst possible means to destroy the board.

The United Farm Workers promptly started circulating initiative petitions to strengthen the existing agricultural labor relations law and to require the Legislature to provide the necessary money for the agricultural board. About 750,000 names, more than twice the number of signatures required to put the proposal on the November 1976 general-election ballot, were collected in two months. Under this initiative, the access rule, then only a board regulation, would be made part of the law. In addition, growers would be required to furnish unions with lists of employees once a union filed notice to seek a representation election, and the board would be permitted to levy triple damages against an employer or a union guilty of unfair labor practices. In short, the initiative would have improved the position of labor unions and farm workers, and its provisions could not have been modified except by another vote of the statewide electorate. Three board members resigned, which the chairman felt increased the possibilities of getting the agency funded for the 1976-77 fiscal year, but the specter of the initiative was the overriding reason for the growers and the rural-area legislators getting behind the approval of agency funds to be available July 1.

Although the Legislature had finally acted favorably, Chavez feared that it would succumb again later to agribusiness. Also, so many initiative petition signatures had been gathered in such a short while that a stronger law that the Legislature could not change seemed a virtual certainty. Chavez therefore proceeded to have the initiative proposal placed on the November 1976 ballot. He gained thousands of volunteers to campaign door-to-door (chiefly in Chicano and black neighborhoods), to make telephone calls, and to gather at freeway entrances and exits to urge an affirmative vote for the proposal, which was Proposition 14.

Jerry Brown entered the bitterly controversial fray as the star supporter of the proposition, giving his words and image to commercial television advertisements and media interviews. Brown spoke very earnestly, almost urgently. In a paid television program, he said that the proposition would lock in the labor law for two years and bring peace and stability to agriculture in the state. And then in a full-page paid open letter in many newspapers on election day, Brown warned, "I hope you won't be misled by the oil companies and the corporations which are buying ads using small farmers. . . . It is time to settle the farm labor issue and get on with other things." Suggesting corporate misbehavior and legislative logjamming that slowed the resolution of other issues, he set up a target for the electorate to riddle.

Harry Kubo, a farmer and the president of the Nisei Farmers League, headed the committee opposing Proposition 14. It hired

William Roberts, a veteran and clever political consultant who organized an ingenious campaign. His strategy included a set of television commercials depicting farmers, including Kubo, claiming the access rule was an invasion of private property rights. There were two implications in the message. Proposition 14 would provide for the access rule. This was true, but it would simply place into initiative statutory law an already existing ALRB administrative regulation. In brief, the implication was that the access rule would go into effect if the proposition passed. In actuality, it already existed. The second implication in the opponents' message was that this "destruction" of property rights of farmers and growers might only be the first step in invading the property rights of nonagricultural groups and individuals.

Considerable money was spent by both advocates and antagonists of Proposition 14. The total for both of them amounted to about $1.5 million. Most of the financing of the "Yes" side came from Chavez's special citizens committee. The opponents' funds were obtained mainly from farm associations and several oil firms.

The proposition was soundly trounced in November 1976, with more people voting on the issue than cast ballots for either Jerry Ford or Jimmy Carter. The proposal gained only 38 percent of the vote. The scare over property rights, a mainstay of much of American society, was a decisive factor in the defeat. The Agricultural Labor Relations Act of 1975 would continue in operation and not be replaced by the stronger pro-labor initiative proposition. Moreover, the ALRB would have to continue to compete for funds through the state's regular budgetary process. Chavez publicly regarded the lost battle as an instrument of farm laborer unification. Speaking to 800 supporters in a Los Angeles area high school the day after the election, he exclaimed, "Our experience in the movement is that we never lose. . . . The work on Proposition 14 was an investment. . . . We've not lost brotherhood, we've not lost unity."

Jerry Brown did not lose either. Although he made some enemies among farm growers, he further solidified his strong friendship with Cesar Chavez and a multitude of farm laborers and others associated with pro-labor causes. (Chavez had recently nominated him for President of the United States and has a strong national following.) In addition, Brown's high status and popularity with the public had not suffered. Mervin Field, director of the California Poll, concluded that the voters had not personally rebuked the Governor by rejecting Chavez's Proposition 14.

Few issues arouse deeper emotions than the death penalty. The premise that a society has a right and an obligation to take the life of an individual convicted of a heinous crime is approved or rejected by people at all levels of society. The ancient principle of an eye for an eye or the more modern contention that this kind of punishment actually deters further criminal activity by others has sharply divided public opinion and has produced loud and endless debate. Yet on the basis of popular votes and opinion polls, it is apparent that the vast majority of people support the concept of the death penalty. On this issue, however, Jerry Brown differs markedly from the public consensus and stands firmly with those opposed to the sanction of "murder" in the name of society. Given the general sentiment and the volatile nature of this issue, the Governor's unyielding opposition demonstrates a commitment to a certain belief that outweighs even the possibility of detrimental political repercussions to him.

In the last quarter century only two individuals have died in California's gas chamber, one during Ronald Reagan's tenure and the other in Pat Brown's administration. Early in Pat's first term as Governor he spent much time and experienced much anguish and indecision about sending the widely-publicized "red light bandit" Caryl Chessman to his death in 1960 after twelve years of appeals and legal and technical maneuvers. The case brought on a worldwide debate over humankind's longtime method of coping with certain enemies of society because Chessman, a talented writer, continued to profess his innocence in book manuscripts that were smuggled out of San Quentin. The pressure from many sources that revolved around the case brought sustained cries for mercy or execution. Pat Brown, a gentle and generally benevolent man, found himself in the center of the controversy. As California's chief executive, he had to make the ultimate decision as to whether Chessman should be executed or have his sentence commuted to life in prison.

Son Jerry, who had been undertaking difficult seminary training, did not lighten Pat's burden. The younger Brown was committed to the belief that no society has the moral right to take the life of any person in the name of justice. This view was discussed by Jerry and his powerful father as Governor Pat pondered his options. Jerry's moral indignation over this case and the death penalty in general played a part in Pat's vacillation in deciding. Finally Pat granted a last-minute sixty-day reprieve to Chessman. This made the Governor seem indecisive to some people and compassionate to others.

Pat Brown called the Legislature into special session on the single item of whether or not capital punishment should be abolished. The proposed abolition lost by one vote in a committee of the state Senate. The Legislature had failed to make the change, the special session adjourned, and Chessman soon walked to the gas chamber. The cyanide pellets that ended another life under the aegis of collective justice firmly solidified a future governor's opposition to a practice he considered barbaric and beyond the legitimate role of government.

Jerry Brown's feelings about the death penalty have remained unaltered over the years while public opinion, in an age of greater violence, has run strongly in the opposite direction. Public support for capital punishment solidly crystallized in 1972 when Californians voted by a two-to-one margin for a sweeping death penalty measure. During Jerry Brown's gubernatorial candidacy two years later the U.S. Supreme Court foretold the fate of this California law—that it would be declared unconstitutional. However, this tribunal found the death penalty not to be cruel or unusual punishment if a state carefully prescribed the causes for which such a penalty could be invoked. At that time Brown told the public that, if elected Governor, he would employ all the political muscle available to him to oppose enactment of a death penalty law that met the U.S. Supreme Court's guide lines. Moreover, he said that if such an act passed he would carry it out.

In 1976 the California Supreme Court declared the existing state death penalty law illegal because it failed to allow for consideration of mitigating circumstances. This judicial verdict set the stage for legislative action. Obviously, in view of the formidable citizen support for capital punishment, death penalty bills would be introduced by legislators in 1977. In the first month of that year, at the conclusion of Brown's State of the State message presented in person to the Legislature, Jerry stressed that he would not sign any bill of this type that reached his desk.

Brown elaborated on the subject several months later while appearing on a nationally televised talk show. To Jerry the death penalty "seems random, arbitrary, and irrational. There are thousands and thousands of homicides and by the time you go through the [judicial] process very few people end up to the point where they get to the gas chamber. Somehow in our society I think we can make people safer, we can make people more secure, if we strengthen law enforcement, if we rebuild our neighborhoods and not put our faith in a process that selects by a very arbitrary manner a very few number of people to pay the penalty for the crimes and sufferings of thousands of other people. . . . That's the way I see it. I realize [many] people don't agree with me." Jerry Brown made it apparent that despite much popular opposition to his view, he would resist any death penalty legislation "as a matter of conscience."

Brown's position on the death penalty issue represented a clear political danger. If the Legislature passed a death penalty bill, Brown vetoed it, and each of the two legislative houses did not muster a two-thirds vote to override his veto, Brown would find this subject had again become a major public controversy. And backed by lopsided public support, it would have become so shortly before Brown's reelection bid for Governor in 1978 and would have placed him at a political disadvantage.

In 1977 George Deukmejian, a hard-working member of the state Senate with persistent aspirations to be the state's Attorney General, spearheaded a successful effort on behalf of the death penalty. With the support of most Republicans and Democrats alike, he pushed legislation through the two houses to impose the death penalty for sixteen types of first degree murder. Late maneuvering by Senator Milton Marks of San Francisco to gain passage of a bill, which Brown favored, to substitute life imprisonment without possibility of parole for the death penalty failed. Brown thus found himself in the dilemma of deciding whether to follow his conscience or the will of the vast majority of the people.

Jerry Brown's judgment was consistent with his moral belief, and he acted promptly and quietly on the matter. He vetoed the bill four and a half hours after its passage by the state Senate, the second of the two houses to approve it. He took this step before only a few aides and away from the media spotlight, thereby seeking to reduce public attention to a generally unpopular action.

Brown's veto message was brief but expressed well the depth of his feeling on the subject: "Statistics can be marshaled and arguments propounded. But at some point, each of us must decide for himself what sort of future we would want. For me, this would be a society where we do not attempt to use death as a punishment." About the time Brown was vetoing the bill, Attorney General Evelle Younger, a Republican candidate for Governor in the following year's election, released a letter to Brown and the media. He declared the veto "would be an irresponsible act which cannot be disguised as a 'matter of conscience.' I believe that you as governor have the responsibility to further, rather than obstruct, the desires of the people of California on this issue."

Deukmejian took another approach in opposition to Brown's decision. The senator contended that Brown had failed to give a responsible reason for his veto. Moreover, the legislator continued, ". . . He [Brown] has ignored the fact that murderers are inflicting death as a punishment upon the innocent. I believe the majority of the people of California want a society where innocent people are not put to death." Deukmejian also argued that Brown had not demonstrated the courage of his position, as he did not try to stop the override of his veto and had the votes to do so.

The death penalty bill was returned to the Legislature for possible overriding of the Governor's veto. This required a two-third majority vote in both houses, the precise margin that had been obtained in the original passage. Brown did not try to persuade particular legislators who had voted initially for the death penalty bill to uphold his veto now. Gray Davis, the Governor's top assistant, advised, "If there is a message it is 'Search your conscience and your constituency and make the best judgment you can.'" Although there was a slight shift in the legislative voting, the successful override tally closely resembled the original vote for passage.

Governor Brown's veto of the death penalty legislation was overridden. This overcoming of executive disapproval was only the third such occurrence in the last thirty-one years in the state and the first during Brown's term of office. The Legislature's decision took place fourteen months before Brown would contest the Republican contender for the governorship. The Republicans who had led the legislative effort to restore capital punishment hoped the voters would remember the political party that had given the stronger support to carrying out the overwhelming mandate by the people. Jerry had shown political courage by following his moral convictions on an emotionally-charged issue even when such a decision might prove to be unpopular with the public. He also demonstrated his political acumen by acting expeditiously on the matter and then making no effort to get the Legislature to sustain his veto. The objective, which was a calculated risk, was to try to make the issue fade away as quickly as possible so that it would not be of consequence in Brown's 1978 gubernatorial reelection bid.

Because no one convicted before the new death penalty law went into operation can be executed, Brown was not faced with the decision of an execution or commuting a death sentence before the gubernatorial campaign in 1978. A murder would have to be committed after the enactment of the legislation and proceed through the long judicial process of trials and appeals before the Governor of the state, whoever he might be, would be faced with a decision that might arouse considerable public controversy.

Jerry Brown's opposition to the death penalty does not mean that he is generally soft on law and order and crime questions even though some of his political enemies seek to lead people to this belief. It is true that on some issues he has stood for personal rights as paramount to a strict law enforcement policy. Here are four examples. First and most significant, the Governor approved a bill decriminalizing private sexual acts between consenting adults of the same or opposite sex. Second, he signed a bill that reduced penalties for the possession of small amounts of marijuana. Third, he sanctioned a measure known as the police bill of rights for rank-and-file officers. The legislation bans the ordering of lie detector tests in departmental investigations, prevents the search of an officer's desk or locker without permission or a warrant, entitles an officer to have a representative present during interrogation, and prohibits the use of offensive language or threat of punitive action while being questioned. Fourth, he vetoed a bill that would have permitted defense attorneys to obtain copies of the complete criminal record of witnesses; his judgment was that the proposal did not adequately safeguard the privacy of confidential criminal records.

On the other hand, Brown has often backed strict—some have said overly severe—law and order propositions. In a time of greater citizen concern over crime and with a personal belief in accountability and punishment for wrongdoing, his frequently strong attitudes in this field have not been surprising. In 1975 Jerry approved legislation that imposed mandatory prison sentences on individuals using firearms in committing a wide range of crimes extending from robbery to attempted murder. At the time of signing this mandatory sentence bill, the Governor pointed out, "I want to send a clear message to every person in this state that using a gun in the commission of a crime means a stiff prison sentence. Whatever the circumstances, however eloquent the lawyer, judges will no longer have discretion to grant probation *even* to first offenders. This may not rehabilitate nor get at the underlying causes but it will punish those who deserve it. The philosophy of this bill is based not on sociology or Freudian theory, but on simple justice." Two years later an extensive campaign began to circulate the slogan "Use a gun. Go to jail" via store signs, billboards, and media announcements as the answer of conservatives to gun-control proposals.

In 1976 Brown sanctioned a law enforcement pacakge of four bills weighted toward stiffer punishment and fixed prison terms. One law made it easier to send persons of sixteen and seventeen years of age to prison for violent crimes. Another required prison terms for persons with two previous felonies who had then been convicted of a violent crime. A third law stipulated a life sentence without possibility of parole for torture killers. The final piece of legislation was the determinate sentence law. This generally replaced a practice of more than a half century that permitted sentencing flexibility by a parole board according to the rate of an inmate's rehabilitation. It provided for the judge to set the exact sentence for a person upon conviction.

In 1977 Brown appeared at a forgotten victims conference sponsored by the state district attorneys' association and presented an eight-point program to get tougher with criminals. (The offering of a multi-point program was unusual for Brown who has often expressed distaste for a laundry list of solutions to problems.) Later in the same year he signed many anti-crime bills, a number of which had been stated earlier in his program. Two bills concerned mandatory prison sentences for ex-convicts who commit violent crimes while on parole or for anyone who violently assaults the elderly, blind, or handicapped. Further bills made it a felony to use minors under sixteen in films, photographs, or live performances of a pornographic nature, and provided state aid to help local prosecutors concentrate their most experienced personnel on cases involving repeat violent offenders.

Still other legislation reduced the number of delays and continuances in criminal proceedings, and compelled criminals to assume the burden of compensating the victims of crime through court-imposed penalty assessments on those convicted of violent crime. Brown stressed that these bills are "tough and make it plain that people who commit serious crimes are going straight to prison."

The most contested criminal justice proposal signed by Brown in the same year authorized up to twenty-six weeks of unemployment insurance compensation for prison parolees who qualify for such assistance through work experience gained while incarcerated. "If they cannot find a job [when coming out of prison], instead of getting [nothing but] the $200 check and a new suit of clothes and a handshake," Brown said, "they will at least have that much of a guarantee that will hopefully keep them on the straight and narrow long enough for them to get back into society."

In Brown's state of the state message of 1978, he recommended two strong law and order proposals. The first urged the allotment of $3 million by the Legislature to fight the use of "angel dust," then accounting for a fourth of all the psychedelic drug abuse in the state. The second asked the Legislature to appropriate money for new prisons. "It is impossible," the Governor warned, "for judges to hand out tough sentences if there are no plans to lock people up."

Despite Brown's support of various strong law and order and criminal punishment laws, some of his critics feel that he is vulnerable in this area. In addition to continued reminders to the voters that Brown opposed restitution of the death penalty when most of them favored the idea, his political opponents attack him on two other grounds. One is the determinate sentencing law, which at the time of its passage was generally viewed as a step toward tightening the criminal justice system and which was opposed by many civil liberties groups. Edward Davis, former Los Angeles police chief and a Republican candidate for Governor in 1978, said that the fixed-sentence law reduced the incentive of .many prisoners to be good so they would be released sooner. Davis then said in dramatic fashion that since good behavior now carried less influence, "inmates no longer have to pay much attention to correctional officers. He [Brown] is going to blow up those prisons before I can take over as governor." Davis has been known for many dramatic—some say outlandish—statements. When police chief, he said that hijackers should be hung from gallows constructed at the airport. In reacting to his failure to get more police personnel, he suggested that the people get guns and dogs in the hope of making up for inadequate law enforcement coverage.

The other point of attack against Brown is more indirect. It centers on Mrs. Pearl West, whom the Governor appointed as director of the California Youth Authority. The director also chairs the board which determines the terms for young criminals sent by the courts to a youth-authority facility. Some state legislators and candidates for state office contend the average term of eleven months is ridiculously short because 42 percent of the inmates are serving time for violent crimes such as homicide, robbery, or assault. Mrs. West generally approves of the length of the CYA sentences, arguing that the agency's job is to treat and rehabilitate young criminals.

Brown has long sensed the importance of being regarded as a supporter of strong law enforcement and criminal laws, but he has also felt the need to protect personal rights. The two concepts are at times difficult to reconcile. In Jerry's campaign in 1974 for Governor, Tom Quinn, his campaign manager, developed some persuasive law and order television advertisements. One featured a San Francisco police sergeant proclaiming his support for Brown. Another showed Jerry complaining about his grand-mother's inability to take daily walks in a park because of her fear of being mugged. Since being elected, Governor Brown has expressed considerable doubt about the possibilities of rehabilita-tion of criminals by governmental authorities and has leaned increasingly toward punishment as the better option. Typical of his comments are "Jails should be made less attractive. A person should have the choice of two years in jail or one year at hard labor." He has pardoned about seventy-five individuals a year, all leading exemplary lives since their release from prison ten to fifteen years ago. His number of pardons is virtually identical to the average of Ronald Reagan during his eight years in office.

California has vast educational establishments at all levels. They include public schools through the twelfth grade, a statewide network of two-year community (junior) colleges, nineteen state colleges and universities (which constitute the world's largest multi-campus system), and the nine campuses of the University of California, which is internationally recognized for research and teaching. The total system, which is tuition free except for the University of California campuses which recently began levying an "educational fee," spends more than $7 billion annually. This represents about 40 percent of all state expenditures and 60 percent of all local expenses.

Most Californians take pride in the magnitude and overall quality of their public educational system from the beginning grades through the university graduate level. In many ways it is a remarkable example of nearly universal and relatively user-free public education. The system, however, is far from free of criticism, particularly in recent years. Repeated discontent has been expressed over the deteriorating results in the public schools as measured by reading, mathematics, and other achievement scores. There has been an increased feeling that while the amount of money invested in both public school and college-university education has gone up, the quality of education has not kept pace. Too much spent on administration and too little on instruction is a frequent expression of unhappiness. Also noted, as early as 1967 in the *Serrano* v. *Priest* case, have been the frequently great differences in the financial resources of school districts in providing the local portion of financing public school education.

Jerry Brown spoke in generalized terms about education during his campaign for Governor. He called for greater educational opportunities for young people through smaller classes, bilingual education, better training in fundamental mathematics and reading, and career education. He also supported restoring the prestige of the higher educational system through renewed commitment to excellence, expanded research, and greater student aid.

Few people knew what specifically to expect from Brown in the field of education, or most other substantive areas, upon his election as Governor. Most residents of the state pegged him as a liberal and expected him to increase state government spending rapidly. His opposition to general tax increases stated during the campaign either had not been heard or had not been taken seriously by most people. Also since he was well educated and an intellectual, the general public feeling was that he would be highly supportive of all levels of public education, particularly in comparison to Ronald Reagan's previous eight years of parsimony.

Soon after Brown took office, it was evident that he was deeply concerned about public education and sensitive and sympathetic to many complaints being made about it. In the first year of his administration, he told Jack Rees, the executive director of the California Teachers Association, "I am going to starve the [public] schools until I get some educational reforms." "What reforms? What do you want?" asked Rees. "I don't know yet," Jerry answered.

Brown made known the specific educational reforms he desired within a short while—all of them for the public schools except one for the universities and colleges. In cutting $27 million from the 1975-76 public school support bill—which is simply one-half of one percent of the amount spent by such schools each year—Brown offered five proposed reforms for public discussion. (1) Focus greater attention on reading, mathematics, and the other survival skills that enable people to think clearly and to cope with an increasingly complex society. (2) Increase local control over schooling so as to enlarge the power of the principal, teachers, and parents at the site of instruction, that is, at the individual local school. (3) Revise the state's master plan for higher education. (4) Bring about changes in school finance. (5) Adopt a fair system of public school funding by minimizing the financial disparities among school districts in line with the mandate of the *Serrano* decision.

Jerry's statements on these points were brief in his message on signing the bill that reduced the legislative appropriation by $27 million. Within a few weeks, they were explained in greater detail by two of Brown's appointees to the State Board of Education who were also advisers on education to the Governor. They were Michael Kirst, a professor of education at Stanford University, and John Pincus, head of the education and human resources program at the Rand Corporation, a think-tank in Santa Monica.

As to the first point on strengthening basic skills, Kirst and Pincus explained that the Governor's emphasis on this did not mean uncritical acceptance of the philosophy of "back to the basics" or a total focus on the 3Rs. Beyond a strong foundation in the survival skills, they continued, there should be locally-developed education programs better adapted to the diversity of people's needs to bring out the talents, capacities, and interests of each young person.

On the second point of greater local control, the Governor sided with the opponents of detailed control of the schools from Sacramento where more than 3,000 bills on education are presented at each session and, if passed, are added to a massive four-volume education code. This proposition of more local autonomy would increase flexibility for decisions by local school boards and by the principal, teachers, and parents at each school location. The transformation of the local school site into the basic unit of management could not take place overnight. Principals and teachers must first learn the techniques of budgeting, community relations, and working together as teams to plan and carry out educational changes. The talents and abilities already present in the schools could thus be concentrated on the children by those who know the problems best—principals, teachers, and parents. Under this procedure, one school might center its attention on basic curriculum and another on science or creative arts. Parents and students should be allowed to choose among schools or among programs within a school in line with their needs.

Concerning the third proposition of revising the master plan of higher education, the age of growth which was operative when this plan had been conceived had given way recently to a period of slow enrollment gains and mounting inflationary pressure. More coordination and setting of priorities among the different elements of higher education needed to be developed in the increased competition for students and state funds. Also, difficult decisions had to be made. For example, how much support should go to adult education as compared with the education of the traditional eighteen-to-twenty-four year old clients? Should the twelfth grade be converted into an optional first year of college or of career training?

Relative to the fourth proposal to produce changes in school finance, some forms of state aid stimulated schools to promote financially profitable programs while others encouraged them to curtail unprofitable ones. Financial aid formulas should be modified to eliminate either profit or loss to school districts for performing required programs. Some existing incentives were similarly illogical. Teachers and administrators should not receive salary increases for simply completing any university courses; instead the rewards should be given to staff members for training pertinent to the particular needs of individual schools and districts. In addition, salary incentives that make required teachers leave the classroom for administrative posts should be reappraised. Salary schedules should be established to encourage good·teachers to continue their teaching.

As to the fifth and final point about installing a more equitable system of educational funding, the judicial ruling in the *Serrano* case was that the existing school finance system in the state was unconstitutional. The reason was that it made the quality of a child's education depend heavily on each school district's assessed property valuation, which sometimes varied greatly and produced clearly unfair situations. As a consequence, districts with high property wealth, like Beverly Hills and Palo Alto, could spend large sums for each student and still keep property tax rates down, while low property wealth districts, such as Compton and Baldwin Park, had to impose high tax rates to offer even minimum support for their schools. A combination of direct help from the wealthier districts to subsidize the poorer units and greater state aid being targeted to them would close the gap in spending between districts and enable them to levy tax rates of closer proximity.

In July 1976 Brown signed a bill strongly backed by educational interest groups that provided an additional $272 million in state school aid for the new fiscal year. His budget for this year also included $260 million in new general support for the public schools, some of it financed from local property taxes. Although the Governor had earlier said that school reform would be a condition of greater state aid for schools, only one significant change was included in this legislation, which increased state aid by 12 percent. The single important reform involved eliminating certain abuses in financing adult education and community colleges.

John Pincus was outraged at this general inaction, calling it "a fiasco in light of his [Brown's] stand on reform." In mid-August 1976, shortly before Pincus announced his resignation from the State Board of Educaion, he wrote a highly critical article about Brown's record on educational reform that was published in various newspapers in the state.

Pincus felt that three factors contributed to the Governor's general inaction on school reform. First, Brown could not withstand the pressure of the school lobby composed of teachers' and school administrators' organizations. Second, in the legislative maneuverings in June, Republican lawmakers, assisted by a Democrat serving his last term, held up adoption of the state budget until the Governor agreed to the school finance bill. Third, the Brown administration was caught unprepared. Jerry had been spending much time campaigning for President. Meanwhile, he had no staff working on school policy. Moreover, neither the state finance department, which helps prepare the proposed executive budget, nor Brown's principal lieutenants in the Legislature received a clear signal on reform policies because there was no one in the Governor's office to give them. "The result of this power vacuum," according to Pincus, "was an opportunity for lobbyists and the governor's political opponents to gather together to raid the [state] treasury in the unassailable name of 'our children's welfare.' "

Brown disagreed with the points made by Pincus in the article. One, the Governor said that the importance of his fiscal reforms in adult education and community colleges had been understated.

Two, it was unwise to go ahead with reforms until the potentially costly *Serrano* solution was determined. Three, it was difficult to know whether any reform ideas were likely to work because of the vagueness of educators about the relation between new methods and results. Four, so-called reforms could be simply a means of transferring money from the taxpayers to the educational establishment. Five, it was probably futile to reform the schools if society itself was in trouble because the underlying problems of the schools are problems of society.

Pincus retorted to Brown's response. He said that the Governor's stand would be more defensible if he had not committed himself to particular reforms eight months after assuming office.

In December 1976 the state Supreme Court reaffirmed the *Serrano* decision, which had declared that the gross financial inequities among school districts violated the equal protection clause of the state constitution. Two weeks later, in January of the following year, the Brown administration submitted to the State Board of Education a school finance plan. Aiming at providing "substantial compliance" with the court order, the plan initially stipulated a $3.3 billion increase in state contributions over a five-year period. The proposal called for no new taxes, use of state surplus funds, and revision of existing state school programs to give more money to poor school districts and less money to wealthier ones.

Governor Brown signed the amended bill in September 1977. It raised the amount of state aid to $4.3 billion but no longer contained a reform provision Brown favored—giving parents more power over neighborhood school operations. However, in anticipation of Brown's approval of the measure, John McDermott, the litigation director of the Western Center on Law and Property who had successfully handled the *Serrano* case before the state Supreme Court, called the legislation "a gigantic fraud on California taxpayers." He contended that the measure did not comply with the court decision. "The money [is to be expended] in such a way," he said, "that I think any court would be embarrassed to accept this as substantial compliance [with the *Serrano* ruling.]"

A few months later, in December 1977, McDermott and his associates filed a new brief with the state Supreme Court, contending that the Governor and the Legislature had not met the court's earlier order to eradicate financial inequities from California's public school system. Brown and legislative leaders continued to argue that the legislation substantially complied with the judicial mandate.

McDermott's brief asked the court for immediate action to require rich school districts to start sharing their wealth with poorer school units. The brief pointed out that if the legislation had narrowed all wealth-related spending differences to within two or even three hundred dollars per student, the petitioners, while lamenting the failure of the law to go further, would never have sought this writ. But, the brief continued, leaving wealth-related spending disparities of $1,200 for each pupil makes a travesty of the court's ruling of December 1976 and cannot be tolerated by the petitioners or by the court.

McDermott believes that "substantial compliance" is destined to take its place alongside "separate but equal" among euphemisms unsuccessfully used by lawmakers to evade their constitutional duties. But, as veteran political observer Ed Salzman has noted, McDermott and others may be taking an overly optimistic view that a strict interpretation of the *Serrano* decision may be forthcoming soon. The state Supreme Court has acquired three new judges, all appointed by Governor Brown, since its four-to-three school ruling of December 1976, and the new court might reaffirm "substantial compliance" or even backtrack on the *Serrano* doctrine.

Also in 1977, Jerry again applied his rule of financial limits to the deliberations of Superior Court Judge Paul Egly who was considering the adequacy of a proposed Los Angeles city school integration plan. Asked on a televised news program about how much the state should pay for the cost of integration, Brown remarked, "The court ought to realize there are certain economic constraints, and money that you take from one program then is not available for someone else. . . . If we give more money for schools, that's less money for state hospitals, less money for fighting smog, for helping old people. That judge ought to realize we live in an era of limits. We want a good program, but we've only got so many cookies in the [state money] jar." As for white flight—when whites leave areas to escape mandated integration—the Governor said such a development must be recognized as a reality. He went on, "Judges can issue their edicts but we are a free country, and if people don't like what they see in the schools they can go to a private school or move [elsewhere and go to another public school.]" Then asked if white flight was all right with him, Brown replied that an integrated society was the only way Americans were going to survive, but the question was when this could occur. It takes much leadership, he continued, a lot of working together in the public and private sectors and that is not easy to realize.

Brown has had a more direct role in public higher education. This has been made possible partly by his ex officio membership on the governing bodies of the University of California (the Board of Regents) and the State University and Colleges system (the Board of Trustees). At the meetings of these boards, he has functioned as an academic iconoclast, an intellectual provocateur, and a moral prodder. Then, too, he has the authority to make appointments to these two governing boards as terms expire or vacancies otherwise occur. And in reviewing the budgets of these two academic giants as part of the state's total financial plan, he has taken on other roles—fiscal slasher of items and general resister of approving new funds to support new programs.

The Governor's method of operations at the early sessions of the Board of Regents and the Board of Trustees established the pattern of his relations with the governing boards of both higher educational systems that he has consistently followed. At the first regents' meeting after Brown's election as Governor, held in January 1975, he arrived at 8:30 a.m., ahead of university officials, other regents, and most of the press. His approach of getting on with the business of government was apparent from the outset of the session. Soon after the start of the meeting he explained, "I have a different time sense. I do not believe this country, state, or university is moving with speed. We need to facilitate change more rapidly—the times are moving faster." Later he said, "Let us raise the energy level of deliberations," and called for "new ideas, new thinking, and bringing a new spirit to the University—more money is not my idea of a new spirit."

After Charles Hitch, then UC President, analyzed the Governor's budget for the University in detail, during which time Brown listened intently and took copious notes, the Governor responded point by point. He made detailed comments in staccato fashion on health sciences, the medical school for the Irvine campus, faculty salaries, the Extended University, admission, affirmative action, inflation, and the economy. A longtime observer termed Brown's performance the most comprehensive extemporaneous response by a governor in twenty years. And at the meeting's conclusion, a university officer characterized the Governor as having been rambunctious, humorous, tenacious, and persistent. At a subsequent press conference, Brown raised a question to which he then gave an answer, "The critical question is what is the role of the university in society. The university is a public service institution and is obliged to assume societal leadership."

At the regents' meeting two months later, UC Vice President C. O. McCorkle, Jr. was beginning to explain the University's proposed five-year academic plan, which had been years in the making. Brown soon interrupted him, remarking, "I find the plan difficult to read and too abstract. I would like to focus on something more concrete and come down from the clouds." He described the document as a product of the "squid process—an abstract statement that tells me absolutely nothing . . . spurts of ink across many pages in patterns that look like words but mean nothing." This procedure, he went on, protects an organism from attack from the outside. The objection by some of those in attendance was not to what Brown had said but that he had not made his remarks in private to the university's president. His method, they felt, showed a lack of manners and represented an attack from within and subjected the University of California to public ridicule.

Brown has attended regent and trustee meetings more often than his immediate predecessors and has participated extensively, seldom letting an agenda item, no matter how minor, pass by without at least raising one question. Some meetings, normally adjourned by mid-afternoon, have extended to the early evening hours. As a moral prodder, he has inquired as to why administrators in both systems should get more money than teachers when the basic objective is teaching. He has told the regents that the salary of the UC President and the director of the UC Davis hospitals are too high.

Jerry has lectured academic administrators and professors, as he also has elsewhere to other public employees, about the psychic possibilities and values of public service as partial substitutes for increased financial benefits. He has pontificated to higher educational administrators and to the regents, some of whom are corporate lawyers and big-businesss executives, that in times of economic limits people in high positions should serve as models of doing without, as they should set an example for the people they lead. A trustee's response to Jerry's moral prodding was that Brown has great materialistic humility but very little personal humility as shown by his limited patience with anyone's position on a subject other than his own.

Two officials—one from the University of California and the other from the State University and College system—have made evaluations of Brown in his role as a governing board member that are comparable to appraisals formed by some people about his performance in other areas of state government. They both find some of his questioning worthwhile, although they judge some of his comments to be uninformed needling. The main difficulty, one of them has noted, is that the Governor is critical without being supportive and does not make positive suggestions. The other official has remarked, "Everybody has been waiting for him to suggest concrete reforms of the type he promised. . . . I don't believe he understands the problems. . . . He's simply making political points by shooting off his mouth." Nevertheless,

Brown has many supporters—in and out of the academic world—in his probings into public higher education. He looks for justification and rethinking of programs. He prods to see if the educational giants contain bloat that should be depressed.

Jerry Brown has had further influence on the University of California and the State University and Colleges system through exercising his power to appoint most members of their governing bodies as openings develop on a staggered basis. The state Senate must approve his nominees. The specified term of office of these members on both boards, (exclusive of a few alumni and student members) exceeds that of the Governor, twelve years for the regents since an initiative law of 1974 and eight years for the trustees. This usually assures the state's chief executive of an impact on public higher education over many years, even sometimes after he has left office.

Brown has made seven appointments to the UC Board of Regents and six to the Board of Trustees, both constituting a minority of the membership. His selections to each board have often been unusual, bringing a different type of representation or background to the deliberations. To the UC Board of Regents he has appointed three women and four men. The former consists of an author of a best-selling book, a Mexican-American activist (the first Chicana ever to be a regent), and an Asian-American community leader. The latter is composed of a renowned anthropologist-philosopher, a wealthy economist, the secretary-treasurer of the California Labor Federation (the first labor appointee in many years), and the former state finance director in the Reagan administration.

In making these appointments, Brown demonstrated that he wanted significant revisions in policy and therefore in most instances had chosen aggressive advocates of change. Brown said he wanted to get away from the practice of most regents being coopted by UC officials. "Once they get on the board, they attend those teas, sit on the 50-yard line, meet the Nobel laureates and begin to become advocates of the university. I want them to be advocates of the people." Gray Davis, Brown's executive secretary, stated Jerry's position about the types of people he wanted on the board in a different way. "[He desires] cage rattlers, thinkers, dreamers, and gadflies." In other words, Brown sought people who would lead the University into a more spirited and open era.

For one, Vilma Martinez, the Chicana member, would assure livelier board meetings. As the general counsel for the Mexican-American Legal Defense and Education Fund, she had previously tangled with the University and its lawyers. Mrs. Martinez had been highly critical of UC's handling of a controversial minority admissions case (the Bakke case). From Gregory Bateson, a seventy-two year old outspoken anthropologist, whom Brown termed as one of the state's leading scholars and intellects, Jerry expected and got stinging comments on a broad range of university life, from the quality of the students through the irrelevancy of stricter admissions standards to the competence of the regents themselves. He has rattled the educational cage and shaken up the Board of Regents which Jerry Brown had regarded as simply a rubber stamp for the administrators of the University of California, particularly in generally approving UC budget proposals without making any major reductions. Bateson's efforts have been aimed chiefly at trying to turn the regents into a debating society that pays attention to more than the financial details of management.

To many people the most surprising of an extraordinary set of appointees by Brown to the UC Board of Regents was Verne Orr, director of finance under Ronald Reagan, Jerry's immediate predecessor from the opposing major political party. More recently Orr had been a Reagan delegate to the 1976 Republican national presidential convention. During Orr's period of service in the Reagan administration he had been an ardent advocate and supporter of that governor's "cut, trim, and squeeze" budgetary practices, which included being an economy-minded critic of the University of California. The recommendation by Orr as state finance director most remembered by UC administrators was his unsuccessful proposal that the University of California sell the rare books in its libraries.

Close observers of Jerry Brown were not stunned by his appointment of Orr to the UC Board of Regents. For one thing,

Jerry had earlier chosen Orr to serve on the state Community College Board of Governors. For another, Reagan and Brown both viewed themselves as fiscal conservatives, and Orr believed in carrying out such a philosophy. Also, about two and a half years before being appointed to the Board of Regents, Orr had let Jerry know of his interest in such a post. Brown remembered this overture, and in making the appointment in 1976 said, "I want to send a message to the university that we want to keep a tight rein on spending."

In late 1977 John Galbraith, the chairman of UCLA's academic senate, warned its members that significant changes were taking place in the Board of Regents. He viewed "with great trepidation" the prospect of more active regental intervention in areas previously regarded as faculty responsibilities. He noted that traditionally the regents had considered their function to be that of trustee, delegating responsibility for basic academic policies to the faculty and usually supporting its exercise of that authority. However, recent discussions of admissions, he observed, made clear that many regents want to assume a more active role in evaluating faculty recommendations. Several months earlier the Governor had indicated that possibly the regents should give considerable time to thinking about the University of California and determining its character instead of relying on the "black box of the faculty."

The Governor's six choices for the Board of Trustees of the State University and Colleges system also represent a variegated group made up of three men and three women. The first includes a Mexican-American who is director of the Chicano Studies Center at UCLA, the Black president of a Los Angeles area restaurant chain, and the executive director of an environmental council. The women members are the corporate secretary to the board of directors of an associated students organization of a state university (and the only student trustee, chosen for a two-year term), an attorney who was a founding member of California Women Lawyers, and a professor of government at a Catholic college in Los Angeles. Mary Jean Pew, the college professor, was a part-time research consultant to Jerry Brown for most of a year when he was Secretary of State and then served as his campaign coordinator for more than a year in his race for the governorship in 1974.

With respect to the annual budgets of the University of California and the State University and Colleges system, Brown made very substantial reductions in his first three years. (He also placed an unprecedented lid on state aid to community colleges.) His general, persistent attitude during this period was stated in late 1975 when he was asked about the chances of the UC and state university systems obtaining substantial increases in state monies in the next year. "Somewhere between slim and nil," he answered. Overall, the "nil" part of the prediction prevailed in each year. Practically all increases in any budgetary category approved by Brown were needed to meet the inflationary costs of continuing current programs. In general, no new money was forthcoming for either implementing new programs or for expanding existing ones in the field of higher education. When a new program was desired, an old one was to be cut back or eliminated.

Brown even sought to apply the principle of finding the money within present resources to an anticipated sizable increase in student enrollment. In January 1976 the Governor, in presenting his proposed budget for the University of California, deleted a request for money earmarked to support an additional 2,388 students expected to enroll the next fall. This was an unpre-cedented action, as state money tied to enrollment had never before been withheld by the state. Brown said that his action was based on the feeling that the university could find the money to support the education of these additional students if it seriously looked for it. University officials denied this could be done and said that for the first time some qualified students would have to be turned away.

Approximately a month after Brown's action, UC announced a downward revision of its fall projection to 1,014. Some people in the Brown administration regarded the announcement as capitulation by the university and obvious evidence that the Governor's position had been taken seriously. One of the

Governor's aides said that the university-wide administration had placed considerable pressure on the chancellors, who are the chief executive officers on each campus, to be more realistic about their estimates. The university's vice president for academic affairs denied the validity of this statement, commenting that the change was simply the result of a routine reappraisal of enrollment projections. In any event, the downscaling pleased the Governor; he inserted the additional money for 1,014 students in his budget.

Public higher education received more sympathetic treatment from Brown in his proposed budget for 1978-79 than in the three previous years. For example, the University of California's total request was cut slightly more than a third as much as in the immediately preceding twelve months—$11.2 million compared to more than $30 million. The Governor's support for research also greatly increased, seemingly because much of it was to be undertaken in areas of interest to Jerry and which he felt could contribute to solving certain problems of the state—energy, the environment, and natural resources. In approving this item Brown specified that one-half million dollars should be devoted to the space sciences, which represent some of his biggest contemporary concerns. Also sanctioned, after being rejected in the year before, was a program to prepare minority teachers for advancement through the various faculty ranks.

But the Governor continued his longtime tough policy on compensation for faculty and administrators, proposing only an increase of 5 percent that excluded those who already earned in excess of $50,000 a year. Although Jerry loosened some of the purse strings in the fourth year of his administration, the university's president concluded that the programmatic improvements were "undone by the problems associated with salary proposals, for it is the people in the university who must carry out the programs."

Jerry Brown has supported a wide variety of environmental concerns throughout his gubernatorial administration, although at times he has not fully satisfied various prominent environmental groups. The Sierra Club, the Planning and Conservation League, and the California Coastal Alliance are included among these organizations. As Brown's term as Governor moved on, he increasingly found himself confronted with making difficult decisions about a proper balance between environmental and business developmental interests.

At first many observers felt that Brown was pro-environment and largely inactive in the realm of business—that is, he did not seek to recruit industrial and commercial firms to locate in California. As will be shown later in this chapter, as time passed the Governor became highly active in business affairs without reducing his support for the environment.

Even before being elected Governor, Brown expressed doubts about locating a liquified gas terminal on the California coast. (Liquified natural gas is placed under extremely cold temperatures for conversion into liquid form for shipment in specially-constructed tankers.) Brown felt the supertankers and their cargoes of LNG could be dangerous and constituted potentially serious environmental hazards. During his administration the controversy over the site of an LNG terminal continued, and the question of tanker safety gained broader interest after a tanker exploded in Los Angeles harbor in December 1976. Then the controversy over the building of the Sohio tanker terminal in Long Beach increased bitterly. A Brown aide pointed out that the tankers expected to use this proposed facility were more than twice as large as one of a half billion-barrel oil capacity that had blown up in Los Angeles harbor. He also complained of the Sohio project's adverse impact on air quality. The oil tanker terminal quarrel over safety and pollution illustrates the kinds of battles that have frequently ensued between environmental and business forces during Jerry's years as Governor.

Early in Brown's administration, the Governor appointed a number of environmentally-minded people to high posts. Prominent among them was Claire Dedrick, placed in the cabinet position of resources secretary. Mrs. Dedrick, a conservation activist, had been national vice president of the Sierra Club, a widely-known conservation organization, and a leader in the 1972 successful initiative campaign to establish strong controls over California's coastline development. In 1977 she became the first woman member of the state Public Utilities Commission. There she supported an order to three major energy utilities to take steps to use waste heat from industrial plants to generate electricity. This process creates no additional air pollutants and in some situations reduces their amount.

Another important environmental appointment by Brown was the selection of Tom Quinn, the Governor's chief political strategist, as chairman of the state Air Quality Board. Quinn and other Brown appointees gave strength to an agency that previously had been waging a weak fight against smog. Quinn emeged as a tough administrator and, as political analyst Ed Salzman has emphasized, under the direction of this Brown appointee, the board "forced recall of automobiles, levied large fines, halted large projects and otherwise let the world know that California [meant] to curb air pollution." In 1978 Quinn announced that the battle to clean up automobiles was being won and this meant the board's attention could be shifted to the contemporary major problem of oil refineries and other stationary sources of pollution.

Richard Maullin, also a Brown campaign analyst, landed another top job that has environmental as well as business implications. He was selected by Jerry to be chairman of the state Energy Development and Conservation Commission. Quinn and Maullin both have raised doubts about the feasibility of nuclear energy as a power source. At one point Quinn wrote a letter to Maullin expressing his judgment that an oil-fired power plant could be an effective alternative, with little harm to air quality, to the $3 billion Sundesert nuclear power facility proposed for construction near the desert community of Blythe. Two months before this letter, Maullin had disclosed that utilities in the state had significantly scaled down their projected needs for new nuclear plants up to 1995. Nuclear power cannot live up to its previously exaggerated potential, Maullin reported.

The Governor has long been dubious about widespread use of nuclear energy, feeling that the storing and transporting of its waste and the possible escape of radiation are dangerous propositions. His obvious preference is to rely on alternative forms of energy if that option can be sufficiently developed. In a speech to a forestry association, he called for increased research into wood products as a potential energy source. "The use of wood chips and wood products . . . is a very old idea," he said, "I see in this state a potential for the use of wood products that cannot be used for anything else to generate steam." According to the state Resources Agency, Brown continued, wood has the potential to generate 2,000 to 3,000 megawatts annually, which is the equivalent of two or three large nuclear plants.

Allied with the Governor's interest in wood as an energy source is his current proposal for a major program of reforestation in California. Although the complete details of the proposal have not yet been developed (the program has just recently been suggested), the state's resources secretary has suggested the replanting of more than 4 million acres of public and private forests and an ambitious tree planting program in cities. In the mountains the program would generate jobs, improve the environment, and create lumber and energy resources. In urban centers it would beautify the land and be a natural remover of pollutants.

Brown's aspirations for a predominantly nonnuclear society for California have gone beyond his expectations for wood as an energy source. In the Governor's proposed budget for 1978-79 he included an item of approximately $200 million for developing certain other sources—coal gasification, geothermal, solar, and biomass conversion. Earlier in the Brown administration he had signed a bill that gave a financial credit to those installing solar heating.

In the summer of 1976 when the life of the coastline conservation initiative was about to expire and new legislation was an absolute necessity to protect the California coast from further excessive development, Brown interceded. At the eleventh hour his aides, using the threat of the Governor calling a special session, strongly lobbied certain state senators who then voted in favor of the bill.

About three months earlier, in June 1976, while Brown was campaigning for President, the nuclear safeguards initiative was on the ballot. The measure, which was decisively defeated, would have made the nuclear industry completely responsible for paying victims for damages from nuclear accidents and would have sharply curtailed the operations of nuclear power plants in California unless the Legislature conclusively found them to be safe. Brown took no stand on the highly controversial initiative which drew 300,000 more votes than did the total candidates in the presidential primary races on the same ballot. In the month preceding the election, Brown had belatedly endorsed a package of three bills that before election day gave the state strict but less severe nuclear safety laws.

In line with Brown's many environmental-minded appointees to ecological positions, about a year after Jerry's sanction of these three bills and voter defeat of the proposition, he made a "bombshell" choice. He selected for membership on the state Board of Forestry David Pesonen, an environmental lawyer, strong antagonist of nuclear power development, and chairman of the committee that had drafted the nuclear safeguards initiative. The forestry board is a rule-making agency for the timber-cutting industry. Its lobbyists said that the appointment of Pesonen would result in "sheer open warfare."

Brown also picked up an environmental idea from his predecessor Ronald Reagan. Renaming Reagan's Ecology Corps and expanding its purpose and size, Jerry moved ahead with the California Conservation Corps which he lobbied President Carter to use nationally. The first corps of sixty-three members, including eighteen women, was organized in early 1977 and undertook a year-long program of work on ecology-oriented projects. The eventual goal is to establish eighteen camps and employ 1,200 youths.

In 1977 the Governor also demonstrated his interest in enlarging state park acreage. He signed a bill that provided for spending more than $52 million to buy twenty-five coastal sites. Most of the money to be used to expand existing state parks and to purchase new ones was derived from a park fund approved by the state electorate in the preceding November. The rest was obtained from the general fund surplus. Brown lopped about $13.6 million from the proposed legislation before signing it.

For two years the Governor has been trying to gain legislative approval of a $3.5 billion program to complete the state water project, which had been started many years before. Some opponents of the original recent bill felt it had too much protection for water quality and fish in the Sacramento-San Joaquin Delta—both environmental features. At the same time, they contended that no real assurance existed that the peripheral canal, which would be built around the delta and be a more efficient device for transporting water to the Central Valley and Southern California, would ever be constructed.

In 1977, as Brown increasingly realized the need to bring the interests of environmentalists and business into greater consort, he turned the era of limits theme around on the environmentalists. Up to this point environmentalists had been applauding the concept as a recognition of the need for conservation. The Governor now said that conservationists had to realize the theme pertained to them as well. Our expanding technology, he warned, is running up against certain limits—physical, political, technological, and foreign policy—and these limits apply not only to business and government but also to environmental groups. Environmentalists, he stressed, must pay attention to jobs and the economy in evaluating all their programs.

Starting mainly in the third year of the Brown administration, the Governor expended much effort to counteract the widely circulated opinion that he opposed economic expansion in California. In part this attitude grew out of three factors. One was Brown's rhetoric about an era of limits and "small is beautiful," which was despised by many business people. Another was his support of Chavez and the establishment of an agricultural labor relations board, which brought forth antagonism from agribusiness and various farmers. Still another was Brown's opposition to construction of the Melones Dam, which agitated the building-trade unions and the construction industry.

More important to the emergence of this negative image of Brown, including blaming him for preventing industrial growth and the creation of more jobs in the state, were three other pieces of evidence, none of which stands up well under close scrutiny. The first claim was that California had an extremely bad business climate. This statement was based chiefly on a study by a Dun and Bradstreet subsidiary, which ranked California next to last of the forty-eight contiguous states as a favorable location for a new business plant. The report, however, had used 1974 statistics and Ronald Reagan was then Governor. Moreover, the analysis had been prepared for a confidential client and was never made available for public scrutiny.

The second claim was that the Brown administration was responsible for the Dow Chemical Company's decision not to build a $500 million petrochemical plant in northern California, strongly opposed by leading environmentalists. Actually Brown's Office of Planning and Research held unprecedented public hearings in December 1976 in an attempt to clarify the complex technical problems centering on the project and to speed up the hearing process. The company needed to obtain sixty-five permits (only four of which had been acquired), many of them requiring local or regional approval rather than state sanction. If Brown and the Legislature had sought to waive the necessity for obtaining the permits, they would have overridden local and regional authorities and the action would have been tied up in the courts for years.

The third claim against Brown was that he was responsible for the state's unemployment rate being consistently higher than that of the rest of the nation. The facts were that in early 1977 California's rate was only seven-tenths of one percent higher than the national figure and that approximately 360,000 new jobs had been created in the previous year. By June of 1977 the state's rate of employment was lower than the nation's—by one-fifth of one percent—for the first time in seventeen years.

In typical whirlwind, intensive fashion once Brown has decided on an objective, the Governor set out to replace this negative image with a positive one. He began talking about the era of possibilities, a much more pleasant phrase to business interests and labor unions, saying that the era of limits makes the era of possibilities a reality. He appointed Alan Rothenberg, an executive of the Bank of America, as interim secretary of business and transportation, and then chose as his successor Richard Silberman, a San Diego investor-banker-entrepreneur, who had been treasurer of Brown's 1976 presidential campaign.

Jerry divided the state's Agriculture and Service Agency into three parts; gave cabinet status to one of its divisions, the directorship of the department of food and agriculture; and selected as director a dirt farmer, Richard Rominger of the small community of Winters. Brown supported legislation to make the plant-construction permit process easier. He went to Japan to try to interest automobile manufacturers there in locating an assembly plant in California. He was accompanied by Silberman, who had sold his bank to the Bank of Tokyo of California two years earlier and had important business contacts in Japan.

The Governor traveled to Canada to talk with its prime minister and to Mexico to discuss with its president the transmission of gas from their countries to California. On Brown's trip to England to speak at the memorial service for British economist Ernest Schumacher, author of *Small is Beautiful*, he conferred with and impressed English financiers and businessmen. After these foreign trips the Governor asked the state Franchise Tax Board to consider exempting some multinational businesses from a tax method that reportedly discourages their expansion in California.

The Governor journeyed to New York City after a day's stopover in New Jersey to campaign for reelection of that state's chief executive Brendan Byrne who had been helpful to Jerry in the 1976 presidential primary there. In the "Big Apple" Brown met with corporate executives, investment bankers, and broker-age-house leaders. He developed several themes in a talk with these influential people. California is on the cutting edge of the new technology. Fifteen percent of the nation's new jobs in the last year were created in California. Corporate and sales taxes had not increased since he took over the gubernatorial office. Consumerism and conservation are important in his thinking but so is business growth. He told, too, how he supported elimination of the business inventory tax—a levy applied annually to goods being held by businesses for resale—but how he did not favor packages of incentives that would place newcomers at an advantage over corporations already operating in the state.

Jerry even attended a ribbon-cutting ceremony breaking ground for a new brewery in southern California. "I have never done this before in my entire life," he said, "but I am doing it because it symbolizes the attractive business climate here in California. Besides, this beer is compatible with life in California." (Brown's two uses of "life" apparently were merely coincidental with the fact that the brewery involved makes Miller high life beer.)

Before a meeting of labor unions, church groups, and civil-rights organizations, Brown reaffirmed his support for the proposed Humphrey-Hawkins Full Employment and Balanced Growth Act, which some business leaders opposed. That measure would provide for considerable financial underwriting by the national government of the goal of jobs for practically all of sixteen years of age (later changed to twenty) and over who want them. Jerry had first supported this proposal in his run for the presidency in 1976.

Brown also enlisted the National Guard in a plan to relieve the massive unemployment problem in the city of Oakland. Under the plan, which was praised by local business representatives, 200 to 500 recruits would be trained each year for about five months at armed forces locations and then return to Oakland with their acquired skills to jobs awaiting them. Jerry pointed out that no limit existed on the number of recruits who could be trained after the initial stages of the plan got under way. The Governor's chief aide further noted that the program could be a model for other cities, saying that there was no reason why every community should not have National Guard links to community needs.

Finally Brown identified himself with an economic future for

California that was truly big—the concept of space—which one writer has identified as "the era of the illimitable." Rusty Schweickart, the first American astronaut to maneuver in space without being attached to a spacecraft, went on loan from the National Aeronautics and Space Administration to the Governor's office. Rusty explained that his concern was with space as an extension of the human environment.

Brown began talking about the possibilities of space colonies and California putting up a satellite alone or in conjunction with other states. In December 1977, the Governor signed the first state-NASA agreement on the application of space technology to state problems. In his 1978 state of the state message, delivered in the following month, he said, "When I speak of space, I don't think of movies. I see the future of our species penetrating the universe." In this speech he proposed the state invest $5 million in the practical application of satellite technology for communications and the monitoring of natural resources.

Brown certainly had become aggressive in seeking to recruit new business and to bring people out of the ranks of the unemployed. Moreover, in philosophizing and making proposals about space, he could not speak in bigger terms and much of business likes the idea of bigness and expansion. Through Brown's pro-business and pro-labor pronouncements and activities, he had vigorously sought to create a positive image to replace the negative one that had confronted him.

Jerry Brown has successfully held to his early pledge of no general tax increases (as in state income and sales taxes), and in December 1977 expressed optimism that, if reelected to a second term, he could avoid such increases in the next four years. Such a hold-the-tax line attitude, accompanied by some drastic budget slashes over the years and well-publicized examples of personal frugality, have given substance to Brown's advocacy of fiscal conservatism. Brown prefers to state the matter another way. "I'm not a fiscal conservative; I'm just cheap."

Despite the absence of general tax increases, Californians have been paying more state taxes. In times of inflation, the income of people tends to rise and they move into higher income brackets that take a larger percentage of their income. However, unlike the federal income tax, the California state income levy has a percentage ceiling, which produces a heavier tax burden on those at the low- and medium-income levels in an inflationary period. Annual adjustments or indexing of income-tax brackets to compensate for the effects of inflation have not been enacted. The state government thus continues to reap an inflationary dividend.

While the rates of general taxes have not risen during the Brown administration, the annual state budgets have gone up considerably. The Governor's budget total has increased each year—$11.9 billion in 1975-76 to $12.6 billion in 1976-77 to $15 billion in 1977-78 to a proposed $16.2 billion in 1978-79. His latest proposed spending program amounted to $17.4 billion, tapping part of the state's $3.2 billion surplus, which has expanded considerably since the Reagan years. Some legislators wanted a portion of this surplus returned to the people, arguing that it is their money and should not be withheld from them.

A study by the state Legislative Analyst's office shows that state spending during the Jerry Brown years, including his most recent financing proposals of January 1978, represents an annual increase of 5.2 percent. By adjusting for inflation and population growth to make the figures comparable, the average increase during the eight Reagan years (1967-74) was 3.1 percent and in Pat Brown's two terms (1959-66) was 5.7 percent.

According to Finance Director Roy Bell, who has served under all three of these governors, major reductions in state spending can be achieved only by curtailing big state programs. However, since most programs have been created or sustained by powerful special-interest groups, eliminating or substantially reducing them is extremely difficult. When asked about Jerry Brown's relatively high rate of spending, Bell attributed it chiefly to cost-of-living increases that the Legislature had incorporated into welfare and other state activities. After living-cost adjustments are written into laws, he remarked, financial control becomes more difficult. The Governor, in his fourth year in office, lamented, "It is very hard to cut government. The appetite is strong, continuing, and inexorable." In general, over the years Brown has talked about slowing the growth of state government and deciding upon the direction that government should take rather than reducing its size.

Brown and the Legislature tried in vain in 1977 to agree on property-tax relief legislation. Their interest was stimulated by discontent among many taxpayers whose bills had skyrocketed because of great increases in the assessed value of their property. Also prodding these state officials was the circulation of an initiative proposal by longtime tax reformer Howard Jarvis that would severely curb local property taxes by limiting them to a fraction of their present level. The Brown-backed tax relief bill, which was only one of several on the subject, provided for using state surplus funds for homeowner and renter relief, limiting the growth of local property revenue, permitting a different level of assessed value for business and residential property, and taxing property on the circuit breaker principle—that is, personal income as well as home value—thereby benefiting the poor and those of medium income. Immediately before adjournment of the 1977 legislative session the bill was killed in the state Senate, principally because of its circuit breaker feature and the cramming of too many features into the package. Some also judged the bill to be loaded with attempts at social reform and to be "too gimmicky." Brown suggested that legislators who had killed the bill should go home, meditate, and be educated by the voters.

In December 1977, slightly more than three months after the legislative session had ended without the passage of property-tax legislation, the Jarvis initiative officially qualified for the June state election ballot of the following year. The initiative was filed with more than twice the number of signatures needed to place it before the voters—an indication of the extensiveness of opposition to the existing property-tax arrangement. It was a sweeping measure, specifying the amending of the state constitution so that annual property taxes would be limited to one percent of market value. This would produce about a two-thirds cut in local property taxes.

In the words of Assembly Speaker Leo McCarthy, the initiative would be a disaster for local government, requiring a major decrease in basic city, county, and school services (unless, of course, the state government enlarged state aid, took over certain local services, or authorized local governments to levy new types of taxes). Jarvis' response to McCarthy was that the initiative would bring relief to overburdened taxpayers and force local governments to reexamine their priorities.

In January 1978, as the Legislature reconvened, Jerry Brown in his traditionally short state of the state message called that body into special session to develop a $1 billion property-tax relief measure. A major advantage of the special session, which would run concurrent with the regular session, was that legislation passed by majority vote would be in effect ninety days after being signed by the Governor, whereas if enacted in a regular session it would not become operative until the following January unless passed by a two-thirds majority. Brown urged the Legislature to have the bill on his desk by January 27. This was a key date. It was the last day for filing arguments against the property tax initiative, arguments that might be more persuasive to the voters if they were able to state that recent legislation made this initiative unnecessary. Important legislators expressed skepticism about the Legislature's ability to reach a consensus by this early date. And they were right. Some observers believed that the people would favor the initiative regardless of what the Legislature did about property-tax reform.

Brown has ranged widely in programs and controversies of state government. When he has felt strongly about an issue, he has plunged deeply into the fray and risked the possibility of tarnishing his political image if the cause suffered defeat. This was the situation with regard to agricultural labor relations. When his conviction has been part of his moral fiber, he has opposed a proposition widely sanctioned by the public while supporting programs that seemed contrary. The subject of capital punishment and anti-crime bills illustrate this stance.

In public school and higher education he has tended to employ a different style—one of attacking and questioning present conditions but not putting forth new ways of dealing with the problems or not following through on them. In addition, in higher education he has chosen a number of appointees to governing boards who have acted as agents of change. At other times, after initially favoring one side of a controversy (for example, environmental protection), Brown has seen the necessity of developing a balance with the other side (economic growth) and has embarked on a vigorous program on behalf of the latter. And on further occasions, as in the field of public finance, he has generally sought to hold to a position of fiscal conservatism while realizing the great difficulty of slowing the growth and cost of state government in a period of inflation, greater consumer demands for services and facilities, and formidable special-interest groups.

Chapter Eight

Brown and His Governmental World

For an individual who campaigned for Governor in support of a one-house legislature and hurled a negative broadside at the state government establishment, Governor Brown has had surprisingly good relations with the Legislature. Such a relationship is, of course, basic to a governor's success.

There are several major reasons why this positive condition has prevailed. The Democrats, in strong control of both houses, were pleased to be free of Ronald Reagan after his eight years as Governor; they would now have a much better possibility of enacting many measures that had long been bottled up. From the start Brown did not present the Legislature with a long list of proposals. Believing in coequal branches of government, Jerry has allowed the Legislature wide latitude.

Brown also supported the winner of the powerful speakership of the Assembly, Leo McCarthy, over Willie Brown (who regularly calls himself "the good Brown"). A governor in California can make little progress unless he has the cooperation of the Speaker. Brown's liaison staff members, particularly Mark Poche in the first two years, learned not to bother the Speaker of the Assembly with every problem, but instead to visit the chairperson and members of various committees. They similarly learned at an early time about the individuality of senators and the necessity of approaching them on a one-by-one basis.

Leo McCarthy, second only in power to the Governor in state government, is a formidable politician because he alone has the authority to appoint committee chairpersons and members and to assign bills to particular committees. In contrast James Mills, the Senate President Pro Tem, has less clout because in this legislative house a five-member Rules Committee, which he chairs but has simply one vote, shares the power concentrated in the Assembly Speaker.

McCarthy, a native of New Zealand and forty-four when elected Speaker, has much governmental experience—deputy to a state senator, member of the San Francisco Board of Supervisors, and assemblyman since 1968. He is a thoughtful, mild-mannered, hard-working individual possessing what his colleagues term "a tough streak." That toughness often enables him and his major lieutenants to round up necessary votes, as was the case with the agricultural labor relations bill in which Brown and his aides also took part.

Brown and McCarthy present the appearance of close cooperation, and it is evident that on a number of measures they have worked together successfully. Various legislators, however, feel that the alliance is based on expediency and necessity and not on mutual admiration. They do not believe a close personal relationship exists, but as one of them said, Who is personally close to Jerry?

Although McCarthy accepted the campaign chairmanship of Brown's 1976 presidential campaign, he has been displeased with Jerry from time to time. Late in Brown's first year, McCarthy told a reporter, "We're protecting him now. I'm killing . . . bills that could embarrass him. . . . At least he could let us know when someone from our counties is being appointed to a judgeship or a state job." Since that time Brown has broken the habit of not informing individual legislators. However, more than two years later, as Jerry's third year neared an end, McCarthy still expressed dissatisfaction, "If Brown has a fault it is that he cannot look at more than one thing at a time. He is introverted. He has come about one-third of the way in understanding the legislators and their concerns and problems." At times McCarthy has shown considerable independence, as in opposing the agricultural farm labor initiative (not the previous legislation), which Jerry wholeheartedly supported. An assistant to the Governor stated that McCarthy had done this because he preferred to see measures enacted through the regular legislative process.

In an age when governmental chief executives have generally been becoming stronger, Brown's belief is that the public interest is best served when the executive and legislative branches can perform their responsibilities without undue pressure from each other and when there can be a reasonable separation of powers. He has sought to realign the relationship of the two branches by having the Legislature take on a greater leadership role in lawmaking.

This gubernatorial effort to increase legislative leadership has met considerable criticism and negative reaction, much of it from legislators. As a prominent state senator has pointed out, "What Jerry does is very frustrating. We legislators work hard but we really don't know what he wants and what he doesn't want. How can we do our work when the leader of our party will not provide the type of guidance we need?" Other legislators have a contrary view, believing that their smaller constituencies place them in closer touch with the people and thus make them more able to formulate legislation that meets public needs. Still other law-makers feel that although Brown encourages the Legislature to propose legislation he takes too much credit for some new laws.

Occasionally Brown has made exceptions to his philosophy of a stronger role for the Legislature. On a few pet projects such as conservation, medical malpractice insurance, and certain budget items, he has directly lobbied legislators even to the point of getting an aide to go to individual legislative district offices. As a legislative staff member warned, "When Jerry really gets interested in something, watch out." In some instances his staff has actually gone on to the floor of a legislative chamber to talk with and pressure particular members. Since lobbying in a legislative house is prohibited these people have been ordered to leave, which is a delicate and embarrassing situation.

The normal procedure followed is for Brown and his executive secretary Gray Davis, who eventually also became known as chief of staff, to comment on no more than about 20 percent of the bills that are introduced. In speaking about this support-oppose system, Davis has said, "We wait until the other bills come our way. Let's face it, with thousands of pieces of legislation being introduced during a session, Governor Brown can only give so much time to approving or disapproving bills if he ever expects to be involved with anything else. We have drawn a line and the legislators are well aware of our concern for good laws and the impossibility of our turning our attention to every proposal that is presented. While many legislators would prefer that the Governor get more involved, we believe we are conducting ourselves in the most serviceable fashion possible by making the Legislature accept its own responsibility."

Vetoes of bills by Brown approximate the same proportion as those Reagan killed. Reagan turned down 171 bills in his first year and 198 in his last. Brown vetoed 148—about 10 percent of the total in his initial year—184 in his second, and 126 in his third. At first glance, this similarity between these two men seems strange since Reagan was from the opposite party than the majority of the legislators while Brown and most assemblymen and senators are from the same party. The main reason is that Reagan rejected a number of bills on the basis of partisanship while Jerry disapproves certain proposals that he finds only mildly distasteful. Brown examines many bills very closely and rejects some of them on a minor point without fear of offending particular legislators.

Many bills are vetoed by Brown because he considers their subject matter improper for state government to handle. He regards their substance as more appropriate to the province of another level of government, an administrative agency, or the private world. He rejects other bills because they will produce bureaucratic growth or increased spending. The Governor personally writes many of the messages accompanying the vetoed bills.

Here is a sample of Brown's veto messages. In turning down a legislative proposal to permit Los Angeles County to remove about 60,000 of its employees from the social security system, Brown's message was that while social security had its problems, it offers needed portable pension benefits to "a mobile and restless society." His message in rejecting a proposal to create a state department of tourism and motion picture development: "There is no credible evidence that a special state bureaucracy . . . can promote tourism more effectively than the Chamber of Commerce and local business." Regarding his opposition to a bill calling for the establishment of a nominating committee for gubernatorial appointments to the Board of State University and College Trustees and the state Community College Board of Governors: "I just don't see the public good is to be accomplished by creating yet another advisory council with no binding power and therefore no final responsibility."

On a measure to establish a state recreation fund for grants to local governments for special recreation programs: "I am not persuaded that the state, as opposed to local government, should assume the leadership role with respect to the leisure time activities funded by this bill." And at times Brown's reason for turning down a bill is that he believes its language is muddled. For instance, in dealing negatively with a bill declaring that the public retirement fund "is a trust fund for the benefit of members and retired members and their survivors and beneficiaries," Brown said that the proposal would "add certain language to the government code, the legal effect of which is not clear." Brown's uncanny ability to sense the temper of the times and to reflect correctly public feeling is evident in such messages which support the consumer, accountability, and local government but attack expanded bureaucracies, bigger government, and ambiguity.

Some legislators who have had bills vetoed by Jerry have made interesting interpretations of why he took such actions. In a philosophical and tolerant vein Assemblyman John Vasconcellos, a liberal Democrat from San Jose, has observed, "There is a curious convergence of the new left and the old right. They both have a certain anti-establishment bias. . . . I think Jerry Brown carries some of that same bias against institutions that Ronald Reagan had, but for different reasons. I don't think Ronald Reagan had a lot of concern about people. Jerry Brown has a lot of concern but seems unsure how to see that assistance truly gets through to them. That's a problem all of us have at this point."

Another assemblyman, from the other side of the political fence, Jerry Lewis, a Republican from Redlands, was more biting in his comment. He said, "I think the governor is attempting to communicate to the public a posture of fiscal conservatism—the knight on Ronald Reagan's white horse challenging the bureaucracy." And then Lewis added enigmatically, "But the problem is that the saddle is kind of tilted." Brown probably would not deny the general validity of Vasconcellos' statement nor even part of the Lewis remarks but he would object to words like "posture" and "tilted saddle."

Although Jerry has worked in general harmony with the Legislature, he is not warmly liked even by most Democratic party members. This could have been expected, as he talked against locker-room politics during his campaign and his personality makeup is such that he does not want to be "one of the boys." He antagonized a number of lawmakers by catapulting over a generation of older, more experienced Democrats, a number of them in the Legislature, who aspired to be Governor. Some dislike him because at times he seems too brash, egotistical, and noncommunicative. His vagueness, which is sometimes purposeful, and his general refusal to propose multi-point programs are also sources of legislative irritation. Many politicians do not like to be left without direction and in the dark.

Despite the hostility, dislike, or personal indifference of various legislators toward Brown, most lawmakers respect him for his intellectual prowess or fear opposing him because of his great power, particularly in appointments and the authority to veto individual items in the budget. Generally, too, they admire what one of them has described as "Brown's uncanny ability to put complex issues in perspective, disarm even the most aggressive opponent, and make the most mundane matter sound profound." Moreover, legislators know about Brown's continuing very high level of public approval. Members of the same party would seldom run the political risk of bucking a governor possessing extraordinarily broad voter sanction.

In turn, Brown recognizes the importance of maintaining cooperative relations with the Legislature. In 1976, for example, he hit the campaign trail in support of various Democratic candidates for legislative office, a gesture not soon forgotten by those who won. Jerry further tries to gain bipartisan support, seeking out Republicans as well as Democrats. Illustrative of Brown's sensitivity to the retention of good relations with the Legislature was a reason he stated in 1978 in ordering the firing of Dr. Josetta Escamilla-Mondanaro, a pediatrician and chief of the state's drug-abuse program.

The dismissal case centered on a letter Dr. Mondanaro wrote to a friend on official stationery that contained vivid—some people said obscene—language. The Governor indicated that his desire for good relations with the Legislature may have played a part in his decision. In her letter, she referred to Assemblyman John Vasconcellos as someone with "his head (or something) screwed on wrong." Brown said this reference to a legislator was "improper and totally unnecessary. It undermines the relationship between the executive and legislative branches, which is essential to carrying out the goals of my Administration." Whether or not Brown's reference to executive-legislative relationships was an afterthought (it was made at the time of the appeal of the dismissal) is not significant here. The important point is that he felt it was worth saying.

Jerry Brown's impact on the judiciary was apparent from the

inception of his administration. The Legislature, with both houses controlled by the Democrats, quickly created forty-nine new judgeships, and deaths and retirements soon made another fifteen posts available. But the Governor did not fill a single one of these sixty-four vacancies during his first seven months in office. Some judges argued that many court calendars were already crowded and the positions should be filled. Brown's frank reply was to question bluntly whether all judges were giving full value for the money spent on them, meaning that some did not work full time.

Jerry's aides pointed out that Brown was giving thorough review to the need to fill each vacancy because every trial judge, including office, bailiff, clerk, and law library, cost $200,000 to $250,000. The Governor and his legal affairs secretary J. Anthony Kline also noted that the problem of overcrowded court dockets was traceable to an increasing public tendency to utilize the courts for every social and economic malaise. "We can no longer address court congestion," suggested Kline, "by throwing more judges into the system."

The Brown administration suggested two particular judicial changes in its early months that it pursued for four years. One is court consolidation. The other is the substitution of arbitration for the judicial process in certain matters.

Brown finally started filling some vacant judgeships, many of them from outside the dominant white-male club atmosphere that existed. By the end of his first year, he had made fifty-seven selections to positions below the level of the state Supreme Court. Twenty-eight of them, that is, slightly more than half, were from minorities—9 Mexican-Americans, 9 Blacks, 6 white women, and 4 Asian-Americans. Caucasian males made up the remainder. Some of the minority and majority appointees were different in another way. They were night law school graduates (a number having worked a long time to earn a law degree while carrying a fulltime job), individuals practicing in inner-city neighborhoods, or attorneys with public-service legal experience. During Jerry's entire term he followed this same general pattern of judicial appointments, thus raising the very low proportion of ethnic minorities and women on the bench.

At times a Brown appointment has involved the elevation of a distinguished minority jurist from one judicial post to another. Bernard Jefferson, a magna cum laude graduate of Harvard Law School, author of the widely used *California Evidence Benchbook,* and the trial-court judge in the famous school integration cases of *Serrano* v. *Priest* is a prominent illustration. He was promoted from the Superior Court of Los Angeles County to the Second District Court of Appeals in the same county by Brown—many years after such action could have appropriately been taken by a previous administration.

The Legislature created thirty-four new judgeships in early 1975 but about the same time in the next year the Governor vetoed a bill to establish forty-five more judicial positions, most of them in Los Angeles County. In the Governor's veto message, he stated, "The demands on the state treasury are escalating while the pace of judicial reform is slow. In addition, the [Los Angeles] County Board of Supervisors opposes this measure."

Another point of successful opposition by Brown pertained to the salaries of judges. Since the Reagan years jurists had been the only type of public employees in the state (except the Los Angeles County Board of Supervisors) who automatically received yearly cost-of-living increases tied directly to the consumer price index. By 1976, as a result of the continuing rise in prices, the range of judicial salaries had far outdistanced that of the other two branches, extending from about $45,000 to almost $67,000. The Governor succeeded in getting a freeze placed on compensation of judges for almost two years and in limiting subsequent pay hikes to not more than 5 percent annually.

Also in 1976 Brown sought a major judicial reform to merge justice, municipal, and superior courts. The objective was to make it easier to transfer judges and other court personnel temporarily to where they were most needed. Although various county boards of supervisors agreed with the Brown-sponsored proposal, some judges actively and successfully lobbied against the legislation. Many legislators are lawyers and have close associations with judges before whom they later present cases.

Brown and Kline have kept hammering away at the lawyers and judges. In view of the monopolistic nature of the legal profession, they sought, through the introduction of legislation by a friendly assemblyman, to require attorneys to donate a specified amount of time. The total time would be forty hours a year given to serving the poor. The statutory effort failed. Kline and the State Judicial Council, an administrative arm of the state's judicial branch, tangled in mid-1976 when a report by the latter said that judges were working harder but the court backlog was growing. Kline retorted that the report was of dubious merit because it accepts certain deficiencies in the judicial system such as five and a half hour work days for many judges. Kline added that his personal research, during which he sat in courtrooms unannounced, revealed a judge leaving at 2 p.m. on a Friday afternoon.

The battle by Brown and Kline with lawyers' and judges' groups continued in 1978 when they announced their intention to have legislation presented that would move some lawsuits and criminal cases from the courts to arbitrators. The decisions of the arbitrators could be appealed to the courts. Kline remarked that some lawyers were part of the problem and not part of the solution because they opposed such reform. A resolution by the State Bar Board of Governors, adopted by an eleven-to-five vote, took sharp issue with Kline. It accused him of possessing nihilistic views and referred to a know-nothing element that rises up for brief intervals to claim that lawyers and judges are unnecessary obstructions to some form of pure, simple, and elementary justice. The resolution then became ever harsher: " 'Models of courts' without laws, judges, or lawyers are well known in the people's courts of Nazi Germany and the peasant courts of the People's Republic of China. We doubt that California wants to copy these models."

Kline replied politely but firmly, saying that he was sorry some members of the board of governors had taken offense when none had been meant. He was merely trying, he said, to express his conviction that because of the increasing number of lawyers in the state and the greater competition for legal business, there was resistance to needed court reform. Kline warned, "Those lawyers who demand more judges as the answer to our problems are precisely the same people who have consistently opposed reforms that would decrease the need to repeatedly enlarge the judiciary in this state, which is already the largest in the world."

During a short span of time in 1977, the Supreme Court of California felt the influence of Jerry Brown—one of long-lasting importance. In less than eight months of that year, two members retired from this court and a third, eighty-three years of age, was forced to leave because of senility. This gave the Governor the opportunity to nominate three persons to be justices of the seven-member judicial body, subject to confirmation or disapproval by the Commission on Judicial Appointments.

The first two selections by Brown broke an all white-male tradition for this court. For the chief justiceship Jerry chose Rose Elizabeth Bird, a relatively young woman of forty years who had been serving as secretary of agriculture and services, where she had been the first woman cabinet member in the state's history. Brown could have nominated for the chief justiceship an associate justice of the Supreme Court or a judge from a lower judicial level, but he decided against doing so.

Rose Bird, unmarried and living with her mother, had first met Jerry seventeen years earlier when both were students at the University of California, Berkeley. She had served as a legislative intern in Sacramento, a law clerk to a justice of the Nevada Supreme Court, a staff member in the public defender's office in Santa Clara County where she obtained much experience as both a trial and appellate lawyer, and a law professor at Stanford University. She had also worked in both Brown campaigns for Secretary of State and for Governor in 1970 and 1974, respectively, before accepting the state cabinet post which she occupied for more than two years.

Wiley Manuel, a black, was Brown's second nominee to the state's highest court. Although Ms. Bird's selection was not a great surprise, that of Manuel was unexpected by him and by many other people. He was comparatively unknown and speculation had focused on Black and Mexican-American judges and lawyers of greater prominence to be tapped for the position. The forty-nine year old Manuel had been appointed by Brown the year before as a superior court judge in Alameda County (Oakland); previously he had spent twenty-two years as a lawyer with the state Attorney General's office, finishing his tenure there as chief assistant attorney general in charge of the civil division. He was lauded by a spokesman for that office when nominated to an associate justiceship by Brown as "probably one of the best attorneys the state has had the good fortune to have in its employ."

Controversy raged around the nomination of Rose Bird, while the reception given to the choice of Manuel was the exact opposite. Some people disliked her nomination because she was a woman. Others found her liberal outlook distasteful, particularly the prominent role she had played in the drafting of the agricultural labor relations act and some of her actions as an assistant public defender. But these would not be sufficient reasons for the Commission on Judicial Appointments to turn down the nomination.

The opposition therefore concentrated its fire on her lack of judicial experience—a characteristic, it should be noted, that also applied to California Governor Earl Warren upon his appointment as Chief Justice of the United States. Ms. Bird's response was "I think I have done my time in the trenches. I've spent most of my professional career in the jails and in the courts of this state." Her supporters counterattacked, stating she was a superb criminal lawyer who possesses intelligence, a keen analytical mind, administrative ability, and human sensitivity. The trial lawyers' association of the state, which rated her as highly qualified for the appointment, also praised the nomination.

The Commission on Judicial Appointments consisted at this time of the acting chief justice of the state Supreme Court, the presiding judge of the second district state appellate court, and the Attorney General of California. The first named, Mathew Tobriner, who had been appointed to the state Supreme Court by Pat Brown, soon made his support known, while the second individual, Parker Wood, acted to the contrary. This put the swing vote in the hands of Evelle Younger, the Attorney General and then the front-running unannounced candidate for the Republican nomination for Governor in the following year.

Considerable pressure was placed on Younger, especially by the conservative wing of the state's Republican party, and for a while he vacillated. Younger felt it was a bad appointment but that his assignment was to determine whether she was qualified. His final decision was that she was qualified, and he voted to confirm her appointment. With the swearing-in of Ms. Bird in March 1977, she became merely the third woman in any state to become chief justice of a state supreme court. (The first had been in Arizona in 1965 and the second in North Carolina ten years later.) At the Bird ceremony Brown predicted that among his administration's activities, her appointment would be remembered as "an act of lasting significance."

Younger's unhappiness over the Bird appointment had not yet run its course. Later in the same year he announced that he would have legislation introduced to limit the term of chief justices. A chief justice technically serves a twelve-year term, but as that time is about to expire the name of this justice is placed on the ballot without opposition to seek a vote of confidence. This procedure means that so far each chief justice has served until retirement or death, which in Ms. Bird's case might extend to thirty or more years.

Younger's proposal was to rotate the chief justiceship every three or four years. He said, "I don't care whether it's Rose Bird or anyone else. The fact that a person of that age has, under ordinary circumstances, so many years to serve as chief justice is significant. . . . Rose Bird or anyone else that age will exert more power for good or bad over a longer period than just about anybody else in California." It scarcely seems possible that Younger, a veteran politician, was naive enough to believe that such a bill would gain sufficient bipartisan political support with the gubernatorial election year just around the corner. Some longtime political analysts interpreted Younger's move as an effort to depress the ire of Republican conservatives who opposed his earlier swing vote in favor of her nomination.

Frank Newman, a fifty-nine year old professor of law at UC Berkeley since 1946, was Brown's choice for the third vacancy on the state Supreme Court. He has wide experience in California and national governments. Included are work with the California Constitutional Revision Commission (where he learned much about controversial issues in serving as its principal draftsman), Governor Earl Warren's Commission on Unemployment Compensation, several federal economic and price stabilization agencies, and as a legal officer in the Navy. He has been active in numerous civil- and human-rights organizations, is considered a strong civil libertarian, and is well known for his legal scholarship. In addition to these impressive credentials, Newman had another important factor working on his behalf. He had been a favorite of Rose Bird ever since he had been one of her professors at Berkeley. She drew him to Brown's attention after Jerry became Governor. (Brown and Newman had never met when Jerry was a student at UC Berkeley. Law did not become his main interest until he later went to Yale.)

The American Civil Liberties Union expressed jubilation over Newman's nomination, and the conservative forces in the state knew they had a strong liberal to try to cut down. But there was no way to contest his qualifications seriously. Like Ms. Bird, he had no previous judicial experience but this would be an outmoded weapon to use against him after its failure to stop Ms. Bird. Attorney General Younger, again serving as a member of the judicial appointment commission, received a few letters of opposition to Newman but none contained significant information that warranted voting against his confirmation. Brown's chief aide termed him "a legal heavyweight." Shortly after Newman took office, Younger, in talking to a southern California Republican club, attacked Newman as a "very left-wing ACLU activist" and then strangely said about this man who has an international reputation, "Probably no one ever heard of him before." Younger did not tell the club membes that he had voted in favor of confirming Newman's appointment.

Although predicting the judicial behavior of individuals during their years on the bench is hazardous, the liberal side of the state

Supreme Court seemingly has gained overall strength through Brown's three changes. The liberal Chief Justice Bird replaced the moderate Donald Wright, the moderate Wiley Manuel supplanted the liberal Raymond Sullivan, and the very liberal Frank Newman took the position of the very conservative Marshall McComb. Apparently a solid liberal bloc has developed on the state Supreme Court—Bird and Newman, plus carryovers Mathew Tobriner and Stanley Mosk. Two Reagan appointees, William P. Clark, Jr. and Frank Richardson, are the only conservative members, with Manuel between the liberals and conservatives. Some observers believe that although Ms. Bird has a strong personality she will spend much time managing the state's judicial system and Newman, her mentor, will write the court's most far-reaching decisions in the immediate future.

As the state's chief executive, Brown has considerable power over the executive branch but not to the extent that many people believe. There are about 130,000 employees in California's state government (exclusive of public college and university personnel), most of them working in executive departments and agencies. But more than nine-tenths of these executive employees are appointed by departmental and agency heads and their top aides on the basis of civil-service examinations designed to test merit. Moreover, after a probationary period, they can be removed only for serious cause, with the right of appeal to the independent State Personnel Board, whose members serve staggered ten-year terms.

The Governor has no direct control over these employees. They generally operate with considerable freedom within their own immediate organization. Many of them are in state employment for many years during which they see a number of governors come and go; they have resilience like "a lumpy air bag," a characterization of the Governor's chief of staff. The amount of responsiveness they give to programs of the Governor and the Legislature depends largely upon whether or not their immediate supervisors provide adequate leadership and supervision. To build better cooperation, Brown persuaded a few permanent civil servants to take temporary leaves from their civil service posts and accept positions in his administration. Like many other governors, however, Jerry has expressed a distaste for the bureaucracy in general and certain bureaucrats in particular.

The Governor's influence as the chief executive is further diminished by the fact that a number of other executives who occupy constitutional offices (so designated because they are specified in the state constitution) are elected by the statewide voters. Some of them are the Lieutenant Governor, who is a standby to succeed the Governor in case of his death, resignation, or disability, but also presides over the state Senate and serves as an ex officio member of some important boards; the Attorney General, who is the state's chief law enforcement officer and legal adviser; and the Controller, who approves claims for payment against the state. Others are the Treasurer, who collects, keeps custody of and invests state funds, and also makes payments of claims authorized by the Controller; the Superintendent of Public Instruction, who oversees the public school system; and the Secretary of State, who is the chief election officer, administrator of laws concerning business and governmental incorporations, and archivist of official state documents.

Although some executive power is dispersed and set apart from the Governor because of these independently elected officers, the nature of their duties makes them of little consequence to the Governor. The Lieutenant Governor, Controller, Treasurer, and Secretary of State simply are neither important policymakers nor the heads of large executive departments. On the other hand, the Attorney General and the Superintendent of Public Instruction can play important policy roles, which are far more independent of the Governor than if they were his appointees.

None of the six individuals holding these constitutional offices has maintained a close relationship with Brown even though only one, Attorney General Younger, is of the opposite party. Dr. Riles is elected on a nonpartisan basis. In view of the arguments between Younger and Brown when the latter was Secretary of

The current official photograph of Edmund G. (Jerry) Brown Jr. distributed by the Governor's Office. It was taken in October 1974 when he was campaigning for the governorship.

ABOVE:
Jerry Brown in 1970 during his term on the Los Angeles Community College District Board of Trustees.

TOP PREVIOUS PAGE:
A family portrait in the late 1950s when Jerry Brown (top left), born in 1938, was studying for the priesthood. To Brown's right are his three sisters—Kathleen, Barbara, and Cynthia. Parents Pat and Bernice are in the front.

BOTTOM PREVIOUS PAGE:
A meeting in 1970 on a college campus of the original Los Angeles Community College District Board of Trustees. Shown are four of the seven members: (l to r) Kenneth Washington, Jerry Brown, Robert Cline, and Michael Antonovich. The latter two later became Republican members of the Legislature, and Antonovich ran for Lieutenant Governor in 1978.

ABOVE:
Jerry Brown waves to crowd in Los Angeles as he claims victory in California Governor's race in 1974. Father Pat and mother Bernice at center, newly re-elected U.S. Senator Alan Cranston at right.

TOP PREVIOUS PAGE:
In January 1971, at the age of thirty-two, Jerry Brown is sworn in as Secretary of State for California by retired Chief Justice of the United States Earl Warren, former three-term Governor of the state. Witnessing the ceremony are Mrs. Warren and former Governor and Mrs. Edmund G. (Pat) Brown Sr.

BOTTOM PREVIOUS PAGE
Two Moods—Houston Flournoy, the Republican contender, laughs while Democrat Jerry Brown makes a point during a debate for Governor in 1974.

Edmund G. Brown Jr. greets other top elected and reelected state officers immediately before taking oath as Governor in January 1975. From left, Jesse Unruh, Treasurer; Evelle Younger, Attorney General; Lt. Gov. Mervyn Dymally; Kenneth Cory, Controller; Brown; March Fong Eu, Secretary of State; Wilson Riles, State Superintendent of Public Instruction. Rear left, Chief Justice Donald Wright; center, Assembly Speaker Leo McCarthy; right (partially hidden), Senate Speaker Pro tem James Mills.

In 1978 all these officials, with two exceptions, sought reelection to the same positions. Younger ran for Governor and Wright had retired.

Governor Brown's first appearance to aid his sister Kathleen Brown Rice (second from right) in her successful campaign in 1975 for the Los Angeles Board of Education. She entered politics largely on her brother's name just as he earlier had come in to politics on the name of his father.

ABOVE:
Governor Brown, celebrating his thirty-eighth birthday in April 1976, tells capitol reporters that Democratic party is still looking for a presidential candidate and he "may be it."

TOP NEXT PAGE:
Jerry Brown addressing a capacity college crowd in Baltimore in late April 1976 while campaigning in the Maryland presidential primary.

BOTTOM NEXT PAGE:
California Lieutenant Governor Mervyn Dymally, Governor Jerry Brown, and Mayor Tom Bradley of Los Angeles at Brown for President office when Dymally and Bradley endorsed him as presidential candidate in 1976.

TOP THIS PAGE:
Governor Brown (center) responds after receiving endorsement for President in 1976 of four of the six Mexican-American members of the Legislature. The legislators are, left to right, Senator Ruben Ayala, Assemblyman Peter Chacon, Assemblyman Richard Alatorre, and Senator Alex Garcia.

BOTTOM PHOTO THIS PAGE:
With his father, left, and his mother looking on, Governor Jerry Brown, at microphone, on the floor of the 1976 Democratic convention turns over to Jimmy Carter all the California delegate votes pledged to Brown.

NEXT PAGE:
Brown campaigning for President in commuter train in New Jersey in May 1976.

Jimmy Carter is greeted at microphone by Governor Jerry Brown, who introduced him at Los Angeles County Fair while Carter was campaigning against Gerald Ford for the presidency in the fall of 1976.

In Baja California in November 1977, Roberto de la Madrid, newly elected governor of Baja California, and Governor Brown told a news conference of their desire to develop a close working relationship.

Governor Brown in March 1978 signed a 30 percent tax property tax reduction bill and called on voters to reject the Jarvis-Gann initiative in June. Senator Peter Behr (left) watches the signing of the bill he authored. Assembly Speaker Leo McCarthy is on the right.

GOVERNOR OF CALIFORNIA

The unusual signature of the extraordinary Edmund G. (Jerry) Brown Jr. This signature is reproduced from a proclamation of a state emergency resulting from a disaster.

NEXT PAGE:
Rose Elizabeth Bird, first woman chief justice of the California Supreme Court, at a press conference in March 1977 after her nomination had been confirmed by a two-to-one vote of the Commission on Judicial Appointments.

Farm labor leader and folk hero Cesar Chavez picketing the headquarters of a grocery chain in San Diego in October 1973 in protest of earlier arrest of twenty-nine workers at a Delano, California, location of this chain.

State, a continuation of their accusations and spats was anticipated when Brown became Governor. Such did not prove to be the case until Younger got ready to make a now-or-never run for the governorship in 1978 and Jerry prepared to seek a second gubernatorial term. The attorney generalship is frequently tried as a stepping stone to the governorship. Earl Warren and Pat Brown were two who were successful. Younger contemplated the effort in 1974 when the polls showed him far in the lead as the Republican nominee but then withdrew because of the smell of Watergate.

Controller Kenneth Cory, a former assemblyman, has been mainly a silent administrator who says little about Brown. Jesse Unruh, previously Speaker of the Assembly and defeated candidate for Governor and Mayor of Los Angeles, has not publicly deprecated Brown and calls him a masterful politician who even surpasses Ronald Reagan in use of the media. Also, Unruh waits in the wings while serving as Treasurer in the hope that he may yet become Governor, a prospect growing more remote. Jesse said on a Los Angeles television program that he had outlasted one generation of Browns and might be able to outlast another.

Superintendent of Public Instruction Wilson Riles has expressed considerable disaffection for Brown because the Governor vetoed the proposed RISE (Reform of Intermediate and Secondary Education) program on which Riles had worked diligently. Although some disagreed, Riles was enthusiastic about the program saying, "I'm concerned about equity as well as adequacy; bring up the low-wealth districts so that at least they have the opportunity to have adequate programs." Many millions of dollars were required to implement the RISE program and, although many, but not all, educators and legislators had thrashed out and had reached agreement about the contents of the bill, the Governor had not commented on its drafts or suggested changes. Instead he remained silent.

The measure passed the Legislature, but Brown vetoed it. Riles bitterly declared that "after this long arduous road of open debate and support, to be derailed at this last step by a single individual—even though he is the Governor—is unconscionable. Declining test scores, vandalism, violence, boredom . . . I'm tired of hearing about them without doing something about it." The opportunity for the Governor and the Superintendent of Public Instruction to work together on developing imaginative educational policymaking had ended for at least the foreseeable future. A year later Riles was still angry. When asked by a television reporter about Brown's replacement of a Cadillac with a Plymouth for his personal use, Riles responded that it made no significant difference in cost.

Secretary of State March Fong Eu, the first Asian-American holder of a constitutional office in the state and a former assemblywoman, has been a strong critic of Governor Brown. Much of this attitude is rooted in budgetary cuts, particularly his elimination of money for a special staff to oversee more closely the work of notaries public. Brown had earlier advocated this change after he had discovered the backdating of the Nixon vice presidential papers by attorney and notary public DiMarco. There is no communication between the offices of the Governor and the Secretary of State except for legally required matters, such as her cosigning of all legislation.

The Lieutenant Governor, although not second among constitutional officers in power (the Attorney General is), stands as the second-ranking official in the state. He is simply a heartbeat or a resignation for a higher office away from the governorship. However, it has been as long ago as 1953 since a California Lieutenant Governor, Goodwin Knight, succeeded to the governorship when Earl Warren was appointed Chief Justice of the United States. In contrast, Lieutenant Governor Edward Reinecke failed dismally to become Governor in his bid in 1974. In addition to presiding at the sessions of the state Senate, the Lieutenant Governor, by virtue of his position, is a member of the University of California Board of Regents, the Board of Trustees of the State Colleges and University system, and the State Lands Commission (the last named dealing with tidelands oil).

Unlike the President and Vice President of the United States, the Governor and Lieutenant Governor of California do not officially run as a ticket for the two posts. And informally the same situation generally prevails, as it did in both the Democratic and Republican races for the two positions in 1974. Jerry Brown and Mervyn Dymally, both Democrats, carried out successful campaigns independent of one another. This means that the possibility exists for the Governor to be of one party and the Lieutenant Governor of the other, with the second party taking

"Amazing, Dad, how much smarter you've gotten in the last three years!"

over the top executive position, as well as the authority to appoint many persons in the executive branch, in case of the death, disability, or resignation of the chief executive.

Dymally, the state's highest black officeholder, is a Trinidad-born former school teacher who was in the Legislature for twelve years before being decisively elected Lieutenant Governor. Dymally, the politician extraordinaire with broad-based support from labor, teachers, government workers, and minorities, including Chicanos, and Brown, who portrays the anti-politician, continued to be far apart from the time of their inauguration into office. And Dymally's efforts on behalf of Brown's 1976 presidential candidacy made no real difference. Later the gap widened even more. In the first part of 1977 Dymally became so angry with Brown that he ordered disconnection of the hot line between their two offices in Sacramento. Brown's aide Gray Davis talked Dymally out of making the phone disconnect, however.

Some insiders have reported that Brown, always sensitive to possible scandal, particularly wanted to stay far distant from Dymally because of a state Attorney General's eighteen-month probe into the alleged misuse of funds by a nonprofit institute Dymally had formed to bring minority youth into government service. The Lieutenant Governor had requested the investigation after an article in the *Los Angeles Times* in July 1975 accused him of misusing funds over five years while he was in the state Senate. Dymally said the Attorney General's report cleared him of any wrongdoing, and he paid $750 in back salary, plus $600 interest, to a brotherhood crusade.

Brown and Dymally grew somewhat closer in late 1977 and on into January 1978 when the Lieutenant Governor announced for reelection, being the first state constitutional officeholder to do so. Examples of a closer working relationship were Brown's approval of improved financing and staffing of the Commission for Economic Development, which Dymally chairs, and Jerry's appointment of the Lieutenant Governor to the Southwest Regional Border State Commission and to the White House Conference on Economic Development. Nevertheless, the split was still apparent when the Lieutenant Governor at news conferences about his reelection candidacy pointed out that he would run an independent campaign and that "The governor has a style that's unique. It's not my kind of style. . . ." Dymally further said that he expected Jerry to remain neutral in the primary and then work very closely with the entire Democratic ticket in the November general election.

Jerry Brown is a political loner and has purposely not worked closely with any of the state constitutional officers. None of them other than possibly Dymally could give him additional political strength and all the Democrats holding constitutional offices are in jobs that almost always have been political dead-ends. From Dymally, Jerry might have gained a broader base of support and a willing worker ready to take on assignments from the Governor. But Brown does not like to share credit with others, apparently fears the possible consequences of the notoriety that Dymally received, and is too different in political interests and style from the man standing-in-waiting.

The heart of Brown's power over the executive branch is his broad-ranging appointment authority (in addition to his ability to veto any specific items in a proposed budget). The Governor is empowered to make about 2,200 appointments (called exempt positions) outside the civil service system, mostly in the executive part of state government. Some of them require the approval of the state Senate, which is usually but not always perfunctory, while others are his to make by himself.

These executive positions are of three types. First is the Governor's personal staff, known officially as the Governor's Office, which includes such individuals as an executive secretary-chief of staff, a press secretary, a legal affairs adviser, a legislative assistant, and an appointments assistant. The second kind of appointment is made up of the heads of the state administrative superagencies (Health and Welfare, Resources, Business and Transportation, and Agriculture and Services), the directors of most departments subordinate to these agencies, and the state director of finance. Many of these people are important policymakers as well as managers of their particular operations. The Governor generally appoints them with the approval of the Senate and may remove them solely at his discretion.

The third type of position for which the Governor is authorized to make selections consists of membership on a great many boards and commissions. Some of these are highly significant, dealing with air resources, water quality, energy, employee relations, personnel, political practices, agriculture, and education. The members of other boards and commissions appointed by the Governor oversee the licensing of professions and trades, like contracting, medicine, dentistry, and pharmacy. Still other boards and commissions conduct local agricultural affairs or are advisory in nature. Senate sanction may or may not be necessary. In total, Jerry Brown's power to make executive appointments (as well as judicial ones discussed earlier in this chapter) is both formidable and extensive.

Far more minorities—both racial and ethnic and women—have been appointed to positions in the executive branch by Brown than by any of his predecessors. Through late August 1977 Jerry had made 1,862 appointments, both executive and judicial. The minority breakdown (with the percentage rounded) is women, 31 percent; Chicano, 10 percent; Black, 8 percent; Asian-American, 3 percent; Indian, 2 percent; and Filipino, one-half of one percent.

Some minority people were selected for very high positions. Here are a few examples. Mario Obledo, a Chicano, was made head of the Health and Welfare Agency. Leonard Grimes, a Black, first served as director of the Department of General Services and then became head of the Agriculture and Services Agency. Rose Bird, who had managed the latter agency, was made chief justice of the California Supreme Court. Claire Dedrick directed the Resources Agency and then became the first woman member of the state Public Utilities Commission.

With the departure of Bird and Dedrick from the Governor's inner circle, certain women in the administration began to make certain claims. They complained that they were not given authority to carry out their responsibilities, had no political clout, and none of them had Brown's ear on any important issues. A woman deputy department director said she did not even have influence within her own department, noting that she had been excluded from hundreds of meetings dealing with her division, which did not happen to men holding equivalent jobs. Another woman, who had been part of the Brown administration before resigning to run for the Legislature, said that Brown and his aides are intellectually committed to the idea of equality and equal opportunities for women; however, she continued, intellectual recognition of the fact and the actual ability to cope with such equality are not always the same. She stressed that many males in the Brown administration are similar to the Governor—bachelors, ex-Jesuits, or those of comparable backgrounds or values. She went on, "I found in terms of personalities, age levels, and experiences of the [men] in the Administration an inability to work with bright, aggressive, capable women."

Brown, who has received a high rating from representatives of the National Organization of Women (NOW) for his female appointments, responded that the charges were unfounded. After replying that he relates well to women in his administration and that it was intellectually dishonest to say otherwise, the Governor remarked, "I don't think there is another place in the world where women have taken positions of power at a more rapid rate."

Although there may be discontent among some women who are past and present members of the Brown administration,. their extensive inclusion certainly does not represent tokenism. For example, late in 1977 the Governor organized a "town hall" brigade, which is a large complement of important advisers to him, that held public forums throughout the state. At a meeting of this group on November 30, 1977 in Sacramento, twenty-eight top-level gubernatorial aides sat on the auditorium stage of the local city college—19 men and 9 women, including 9 Blacks and Chicanos.

A number of Brown appointees to the state executive branch also have a strong clientele orientation. In part this grows out of the Governor's attachment to people with such concerns but it also emanates from the passage of public-member legislation during his administration. This law calls for representatives of the public to be appointed to various boards and commissions. Included are those in the fields of regulation and licensing and the State Bar Board of Governors. Rose Bird, who lobbied successfully for this legislation, felt the law was very significant because it opened up government to the citizen. And the president of the State Bar Board of Governors appraised the change as positive, saying that the public members bring a new, different, and lay perspective to the board and raise such questions as who will benefit from a specific proposal. By August 1977 Brown had appointed sixty-five public members to boards and commissions.

The infusion of youth into the Governor's Office, executive agencies and departments, and boards and commissions by Brown is similarly very evident. Many of his appointees were either in their late twenties or in their thirties when chosen. Of Brown's first set of close advisors only Claire Dedrick was more than forty. And as late as January 1978 the accent on youth was still continuing. At that time a woman of twenty-eight was chosen by Jerry to be director of the Department of Alcohol and Drug Abuse and a man of thirty-five was selected as director of the state Office of Economic Opportunity.

A close aide of Brown has made it clear that the proclivity to favor youth is deliberate. This assistant, also young, has emphasized, "The public is better served by the energy that comes from youth. The Governor believes that there is no evidence that older experienced individuals can provide any better service; to the contrary, we believe that the energy of the young provides more benefits." When asked whether some wisdom and knowledge might not be lost through bypassing certain older people, this individual responded, "Wisdom has its place but who is to say that a young person cannot be wise? But if it gets down to a trade-off between wisdom and energy, the state would be better served with youth and what it brings." This strong accent on youth is highly arguable. It brings energy and possibly a higher degree of purity in decisionmaking; however, it also brings naivete and a tendency to try certain things thought to be new but that have been previously tried and found to be of little value. In addition, too strong an emphasis on youth means the loss of much of an older, but not ancient, and talented generation.

Many Brown appointees in the executive branch also differ in another key respect from a large number of their predecessors. Many appointments in previous administrations came from the world of private business, persons with considerable experience in the economic marketplace. Still others were rewarded with posts because of their political service or financial contributions. Some business and political types (Charles Silberman and Tom Quinn are examples) have found their way into the Brown administration but the vocational backgrounds of others have often been dissimilar. Brown has selected many more individuals who have not had major business experience.

In a sense Jerry has chosen to appoint far more people from the other side of the financial tracks. They are individuals who have served as public defenders for those unable to pay regular attorney fees in court cases; public-interest lawyers who have fought particular governmental policies, sometimes in class action suits; civil-rights and consumer advocates; and officers and staff members of controlled growth and environmental organizations. A number of these people have gone into highly influential positions in the Governor's Office, executive agencies such as Resources and Agriculture and Services, the state energy and coastal boards, and the utilities and other regulatory commissions. Such persons commonly bring a different philosophy and outlook to the public problems they face and the decisions they make. These appointees are producing a great change in state government, one largely unnoticed by the general public since its strong impact is only apparent when viewed in total.

The responsibility for final decisions is retained by Brown, who does not like to delegate authority, but much discussion and decision-making take place among a small group of top staff people who make up the executive cabinet. They include four heads of superagencies—Huey Johnson, secretary of the Resources Agency; Mario Obledo, secretary of the Health and Welfare Agency; Leonard Grimes, secretary of the Agriculture and Services Agency; and Richard Silberman, secretary of the Business and Transportation Agency. The others come from a variety of posts—Richard Rominger, director of Food and

Agriculture; Donald Vial, director of Industrial Relations; Roy Bell, state finance director; Tom Quinn, chairman of the Air Resources Board; and Gray Davis, the Governor's executive secretary and chief of staff.

These decisionmaking meetings, in which other people may take part from time to time, are often done in a free-form fashion. Informal and direct, the conversations may be extremely lengthy, individuals may assume adversary positions, and strong debates may ensue. Some of these sessions have run from early morning long into the night. The thorough thrashing out of all viewpoints of a subject, it is believed, leads to sounder judgments and decisions.

Gray Davis is one of the brightest luminaries in the Brown administration. He graduated with honors from Stanford University and is an alumnus of Columbia University Law School. He served as finance director and treasurer of Tom Bradley's successful campaign in 1973 for mayor of Los Angeles, advised him in his new job on ways to improve the city's investment and budgetary policies, and specialized in the practice of corporate law and litigation in a firm of attorneys. In 1974, at the age of thirty-one, he went on the campaign trail to try to win the post of State Treasurer. He might have been successful in reaching this goal but for the late entry into the same contest of a well-known political figure, Jesse Unruh, a former speaker of the Assembly. Although Davis lost this bid, he met Jerry Brown a number of times while campaigning and impressed Brown to the point that he was immediately offered the executive secretaryship in the Governor's Office after the election.

Davis is the Governor's right-hand man who is an accessible, capable, and intelligent administrator and policymaker. He has many discussions with and makes numerous recommendations to the Governor and strongly influences how Jerry can best spend his time. Gray manages the staff of the six divisions of the Governor's Office—press, legal affairs, cabinet, appointments, legislative affairs, and administrative affairs. He acts as an excellent buffer for the Governor and is totally dedicated to his arduous and seemingly never-ending work.

Gray Davis has the look of a polished reflection of Brown's own quiet elegance. Other similarities exist in their physical size, height, and build and in their style of grooming and clothes. And they are both handsome bachelors.

There is another important similarity. Davis thoroughly knows the philosophy and thoughts of Brown. Statements Gray makes about Brown's views and positions are virtually identical to those Jerry would have made or has uttered earlier. Never in the entire span of the Brown administration has Davis had to retract a statement he made on behalf of the Governor. And never has Davis been publicly criticized, even in a minor fashion, by Jerry who is a demanding perfectionist. This is a far cry from the experience of individuals occupying comparable positions in various other states and national administrations.

J. Anthony Kline, the Governor's legal affairs adviser, is another important figure in the Brown administration. Bearded and casual in his attire and manner, Kline was a classmate of Jerry's at Yale Law School. Tony founded and was heading Public Advocates, Inc., a public-interest law firm that had often sued the government, when Brown picked him as one of his first staff members. Kline spends considerable time on proposed judicial appointments and other court and legal matters. He is young, bright, aggressive, tough, and highly sophisticated in the art of political maneuvering. Although not universally liked by people in government and legal circles, he is well respected for his competence.

The executive branch has not been free of criticism, discontent, and dismissals in the Brown administration. These outbursts are to be expected in any large organization; what has been surprising is that there has not been more discord in view of the frequently unusual types, such as anti-establishment people, whom Jerry has recruited.

The first major dissatisfaction to surface publicly involved James Lorenz, a cofounder of the California Legal Assistance

League, which had been a constant adversary of the Ronald Reagan administration. Lorenz, who had worked in Jerry's 1974 campaign for Governor, was appointed by Brown as director of the Department of Economic Development. Regarded by some people as a great liberal hope and by others as a radical, Lorenz felt that his appointment meant he could proceed to develop innovative solutions to employment problems. He proceeded as a hard-hitting free thinker who on occasion bypassed established procedures. In dealing with private and public leaders he tended to alienate rather than bring together the elements needed to deal with the problems. While Brown in the early months of his administration was concerned with developing a process of governance, Lorenz's objective was public action.

The breaking point occurred when a working draft of a controversial jobs plan prepared by Lorenz and his staff was obtained and released by a newspaper. The plan called for business cooperatives and collectives. The banner headline on the *Oakland Tribune* announced "Governor's Secret Workers State Plan" and some business leaders labeled the proposal socialistic and anti-capitalistic. When Lorenz was asked to resign and refused to do so, Brown fired him. Lorenz was only in the seventh month of his employment. After the firing, an aide to Lorenz made a very revealing statement that showed the intense action orientation of his chief in a time when to the contrary Jerry was letting issues emerge. The aide said, "In retrospect, I should have noted more carefully that—with the exception of Lorenz—the Governor had appointed individuals who, while they had worked with public-interest groups, brought with them no particular commitment to positive programs of action. I had forgotten many lawyers were attracted to public-interest work more for a chance to try interesting cases than out of any deep philosophical conviction."

Lorenz licked his wounds for a long time. Finally, in 1978, almost three years after his discharge, he sought his revenge by writing a book about Brown, which was first excerpted in *Esquire* magazine. Lorenz particularly attacked Brown for techniques he says Jerry employed in the 1974 Governor's race. One is the use of "buzz words," phrases designed to appeal to an audience for what they imply rather than their specifics. Another is the spending of hours on devising the right theme or phrase for a short talk and then taking further time to give it an extemporaneous appearance. It is not these revelations that are shocking but Lorenz's naivete in believing so. He apparently does not know that many public and private figures employ these practices. Words that appeal to the media are constantly sought. The appearance of spontaneity instead of stiffness or awkwardness is a steady objective. Also, some critics of Lorenz believe he lacks ethics for revealing information drawn from his experience as a confidential campaign aide, much in the manner of the tattletales of a maid or butler in the White House. But an even more central point can be raised. If Lorenz thought so poorly of Jerry Brown when working in the gubernatorial campaign, why did he accept a position in his administration?

The sprawling Health and Welfare Agency has experienced the most administrative headaches during the Jerry Brown years. Mario Obledo, who is the agency's secretary, is the first Chicano in a California Governor's cabinet and was previously director of the Mexican-American Legal Defense and Educational Fund. Obledo has been criticized for mismanagement. Putting the matter in polite terms, Assembly Speaker Leo McCarthy said in November 1977 that Obledo, while being a superb human being, lacked administrative experience to run the state's largest agency. At the same time, McCarthy pointed out that not only this agency secretary but some department heads as well were without management skills, "the Health Department [in the Health and Welfare Agency] being the most notable." McCarthy's reference was to Dr. Jerome Lackner, who had earlier described himself as a poor administrator but a good doctor. The Health Department had recently been rated by far the worst state unit by participating legislators.

Obledo was also charged with favoritism in the hiring and promotion of Mexican-Americans, and the November 1977 issue of *Reader's Digest* carried an article that purported to show that he was a supporter of a person allegedly connected with the so-called Mexican Mafia, a criminal organization. Obledo strongly denied the contents of the article and asked for a retraction. Mexican-American leaders viewed the attacks on him as criticisms of all Chicanos and piqued by Brown's silence on the subject, one of these leaders sent a telegram to the Governor, giving him five days to support Obledo clearly and publicly. According to this leader, political warfare against Brown would develop unless he expressed total support for Obledo.

In that same week Brown walked into the large exhibition hall at the Sacramento Convention Center during a dinner attended by 1,400 people to honor Mario Obledo. The Governor strongly endorsed Obledo, declaring, "I can't think of anyone in my Cabinet or anywhere else who better represents what we're trying to do in goverment. He's a good man. He's a great man. He's in the eye of a political storm, and you're there with him, we're all there together. You're on the move because he's on the move." To shouts of "Viva el gobernador," Brown had solidified his relations with a large ethnic minority on whose support he was counting heavily for reelection in the following year.

Other problems have plagued the Health and Welfare Agency. Cost overruns in the Medi-Cal program is one. Another centers on suspicious deaths in the state mental hospitals; as a result, Jerry made many personal visits to several hospitals and bolstered support for them in his proposed 1978-79 state budget.

Still another problem grew out of the firing, on order of the Governor, of Dr. Josette Escamilla-Mondanaro, a thirty-two year old pediatrician serving as deputy director of the state division of substance (drug) abuse. The action was taken on the last day of her probationary (non-tenure) status. Angered by an article sent by a friend that said the evidence was incomplete on the harmful effects of child pornography and pre-puberty sexual abuse, she wrote the friend a frank letter containing some vivid language of questionable taste. In the most provocative paragraph, she wrote facetiously about fantasizing that a giant forces a tiny baby— whom she imagined as the article's author—into a sex act and then asking if the infant's sucking urge had been satisfied.

The letter was a personal one to a friend, but it was brought to the office, typed by a government secretary on state letterhead stationery, and placed in the office files. A copy of the letter eventually went forward to Obledo, who found it "so filthy, obscene, and disgusting" as to feel it was his responsibility to transmit it to the Governor. Brown, who decided within hours to get her to resign or to have her fired, concluded that writing the letter on state department stationery—a letterhead bearing his name in the upper right hand corner—was sufficient reason to discharge her. But the convincing factor, he said, was placing her official title under her signature. If she was that dumb, he reasoned, what other poor judgments had she made on the job?

Brown asked the department deputy director to persuade her to resign, but Dr. Mondanaro would not do so and Brown ordered the department head to fire her. She then appealed the dismissal to the State Personnel Board in January 1978. At this time Jerry testified before a board hearing officer in the Governor's office, the first time any one could remember a governor giving a deposition in the firing appeal of a state employee. He remarked that he found the letter "shocking and totally incompatible with the standards of propriety for high office in my Administration." He denied that she had been dismissed for her avowed lesbianism and because she had refused to hire an alleged crony of the agency secretary. Dr. Lackner and his deputy director contended that the reprimand she had received was sufficient and that she should not be fired. The State Personnel Board reinstated her by a four-to-one vote in February 1978. This was the most sensational dismissal case in an administration generally devoid of personal sensationalism.

As a result of realizing that the growth of government could only be slowed if more voluntary help could be acquired in public services, Jerry Brown set up in August 1977 the State Office for Volunteerism with Charles Baldwin, a former Senate Committee aide, in charge. The agency is designed to prompt more people to be government volunteers and also to provide a focal point of support and information for volunteers in private but publicly-related activities. The stimulant for establishing the office was Brown's earlier visit to a state mental hospital where he discovered patients devoid of human contact or sufficient supervision. Brown called on religious leaders and others to motivate their people to come to the assistance of the state government by putting their faith into action.

"The idea of the volunteer program," Brown has explained, "is to try to rekindle the spirit of service that certainly characterized neighborhoods and communities of the past and [does] even today in rural areas." Because of anonymity, mobility, and other fragmenting influences, it is increasingly important for "people to come together in neighborhoods and communities to support each other, whether in matters of mental health, alcoholism, child care or other programs aimed at people in need."

Jerry wants to develop increased volunteerism in government because the public sector is crowding out the spiritual and private elements—churches, businesses, neighborhoods, and families. He fears that the balance between the public and private sectors is tilting too far toward the centralized public bureaucracy, thus endangering individual freedom and society's diversity. The Governor further notes that as the family breaks down, the government has to provide the props and, as these supports become better, the family breaks down more.

About six months after the state office was organized, more than 500 volunteers were active in four state hospitals for the mentally ill in both northern and southern California. Before beginning work with patients, the volunteers complete a twelve-hour training program familiarizing them with the hospital's programs and the management of patients. The volunteers make a commitment to spend at least four hours a week at a hospital for three months. They work under staff supervision in the wards, acting as an outside friend or companion on a one-to-one basis. The expectation is that the volunteer program will spread to other state activities. However, the state bureaucracy is closely watching the movement to make certain it does not reduce the number of state paid jobs.

Governor Brown has spent very little time at out-of-state meetings with his counterparts and other major state officials. What time he has used elsewhere has been largely devoted to talking about California business opportunities with private leaders in New York and Japan and the state's gas needs with high public officers in Canada and Mexico (considered in chapter 7) and to conferring with politicians at various levels of government during his late 1976 presidential campaign (discussed in the next chapter).

Governors have the opportunity to meet informally and often with one another if they wish to do so. They also have an organization known as the Governors' Conference, which is part of an official, government dues-paying association of all the states called the Council of State Governments. The Governors' Conference holds annual and subsidiary meetings and has various study committees on which many governors are active.

Jerry made an early decision to take little part in these interstate activities, preferring to stay at home and learn the job of Governor thoroughly. This judgment irritated various other governors, particularly those in the West who felt they had common problems in such fields as water and agriculture. Brown made an exception in January 1978 when he went to Nevada to confer with the other western governors, the Vice President, and the Secretary of the Interior. He made presentations on the 160-acre per person limitation of farms receiving water from federal projects and national government involvement in the California Water Project. This exception may become a more general practice if Jerry makes another move for the presidency. If he does, he will need the support of many officials outside California, and those in the West, unhappy with the national administration, would form a good starting base.

Before speculating about the future, we will look at Brown's astonishing but belated race in 1976 to be the President of the United States.

Chapter Nine

Now He Belongs
to the Nation

In January 1960 an inner-directed Jerry Brown emerged from
several years of study in a Jesuit seminary to face the secular
calling of his life. As he passed through various academic
classrooms assimilating whatever wisdom was to be garnered from
these university establishments, he quickly matured into a man of
a modern and changing society. Blessed with the good fortune of
name and breeding, he found the magnetism of politics drawing
him to higher and higher political office. Through a succession of
public positions, he reached a point of prominence much earlier
than most other persons in either public or private life. As the
Governor of the most populous and a highly dynamic state, the
former seminarian had come a long way in a relatively short time.

Yet Brown could not rest. The troubled and unsettled political
environment soon drew him into the fray of national politics; the

United States presidency looked like the next step. So it was that Jerry Brown in the fifteenth month of his governorship—less than half way through his term—entered into the national arena as a threat to the frontrunning Jimmy Carter. Brown's decision to campaign for the presidency, which was announced only five months before the convention delegates assembled at their national conclave, made him an important national political figure.

Presidential aspirations were not new to Brown. In 1971, in Jerry's eighth month as Secretary of State, he discussed the presidency with his friend Stephen Reinhardt, a politically-active Los Angeles attorney. After a long Labor Day weekend campaigning throughout California with Senator Edmund Muskie of Maine, then a leading contender for the 1972 Democratic presidential nomination, Brown told his friend of his interest in the presidency. "I think he recognized, even at that stage," Reinhardt has said, that being governor [Brown was looking ahead even then to running for that office about three years hence] might even lead to that [the presidency] and it was the kind of career that might be possible." Brown perceived of himself as a rising political star who might some day take up residence in Washington, D.C., as the nation's most prominent citizen. His presidential aspirations seemed well established even in 1971.

Four years later, in 1975, Brown gave more serious thought to seeking the presidency. At this time he told friends not to support other candidates as he might run and met with state Democratic party officials to analyze his presidential potential. However, Jerry rejected the idea at this time because he was then in his first year as Governor. Moreover, he had purposely not traveled out of the state during his brief tenure (thus showing the voters they were getting their money's worth), which made it difficult to gauge public reaction to him elsewhere. Also, a presidential bid this early might seriously erode his home-state popularity, which was at a high level.

Brown is a bright and cunning politician. He possesses a deep understanding of things political and knows when to move and at what speed toward his eventual goal. Proper timing and environment would be required before seeking the presidency. He recognized that without the presence of these conditions capable presidential candidates in earlier elections had been defeated as early as a significant primary contest or at the national nominating convention. Brown would become a candidate for the United States presidency only when he could make political gains, and as a first-term governor 1976 initially did not seem to be that year.

Jerry's early interaction with national party officials also seemed to preclude any serious presidential effort by him in 1976. One instance in particular served to alienate certain party chieftains. Brown did the unforgivable by openly ridiculing the motives of a committee of the National Democratic Committee in its consideration of a particular site in California for the upcoming Democratic presidential convention. What other person in American politics would summarily attack leaders of his party and soon ask to become its standard bearer? Yet this is precisely what Jerry Brown did.

Los Angeles made a bid to be the locale of the 1976 Democratic national presidential convention, and in April 1975 the site selection committee paid this city a visit. Despite the important political leverage and income for California this series of convention events would represent, Brown did not participate enthusiastically in the negotiations. In fact, the Governor single-handedly derailed the efforts of Los Angeles Mayor Tom Bradley, other politicians, and business and labor leaders. Brown's unorthodox stand alienated party regulars across the nation.

Ordinarily the committee responsible for choosing the national convention site is greeted warmly by local and state officials and private luminaries who are interested in attracting the publicity and revenue of a nominating conclave to their domain. As the Democratic site committee explored Los Angeles as a possible location, its members received this type of courting from public and private leaders—with the exception of the Governor of California. Jerry Brown did not like to promote a series of events he felt exhibited silly self-indulgence. His position was made evident to the committee; he welcomed a national convention for Los Angeles so long as it did not involve ludicrous extravagance. Contending that the committee was interested too much in comfort and luxury, he self-righteously lambasted these national party officials. Brown's earthy solution was that "we [the convention delegates] can sleep in the church basements rather than in expensive hotel suites" and "get to the business of the people's needs by being closer to them." Instead of being met by a glad-handing political accommodater, many of the committee faced what they considered a distasteful and unreasonable maverick.

Brown's attack on prominent Democrats was regarded as personally insulting. Governor Philip Noel of Rhode Island, who was a committee member, called Brown a dude who when a youth had lived in a governor's mansion while Noel's mother was hitting a press in a jewelry factory. The committee decided by an eleven-to-nine vote to hold the convention in a city where all public officials were respectful. Los Angeles lost to New York City. Brown's lackadaisical and caustic activity about the convention site, which took place merely fifteen months before the nominating sessions, seemed to make him one of the party's least likely presidential prospects. But such was not to be the case.

Shortly before Brown announced his candidacy for the presidency, several events transpired that encouraged him to go ahead. Two of them involved elements of the media—*Playboy* magazine and the "60 Minutes" television program on the CBS network—and gave him a national audience and the opportunity for reactions from people throughout the nation. The interview in *Playboy*, which is billed as "the men's entertainment magazine," was based on almost twenty hours of recorded questions and answers. The inquiries made of Brown were direct and sometimes difficult and covered a broad range of personal and political subjects. Brown fielded the nearly endless stream of questions, at times from two reporters in succession, in a skillful, newsworthy, and frequently unique manner. The interview when it appeared in print (covering fifteen pages), was very well received and brought a large amount of favorable mail to the Governor.

The "60 Minutes" program provided an intriguing visual cameo of Brown in a longer segment of time than had been allotted to either presidential hopeful Ronald Reagan or incumbent Gerald Ford. The telecast presented a condensed version of Brown's political philosophy and life style and portrayed him as a new kind of politician worthy of serious attention. When Brown was asked whom he favored for the presidency, he said, "I have no candidate for President. I don't want to meddle in an overcrowded presidential race." Again as with the *Playboy* interview, the public response was extensive and overwhelmingly favorable.

A third event that influenced Brown's decision to enter the presidential race was the poor showing of leading candidate Jimmy Carter in the Massachusetts primary on March 2. Carter ran fourth in that contest. His lack of appeal in this heavily urbanized state, which could be important to the results of the Democratic national convention and the national presidential election, reinforced in Brown's mind a long-held evaluation. In his judgment, no candidate was capturing the enthusiasm of the country, and none was speaking to the concerns Brown regarded as important. In addition to these three pro-Brown events, another fact faced Jerry. Unless he made an immediate decision to run, he would not get on the Democratic primary ballots in Maryland, California, and Nevada.

On March 12, after going to a young people's art exhibit in California's state capitol, Brown strolled back to his office with four news reporters. There, in a manner similar to that used in speaking about the weather, he casually announced that he was going to be an active candidate to become President of the United States. A master of the unexpected, Brown in the timing and manner of the announcement caught many people by surprise. Included among them were members of his own staff as well as Pat Brown who was on his way to a political fund-raiser for Carter when Jerry called his father. Some intimates of Brown have said

NOW HE BELONGS TO THE NATION

that Jerry, who is known for taking a long time to make decisions, had not conclusively decided to run for the presidency until the moment he announced. They cite as evidence of this the fact that he did not have a campaign manager until ten days after his announcement. Jerry's declaration was the start of a short-lived run for the White House that was a remarkable effort filled with surprising successes but also a final defeat—at least for the time being.

As revealed after the convention by Mickey Kantor, Brown's campaign manager, Jerry's campaign was based on several assumptions. First, Hubert Humphrey would eventually enter the race and divert labor and party regulars from supporting Carter. Second, if Arizona Congressman Morris Udall could defeat Carter in the Wisconsin primary of April 6, the liberal vote would be frozen. Third, Brown would then decisively win the California primary in June, thereby positioning himself to be nominated by the convention in the following month on the third ballot or later. Kantor also indicated after the convention that the initial plan was for Brown to campaign only in California as a favorite son to avoid the possibility of alienating many voters in the state who might feel his presidential bid was premature. However, when it became evident in late April that Carter was going to win in Pennsylvania and Humphrey might not enter the presidential race, Brown had to decide to campaign actively in a number of states, particularly in those where his name was already on the ballot or where a large slate of uncommitted delegates existed. The change in strategy meant that Jerry had to try to perform a political miracle, starting with the Maryland primary to be held on May 18, which was very close at hand by the time he decided to campaign in other states.

The Brown campaign faced formidable obstacles from the outset. First of all, Jimmy Carter had been campaigning for President for almost two years—since before Brown had been inaugurated as Governor in January 1975. Carter, who had gone into all state primaries and had sought further support at state party caucuses, already had obtained between 600 and 700 convention delegates. This was more than twice as many as any other contender had and almost half of what he needed to be nominated. In contrast, Brown was not then a national political figure, although more and more people were becoming curious about him. In addition, Jerry had no established campaign organization and few political friends elsewhere; he had to improvise in different ways as he proceeded in various states. Also, he was strongly disliked, some say hated, by many party professionals. His enemies included Democratic National Chairman Robert Strauss whose antagonism toward Brown dated back to the previous year when the convention site was being determined.

Brown named Mickey Kantor, a Los Angeles attorney and a law partner of Charles Manatt, chairman of the California Democratic Central Committee, as his campaign manager. Tom Quinn, who had been the chief campaign aide in Brown's two previous races, was now the Brown-appointed chairman of the state's Air Resources Board and was less active in this political effort. Marianna Pfaelzer, a member of a law firm carrying the name of the late Eugene Wyman, a prominent Democratic fund raiser, was appointed campaign treasurer. And Leo McCarthy, the powerful speaker of the state Assembly and an ally of Brown in various legislative affairs, was selected as campaign chairman.

Jerry's decision to seek the presidency was made too late for him to qualify a slate of pledged convention delegates for the Maryland ballot. Nevertheless, his name would appear on the other portion of the two-part Democratic primary ballot, variously called the beauty contest, popularity poll, or advisory portion. Brown made his first of three trips to Maryland on April 28, only three weeks before the primary there.

A combination of several factors fell into place and worked to Brown's advantage in Maryland. One was that various leaders in the state political organization or machine—including the Governor of Maryland (then under indictment and later convicted), the elected executive of Baltimore County, and a former mayor of

Baltimore—liked Brown and directly or indirectly threw their organization support behind him. Helpful in getting many organizational people in back of Jerry was the recent decline of Henry Jackson's presidential effort.

When Brown was asked how a new-style politician could ally himself with a political machine, he resurrected a quotation from Ronald Reagan who had been endorsed by the John Birch Society in his first run for the California governorship in 1966. Jerry said, "When they come out for me, they are buying my philosophy and programs. I am not necessarily buying theirs."

The work of former New York Congressman Allard Lowenstein, particularly among his many friends in the wealthy Washington suburbs in Montgomery County, was also important. Lowenstein had engineered the successful move to dump Lyndon Johnson as the Democratic presidential nominee almost a decade before and had served on Brown's gubernatorial staff in the summer of 1975. Then, too, he had been the first nationally-known politician to encourage Brown to seek the presidency.

The four major metropolitan newspapers with wide readership in Maryland, two in Washington and two in Baltimore, were prepared to give Brown on-the-scene broad campaign coverage. They were looking for something new to report in the presidential race, and in the same week as the Maryland primary there would be only one other primary to cover—between two old contenders, Carter and Udall, in Michigan.

Carter's mistake in deciding to campaign in Maryland also worked to Brown's benefit. Brown could not win any delegates in the state, but Carter gave Jerry's campaign there significance by making speeches in Maryland and criticizing him. Not content with the strong probability of winning most delegates in the state, Carter was determined to emerge triumphant in the popularity portion of the balloting as well, thus putting a quick damper on Brown's presidential bid.

Jerry launched a whirlwind campaign in Maryland of many personal appearances, including a number on college campuses, and excellent media coverage, much of it purchased radio and television time of a very extensive nature. Some observers called it "media saturation." As Brown had done in winning the governorship in California, he followed his "no promises" approach in the Maryland primary. "I'm no Santa Claus," he said. "I don't want to give you the idea it's just a lot of cotton candy— elect me and all your problems will be over." In contrast, although Carter had been portraying himself as an anti-establishment politician, he had been making many promises during the

"One of you will try to deny me the nomination. . .!"

primaries, including reductions in defense expenditures and the national governmental bureaucracy.

Sometimes Brown spoke in lofty terms. "I offer a new vision based not on America's guilt but on America's pride. . . . The fires of democracy are flickering out across the planet, and it's up to us to re-light them. . . . I come to Maryland to test whether this state and this nation are ready for a new generation of leadership." Other times he became the political pragmatist, attacking Carter in several ways. For one thing, Jerry downplayed the significance of Carter's wins in eight of the first ten primaries as "fractional pluralities in a minority of states with very little enthusiasm." Brown also said that his own belief in the era of limits was more honest and realistic than Carter's "invocation of the economic rhetoric of the 1960s," a statement that placed Carter with the old faces of another generation. Jerry went on to criticize Carter for "overselling the value of excessive reorganization in Washington and overstating the potential for zero-based budgeting."

As for federal reorganization, Brown rejected Carter's suggestion that this idea would save considerable money and then dug in, "It's not how the boxes [in an organizational chart] are arranged but rather it's who are in them that counts. It [Carter's reorganization proposal] kind of reminds me of the secret plan Nixon had about Vietnam." Regarding zero-based budgeting—reducing all agency requests to zero and requiring justification of all proposed expenditures from that point—Jerry proclaimed "it is overblown and oversold, rhetoric, and a form of consumer fraud" that deludes people into believing there is an easy way to decrease the federal budget.

His public audiences, which were frequently large and standing-room only, received him enthusiastically as did many radio listeners and television viewers. Brown also shook a seemingly endless line of hands—a traditional political practice, the pressing of the flesh, he generally avoids. Large numbers of volunteers and party regulars flocked to Jerry's candidacy.

Carter did not handle Brown gently either in the Maryland primary. After calling Brown "a fine young man," Carter questioned the seriousness of Jerry's candidacy, and sought to link him to political bosses who in Carter's judgment were part of the stop-Carter effort. "I don't see how Brown can be a serious candidate," Carter stressed. "He doesn't have a single delegate. I have nothing for him but admiration, but Jerry Brown is not running for President. . . ." (But, as Carter would soon discover, Brown, with his typical terrier-like tenacity once he decides on an objective, was seeking to wrest the Democratic nomination from Carter and then win the presidency.) Also, Carter stated that Jerry had been adopted by the machine politicians who hoped to use their power to pick the nominee themselves at a deadlocked convention. The struggle, Carter continued, is between the people and the political bosses as to who will choose the President.

A poll conducted for the *Baltimore Sun* in early April before Brown began campaigning in Maryland revealed that Carter had a decisive lead. He was favored by 24 percent of those questioned, while Brown with only 7 percent also trailed Wallace, Jackson, and Udall. In a similar poll carried out in early May, after much campaigning and merely nine days before the primary, Carter had 28 percent and Brown merely one percentage point less. But then another sampling for the same newspaper completed four days before the election showed Carter with 31 percent and Brown with 28 percent. Had Brown's campaign peaked too soon or was the sample simply not that precise? In either case a close election seemed likely.

The results of the popularity contest of the Democratic primary in Maryland showed that late comer but vigorous campaigner Brown had pulled off a smashing victory. He outran Carter by about 67,000 votes, beating him in every section of the state except for the conservative Eastern Shore and some small rural areas. Jerry won Montgomery County (near Washington) very handily, garnered about 70 percent of the youth votes (eighteen to twenty-five), and won black electoral support by a small margin. (Late in the campaign Brown had had a rally in the black section of Baltimore where he was joined by black politicians from both California and Maryland.) Jerry received an amazing 49 percent of the popularity vote to Carter's 39 percent, with no other candidate obtaining more than 5 percent. Although Brown could not gain any delegates because his name was not on that portion of the ballot, his outstanding performance slowed the Carter bandwagon for the time being. Jerry had demonstrated that his new spirit politics had widespread appeal not only in California but elsewhere as well.

Brown's political shrewdness and quickness had been clearly demonstrated during the time of the Maryland campaign when he made a sidetrip to Charlotte, North Carolina, to appear before about 1,000 delegates to the Caucus of Black Democrats. Carter, Udall, and Senator Frank Church of Idaho also were seated on the platform to answer questions. Jerry took several actions to set himself apart from the other three. His aides distributed a twelve-page tabloid titled "Sacramento Observer" that extolled the large number of blacks Brown had appointed to important state positions and contained a front-page picture of Jerry flanked by Tom Bradley, the black mayor of Los Angeles, and Mervyn Dymally, the black Lieutenant Governor of California. Dymally had had a great deal to do with putting this publication together. In this tabloid Dymally, the first black to occupy this high state position, proclaimed, "In his outstanding job as governor, in his appointment of many Blacks and [other] minorities to high posts in his administration, in his genuine concern for the problems of the people, and in his unexcelled abilities to restore faith in government, Jerry Brown stands out as no man has since John Kennedy."

When Brown and the other candidates were asked at this caucus why blacks should vote for them, he gave two answers that distinguished him from the rest. Jerry first said, "I represent the generation that came of age in the civil rights movement and the anti-Vietnam war movement" and then, while gesturing toward Dymally, he continued, "When I go to Washington, he'll go to Sacramento." Of course, Dymally was already in Sacramento in the office of Lieutenant Governor and would automatically succeed to the governorship of the most populous state in the Union if Brown vacated the office. The significance of the statement—California would have a black governor—was grasped by the delegates. Although the caucus did not endorse anyone for

President, an informal poll by a Philadelphia newspaper showed that Brown had favorably impressed many delegates and had tied for first place with Carter among those delegates surveyed.

After Brown's dazzling triumph in Maryland, the Nevada and Oregon primaries both faced him a mere seven days hence. The Nevada contest was easy for Jerry. Although he campaigned moderately there, it was probably unnecessary, as Nevada voters were familiar with Brown because California television stations and their wide news coverage of him reached into this neighboring state. Brown picked up 53 percent of the popular vote to 23 percent for Carter and 9 percent for Church. Jerry also received a majority of the delegates, who thus became his first.

In sharp contrast, the Oregon primary was a veritable obstacle course. The Secretary of State did not regard Jerry as a serious candidate and, using his official discretion, he refused to list Brown on the presidential primary ballot. This meant Carter and Church would be on the ballot but Brown would have to undertake a lightning-like campaign to persuade voters to write in his name.

The activity on behalf of Brown in Oregon was the most exciting of the whole presidential race in 1976. Hundreds and hundreds of people from California, many of them state workers making use of vacation time, as well as college students and other young people, poured into Oregon to do door-to-door campaigning and other chores. Youthful supporters wore "Write-In Jerry Brown" T-shirts as they went about their work. Banks of phones were set up and more than 1 million pieces of literature were distributed, much of it including instructions about how to write in Brown's name on the election ballot. This was a procedure difficult to explain because some counties used punch card ballots and others employed paper ballots. Allard Lowenstein, who had helped Brown in the Maryland primary, came in, gave speeches, and rounded up many Democrats who had brought Eugene McCarthy his Oregon primary victory over Robert Kennedy in 1968.

Brown criss-crossed the state in his week-long campaign that cost more than $100,000, about half for television and radio commercials and most of the rest for direct mailing and newspaper advertising. (He had not yet qualified for federal matching funds.) Jerry designed his stops for maximum media exposure and was accompanied by a large press entourage. Generally he was met by large, enthusiastic crowds; for example, about 4,000 students and others turned out to hear him at the University of Oregon campus in Eugene. "Remember," he kept telling people, "the blank space [on the ballot] does not represent emptiness; it represents possibilities. Don't write me off, write me in. Bring a pencil to the polls." At most places he emphasized the same themes—the need for full employment ("my first priority"), the need for a new generation of leadership, and the need to realize that "we are on a very small spaceship called earth and have to conserve our resources." He played to his audiences, mentioning most frequently to college crowds, his civil-rights efforts, help for farm workers, and leadership in campaign and lobbying reform. He closed the campaign with thirty minutes of purchased television time in Portland.

A late break came when the Oregon Secretary of State decided that the electorate could write in either "Jerry Brown" or "Edmund G. Brown Jr." and the vote would be counted. On election day Brown volunteers were available at most of the state's 2,000 polling places—at the legally required minimum distance of 100 feet—to explain the write-in procedure to anyone desiring that information.

Although Brown ran behind winner Frank Church and Carter (the latter in second place by a lead of only two percentage points), Jerry racked up a striking 25 percent, all by means of write-ins. Brown collected 106,366 votes on Democratic ballots, the highest total ever recorded in Oregon for a write-in candidate. He even received some votes on Republican ballots. Because some write-in votes for Brown were late in being counted, many easterners retired for the night, thinking that Brown's effort in Oregon had flopped and Carter had soundly defeated him. With the allocation of delegates based on percentages of popular votes in each of four congressional districts in Oregon, Brown obtained 9 delegates, Church 14, and Carter 11.

The spontaneity of Brown's appeal had again shaken the Carter bandwagon, although during the campaign in that state Carter had tried to cover himself in advance by saying that too much importance was being attached to the Oregon vote. An increasing number of politicians and voters were giving Jerry greater attention as were the various elements of the mass media.

Next Brown moved on to Rhode Island, where the primary took place merely six days after the Oregon contest. Here Jerry had to convince the electorate that a vote for an uncommitted slate of delegates was a vote for him. He quickly constructed a largely volunteer organization to spread the word about what convention delegates to support, bought much television and radio time, and had more than 400,000 pieces of literature distributed.

While Brown was in Providence (Rhode Island, that is) during the campaign, he took out after Church who had criticized Jerry for lack of qualifications and training to be President and cited his own long experience in Washington and on the Senate's Foreign Relations Committee. Brown made a scathing reply, "I don't think twenty years in Washington reading the *Congressional Record* necessarily qualifies you for the highest executive job in the country." Then he condemned what he said was Church's claim to qualifications for the presidency: "This is the same mistake . . . made for too long in this country that foreign policy is a special, private prerogative of the experts and has a mystique all its own that is beyond the ken of the American people, that it requires a seat on the Foreign Relations Committee for an intimate relationship with the various foreign policy think tanks." And Jerry concluded, "This is a dangerous idea. . . . the Dean Rusks [Secretary of State during the Kennedy-Johnson era of the 1960s] of this world, the best and brightest who told us what we were supposed to think about Vietnam." As Carter had in both Maryland and Oregon, he again decided it was necessary to campaign personally in Rhode Island, including marching in a Memorial Day parade.

On the day of the Rhode Island balloting three Brown volunteers worked each precinct in the heavily populated but geographically small state, and Brown handed both Carter and Church a surprising and stinging setback. With only a tiny fraction—a tenth—of the electorate turning out, the Brown-affiliated slate took 31 percent of the vote, being trailed closely by the Carter and Church groups, respectively.

Super-bowl Tuesday, as political commentators dubbed June 8, 1976 now lay simply a week ahead. On that date the final primaries for the presidential race would be held in the three highly important states of California, Ohio, and New Jersey. Together, they had 450 delegates, which was in excess of a third of the total needed for nomination. The strategy of the Brown forces was based on the hope for a close contest in Ohio, predicated on the ability of Udall to hold on (Jerry was not on the Ohio ballot), a decisive victory in California for Brown, and about 40 percent of the New Jersey vote to the uncommitted slate favoring both Humphrey and Brown. If all this fell into place, the Brown camp hoped the convention would make a decision for Humphrey or Brown by the third ballot if Carter did not make it on the first or second count.

About a week before the three primaries, the Field Poll in California showed that Brown was favored by 51 percent of the voters to Carter's 20 percent and Church's 9 percent. Although Jerry seemed headed for a runaway triumph, he took nothing for granted in his home state and campaigned vigorously. On one occasion in San Francisco, he attracted what one political supporter called the biggest crowd ever in Union Square—about 5,000 people. For that meeting, Brown's campaign workers blanketed the downtown area with 20,000 leaflets and symbolic brown bags inviting workers to use their lunch hour to see and listen to Brown and movie star Warren Beatty and to hear rock music. Carter and Church campaigned in California but to no avail. Jerry challenged Carter to a debate, and Church echoed his invitation, but Carter declined.

The final election results showed Brown with a huge 59 percent to Carter's 21, Church's 7, and Udall's 5. Brown had rolled up the largest plurality ever in a contested presidential primary in California. Brown also gathered in 204 of the 280 convention delegates, more than seven-tenths of the total.

In New Jersey Brown had the difficult assignment of wooing an uncommitted slate of delegates that still wanted to see Hubert Humphrey enter the contest. After some meetings of Jerry and his aides with important political leaders in the state, a compromise was worked out. The uncommitted delegates would do the highly unusual thing of favoring both Humphrey and Brown. Jerry accomplished another sparkling victory in New Jersey. The uncommitted delegates—really Brown-Humphrey supporters— got 42 percent of the votes and 83 convention seats to the Carter delegates' 28 percent of the vote and 25 seats.

In Ohio, where Brown was neither on the primary ballot nor had campaigned, Carter, as he had said he would, rolled up an impressive win, particularly in the rural sections. He received 52 percent of the vote to Udall's 21 and Church's 14. Moreover, he acquired 126 delegates to Udall's 20. (Earlier in this primary contest Udall had sought unsuccessfully to get a persistent Church not to campaign there.) All this election proved was that Carter could beat Udall again.

Brown was bouyed by the victories in California and New Jersey and felt the overall results of June 8 had boosted his candidacy. However, the media coverage of the next day focused on the Ohio election results, endorsements of Carter by Richard Daley, the longtime Chicago political boss, and presidential aspirants George Wallace of Alabama and Henry Jackson of Washington, and indications by other political leaders that Carter's win in Ohio meant that he had the nomination.

Carter and Daley had talked by telephone on the morning of June 8. (Daley was one of the first politicians to whom Brown had talked when he decided to run, but Carter telephoned Daley regularly.) On this call Carter stated that he was going to lose in California and New Jersey but would win in Ohio. Shortly after the telephone conversation, Daley held a press conference at which he turned a Carter prediction into a Daley dictum—the election in Ohio was the important one and a win for Carter there would be the "ball game." Moreover, to depress the idea of a late Humphrey draft, Daley proclaimed that the party did not have to knight any man on a white horse by drafting him and then walking him into the convention. In part, Brown, a master in electronic communication, was the victim of the media's decision about what to emphasize but Daley pointed the direction for radio and television as well as the newspapers.

For all practical purposes, the race for the Democratic nomination for President was over, even though Carter had not won any of the six state contests where Brown had campaigned. But Jerry Brown did not concede. His popularity is based to an important degree on being different. If he had quit, he would have seemed like merely one of the political crowd. Also, as a Brown staff member pointed out, Jerry felt he had to follow through on a commitment to those people who had given him such a strong mandate in a number of states.

Brown persisted with his campaign. He spoke to the National Press Club and went to a birthday party for Robert Strauss, the national chairman, in Texas. In addition, he decided to have his name placed in nomination at the Democratic convention and to fight any plan to avoid a full roll call. (Udall also resolved to contest Carter's nomination further.)

About two weeks before the Democratic national convention of mid-July Brown bought thirty minutes of national television time on one of the networks and was seen and heard by an estimated 11 million people at a cost of $80,000. According to Tom Quinn, the reason for making this "last hurrah" speech, which seemed a futile and unnecessary venture to many politicians, was that "this man entered this race because he felt very strongly about some views and principles he has." Unquestionably it was a one-time opportunity to build a broader national image that might be important for the future.

In the taped telecast Brown, attired in a conservative blue suit and staring unsmilingly but speaking earnestly into the camera, pleaded for a "politics of candor, of openness and integrity." He did not endorse Carter, although he said he would support him against the Republican candidate if Carter won the nomination nor did he release his several hundred delegates.

Jerry's television talk contained very few surprises. He used many phrases that had been employed earlier in his campaign— we are entering an era of limits; the President is not a Santa Claus nor a magician with a bag of tricks; the President can set a tone, describe a vision, indicate what is possible in this nation; we are all on Spaceship Earth hurtling through the universe. He also made six specific proposals, mostly reiterations of past statements.

You're a stubborn man, Jerry Brown!

Abolish the federal income tax for single persons making $5,000 or less annually and couples earning not more than $8,000 a year. Authorize the President to appoint a public member to boards of directors of large multinational corporations. Place a ban on new hospital construction until the present excess number of hospital beds is eliminated. Congress should retain tough automobile anti-smog standards and resist the influence and the pressure of car manufacturers. Create a public service corps to furnish jobs for young people. Make a renewed commitment to energy conservation so the nation might reduce its dependence on imported oil.

Jerry Brown did not sleep in a church basement when he went to the Democratic convention in New York City, but his choice of the McAlpin Hotel, certainly not one of the city's prestigious hotels and scheduled for demolition, was in keeping with his life style. Other members of the California delegation stayed uptown at the New York Hilton.

On the day of the roll call of the delegates, Brown repeated that he would not release any delegates, which then numbered about 300, and went to a meeting of delegates from several states to solicit their support. Jerry had in a short while become a national political figure and he was continuing to get more national exposure. In general, the convention delegates viewed Brown's quest with indifference but believed in letting him do his thing. They had different views of him. One said, "I don't think he has a viable chance in 1976 but next time around no doubt the country would be ready for him." Another remarked, "He's evasive on the issues. . . . he is new, young, really evasive, kind of scary."

Jerry knew that Carter had more than enough votes for the nomination but wanted to go through the nomination procedure and a roll call and see the process through to its end. He also was willing after the roll call to move that Carter's nomination be made unanimous by acclamation but to do so from the podium. National Chairman Robert Strauss and Charles Kirbo, Carter's senior adviser, were fearful that if Brown appeared on the podium he might try to address the convention and start something with one shot at television. Black Congresswoman

Barbara Jordan had started something with her earlier address to the convention—piles of telegrams saying she should be the vice-presidential nominee. Although Strauss and Kirbo had brief negotiations with Brown and his aides, the proposal to permit Jerry to appear on the podium was never seriously considered.

Carter and Brown assistants finally worked out a more moderate plan—after Brown had been nominated and the roll had been called. Jerry would announce the first switch of votes of any state, standing at the California microphone on the convention floor. Brown still wanted to go to the podium but, knowing this request would not be honored, finally agreed to make his statement from the floor if Chairman Strauss personally would recognize his request to make an announcement. Strauss on the podium could switch off the floor microphone at any time he began to dislike Jerry's remarks; this action would have been impossible if Brown had been permitted to speak from the podium.

Everything proceeded without incident. The names of Carter, Udall, Brown, and Ellen McCormack, the anti-abortion candidate, were placed in nomination (Brown by his longtime farm labor friend Cesar Chavez), after which Udall formally withdrew his name. The roll was called and the votes tallied. Carter received 2,238 votes, Udall 329½, Brown 300½, Wallace 57, Church 19, and some miscellaneous votes were also cast. Jerry was then recognized at his state's microphone, spoke very briefly, made a call for unity and victory, pledged his support, and announced that all of California's delegate votes were now being cast for Carter. And thus ended Brown's bid in 1976 for the presidency of the United States.

Brown had no interest in the vice presidency and Carter had no desire for him to be his running mate. From early in Jerry's campaign some political pundits said that Brown was actually seeking the nomination for Vice President, a theory that Jerry denied from the outset. Some delegates pledged to Carter stated their preference for Brown for the vice presidency, a feeling that was actually an attempt to block Brown's presidential aspirations. Carter aide Hamilton Jordan drew up a list of promising vice presidential possibilities about six weeks before the convention. It included Brown and two other Californians—U.S. Senator Alan Cranston and Mayor Tom Bradley of Los Angeles. By a week before the convention, all three names had been eliminated.

At least in the case of Brown the process of including him on a list of vice presidential possibilities was meaningless. Carter and Brown simply differed too much in their concept of and approach to governing. Carter remarked shortly before the convention about Brown's very high popularity in his home state. "Approval is there to be used." But most of all, they have widely different personalities—Carter the softball player and picnic tug-of-war participant; Brown the onlooker at such events. In short, they have never liked one another.

Jerry Brown made political gains in his late run for the presidency in 1976 at age thirty-eight. The chief advantage to him was that virtually overnight he became a major national political figure. A determined, persistent, and highly ambitious candidate, he proved to be an indefatigable campaigner who spent about $2 million, some of it federal campaign matching funds.

Brown showed how media saturation by an individual, who is judged by some observers to be even more appealing on television than in person, can be an important partial substitute for a large campaign organization. He demonstrated, too, how charisma and a message can attract large numbers of volunteers regardless of current widespread cynicism about politics. On television Jerry is an expert at makeup and how to sit and move. He can be aloof and detached until the red light on the television camera shows and then he instantly turns on.

Brown further proved his ability to be quick and often clever in his responses on the campaign trail, sometimes to the point of ridiculing his opponents in a scathing or outrageous manner. (Frank Church, for instance, had not spent twenty years in Washington reading the *Congressional Record*.) Jerry showed himself to be a fast learner of new facts, a prompt responder to different situations, an accurate sensor of the mood of a crowd. He was a new face and a person cloaked in mystery, outdoing Carter on both fronts, and making anti-Washington Carter suddenly the establishment candidate fighting to protect what he had while trying to obtain more.

Jerry had sorely embarrassed Carter in some late primaries. Although the two of them would later profess to be on friendly terms and Brown would lend two key aides and would personally campaign in California and some other states for the Democratic nominee, Carter's suspicions and fear of Brown have continued. (Ford defeated Carter in California in the presidential race in November.)

Jerry Brown carried out a brilliantly-executed campaign for the presidency but it had a fatal flaw—he started too late. Some people also say that he stayed in the race too long but to do otherwise would have been to follow the expected, which is not his style. Was this to be only Jerry Brown's first attempt to win the presidency?

Chapter Ten

Today and Tomorrow

The political future of the extraordinary Jerry Brown seems extremely bright. Turning a youthful-looking forty years old soon after becoming a candidate for reelection to the governorship of the nation's most populous state, Brown is a strong favorite to be returned to this very powerful public office. The people continue to like him to a degree unprecedented in the history of public opinion polls in the Golden State.

News is the unusual, and Jerry Brown has a great capacity to generate the unusual. He has been a constant delight for the media during his gubernatorial administration, but never more so than on the occasion of officially declaring his candidacy for a second term. In late February 1978, Brown in an artful but casual manner had his press office distribute to capitol reporters a three-paragraph memorandum that looked routine. The most important information in the release had long been anticipated, yet its form of presentation was a surprise and therefore received considerable news coverage.

The memorandum began, "Gov. Edmund G. Brown Jr. announced today that his chief of staff Gray Davis will take a leave of absence to manage his [Brown's] reelection campaign." And thus Jerry officially acknowledged that he was seeking reelection. The release went on to reveal that Davis would be temporarily replaced as the Governor's chief aide by Richard T. Silberman, secretary of the Business and Transportation Agency, and that after the November general election both would return to their previous posts. The statement concluded that Brown would answer questions about campaign details at a capitol press conference the next morning. A plain Brown news release had astonishingly replaced the four-city, one-day airplane tour taken by Brown four years before and a standard ritual for serious candidates for Governor.

The news conference of the following day also had elements that ran counter to political traditions. Although confounding reporters and political opponents alike, Brown's startling statements were typical of him. The first question asked was whether Jerry would commit himself to serving a full four-year term if reelected. It was an inquiry directly related to whether Brown would again pick up his quest for the presidency at the next opportunity. A customary reply would have been that Brown expected Jimmy Carter to seek reelection as President in 1980 and Brown expected to support him. Such an answer would have left room for later backtracking if it proved advantageous. But, as has often been the case, Brown did not do the customary. He said, "I'm going to take one step at a time and that question I don't think I'll decide today. I'm not locking any doors absolutely shut. To try to plan [two,] eight, or six years down the road is foolish. . . . I'm not going to decide today what I am going to do in 1979 or 1982 or any other year in between." This was a highly candid response to make immediately after asking for voter support to keep him in the governorship.

A second break with conventional political wisdom came when Brown challenged the Republican finalist to debate. "Whoever should happen to be the Republican winner I challenge him this morning to debate after the June primary," Brown said. "I think a debate would be helpful and it would elucidate the issues," he continued. This attitude runs counter to the position taken by most popular incumbents in major offices who do not want to give their principal opponent the benefit of a common forum that thus gives the contender wide public exposure. Moreover, unlike the campaign of 1974, Brown declared he would not place any limitations on the extent of television coverage of the debate (or even a set of debates, as he elaborated later).

At the news conference Brown did something that has become customary for him but is unknown to most politicians. He came to the meeting with no prepared statement to read for the television camera crews and to give to the reporters. After a short prelude of quips, he simply said that it was no secret that he was going to seek another term as Governor and that over the next four years if given the opportunity he would continue in the same spirit of trying to keep California economically, culturally, and politically in the forefront.

Jerry showed further self-assurance at this session. Although appraising the forthcoming campaign as tough and the Republican contenders as intelligent, he expressed shock on being unable to discover recently anything of substance in at least some of the other candidates. "I invite them to come up with a few ideas, maybe just one, between now and June [the month of the primary]. As to whom he would like to face in the general election, Jerry commented, "I'll take whoever stumbles across the finish line." And in answer to a query about the possibility of his running scared as if he could be defeated, he replied, "No. As a matter of fact I am very confident."

The Governor shattered another political tradition about a week later when he dropped a dramatic news bombshell at a meeting for Washington-based reporters for California newspapers and broadcast facilities. In responding to a question, he said that he had ruled out a third term as Governor. This declaration even startled his top aide Gray Davis. Jerry had never mentioned this decision to him even in private, Davis noted.

This "no third-term" declaration is contrary to the widely-held political belief that the effectiveness of a political officeholder declines sharply once it is known that he or she is a "lame duck," a person who will not try or has been defeated for another term. Brown, not yet elected to a second term when he made this remark about a third, disputed the validity of this belief by expressing his own political philosophy. "No. I don't believe that. Because I think ideas pass because they become irresistible, because the moment is right or because the Legislature wants them."

Brown opposed a third term because "From what I've been able to tell, two terms are about the effectiveness time period for a governor. And Governor Reagan made a two-term commitment and it made sense to me. . . . I tend to think that at some period close to about the eighth year [in office], there's a regurgitation process that sets in. And I think I would prefer to bow out gracefully." Jerry's regurgitation statement closely parallels one made by his father in 1966 after his unsuccessful attempt to gain a third term—a campaign in which Jerry worked. Pat said that people "can accept only so much government and then they regurgitate [by defeating the incumbent.]"

Contrary to the President of the United States who is limited by a constitutional amendment to not more than two terms, a person can technically serve an unlimited number as Governor of California. But Jerry's knowledge of the history of California politics or other plans he may have developed very late in his first term as Governor may have helped shape his decision. Earl Warren has been the only governor in California ever to be elected to three terms. And Jerry's father Pat was resoundingly defeated in a third-term attempt by Ronald Reagan who in his successful campaign against the senior Brown promised (and later kept that promise) not to try to be a three-term governor.

Jerry Brown is the decided favorite to win the race for Governor in 1978. He will easily gain the Democratic nomination as he has no serious opponent in the primary. In comparison, as the party out of power, the Republicans have a crowded field of five candidates battling for the nomination in June. They are Attorney General Evelle Younger, recently retired Los Angeles Police Chief Edward Davis, Fresno Assemblyman Ken Maddy,

San Diego Mayor Pete Wilson, and Orange County (Fullerton) State Senator John Briggs. The Field California Poll taken in February 1978 shows their voter support to be in the order just stated but with no one of them possessing a commanding lead. Younger is first with 31 percent but has dropped considerably in six months' time, a development that usually proves irreversible in a primary, Davis has 20 percent, a slight drop in six months, Maddy has 16 percent, a three-fold increase in the same period, primarily because of heavy television expenditures. Wilson possesses 11 percent, which is down slightly. Briggs has a stable but dismal 3 percent. Obviously no Republican contender is a commanding choice of the members of his party.

These five Republican candidates are tending to act as though each of them is already the finalist against Brown, but some internecine warfare has already developed and more will probably emerge in the Republican primary. Wilson has pointed out that as mayor of San Diego he is the only Republican hopeful who has had executive experience similar in type to that of a governor. And Briggs in a public address gave generally negative appraisals of each of the other Republican aspirants, after prefatory remarks that three of them were "nice guys." As a consequence of the wide open nature of the Republican primary, a victor will be found only after much tough campaigning and some political blood letting. Meanwhile Brown will have coasted to a landslide primary triumph.

Not only does the widely scattered support for a variety of Republicans seem a happy sign for Jerry Brown's success in November, but he has a towering lead over all these Republicans. Two California polls, conducted in October 1977 and February 1978, are evidence of this point. The earlier poll revealed that Brown's margin over the five Republican hopefuls ranged from 28 percent to 45 percent. It also showed that Jerry had the support of four of every five Democrats, no matter which Republican he is opposing, and about one of each three Republicans, too. Such strong support from members of his own party plus inroads of this depth into the opposition ranks have to be worrisome matters for his final opponent.

In the poll of February 1978, Brown's lead had declined

somewhat but was still highly impressive. Jerry's margin now ranged from 14 percent to 27 percent. All these margins would be overwhelming victories if they were retained to general-election day. Such broad differences are unlikely to be maintained as four of the candidates who have never run for statewide office (Younger is the exception) gain greater name identification and as eventually the Republican opposition decreases to one person.

"Jerry, my son, I'm giving you a new mantra . . . pres-i-dent!"

Nevertheless the lead of Brown over all five opponents remains strong.

Some words of caution should be expressed about placing great faith in public opinion polls carried out many months before a general election. Broad changes can occur in voter preferences in the later stages of a campaign. A decisive issue may develop or intensify, an event detrimental to a particular candidate may occur, or one of the contenders may develop a type of campaign that catches the public's fancy.

There have been some amazing reversals of public opinion during the life time of the highly reliable California Poll. In 1958 Edmund (Pat) Brown Sr. lagged behind Republican U.S. Senator William Knowland by 12 percentage points early in the gubernatorial race but fought on to win by 20 points—a 32 percentage point reversal. Somewhat similarly, former Vice President (and later President) Richard Nixon contested Pat Brown for Governor four years later and once had a 16-point advantage which became a 5-point deficit on the day of the election.

Another example of a sharp change in public opinion, although not a reversal from victory to defeat, involved Jerry Brown in the battle for Governor in his initial attempt in 1974. In that year about ten months before the general runoff Jerry had a 25-point bulge over Houston Flournoy, the eventual Republican nominee. Brown's lead declined to 8 points a week before the election and was further depressed to simply 3 points in the voting booths.

Because Jerry Brown had a narrow escape in 1974 does not mean the situation will necessarily be repeated, or that he will even lose, in 1978. For one thing, Brown is now running as the incumbent—his first such experience in any public office—who has established a four-year record he is proud to defend. Second, he faces a new opponent, one who unlike Houston Flournoy in 1974 may never have held a statewide office and had statewide voter exposure. Third, Brown plans a much more extensive and livelier campaign than he undertook four years ago. All these factors are likely to work to Jerry Brown's benefit in his quest for a second term as Governor. And recent California political history seems to be on Brown's side as well. No first-term Governor of California has been defeated in a reelection bid for thirty-six years, since Earl Warren turned Culbert Olson out of the office in 1942.

Brown also has the advantage of seeking reelection in a state where the Democratic party has become dominant. The Democrats presently have large majorities in both state legislative houses, most of the congressional seats, all except the attorney generalship among state constitutional offices, and one of two United States senatorships. Although political parties are not strong organizations in California, the minority party needs a great degree of unity to pick up state executive and legislative positions. The registered Republicans are outnumbered by a solid three-to-two margin, and the Republican party in the state is badly split between moderate and conservative wings.

Many prominent Republicans have tied their political fortunes to the activities of Ronald Reagan, either formally through Citizens for the Republic (formerly Citizens for Reagan) or informally through devotion to his continued presidential aspirations. Reagan, who has twice sought and lost the Republican presidential nomination—barely so in 1976—remains a potential candidate for 1980 and continues in the public limelight through a syndicated newspaper column and regular radio commentary. Some political observers believe that so long as Reagan keeps his formal and informal organizations together to serve his own political ends, the Republicans will not generally be able to contest the Democrats formidably and extensively in California. Many Reagan supporters have given scant attention to the primary contest for Governor.

From an early time as Governor, Brown seized hold of the traditional philosophic positions of the Republicans, including fiscal conservatism, opposition to the growth of state government, and stopping expanding social-welfare programs. Although some Republican candidates argue that he had not followed these goals, the important thing in the campaign is that a large number of voters believes that he has done so. In addition, as political analyst Ed Salzman has well noted, Jerry Brown has realized the importance of retaining the support of middle-class suburbia, which the Republicans desperately need, and has taken moderate to conservative stands on various issues despite incurring the wrath of some social activists in the state. Apparently Brown, a masterful politician, has gone into the Republicans' own back yard and taken their bat and ball away from them.

The national political stature of Brown will be greatly enhanced if he wins by a big margin—say by about 600,000 or more votes—in the November 1978 election for Governor. Even if he is victorious by only a narrow margin his political reputation will not be severely damaged, as California is known as a state of the politically unpredictable. And if Jerry loses in the gubernatorial contest his political career will not necessarily have come to an end. After all, Richard Nixon, a former vice president, congressman, and U.S. senator, lost a governor's race in California in 1962 and still landed in the White House six years later. A political comeback for the forty-year old Brown should not be difficult.

If Jerry loses his reelection effort in late 1978 he would not be a candidate for President of the United States in 1980. But he could remain in the political limelight by following the Ronald Reagan practice of becoming a media commentator. Then he could run for the United States Senate seat of the superannuated S. I. Hayakawa in 1982, which would serve as an effective launching pad for a presidential attempt two years later.

The hopes of Jerry Brown are to win the November 1978 election decisively and to place himself in an advantageous position if he decides to make a bid for the presidency in 1980. A widespread opinion is that a winning Brown in 1978 will make the presidential race in 1980, particularly if Jimmy Carter's popularity continues at a low ebb or the public seems ambivalent about him. Challenging an incumbent President of limited popularity is not an anathema, as Estes Kefauver proved to Harry Truman in 1952 and as Ronald Reagan made clear to Gerald Ford twenty-four years later.

Some people are convinced that Jerry Brown is already running for the presidency before being elected to a second term as

Governor. Some feel that his presidential campaign started as early as April 1977 when his foreign travels and contacts began. He has since made trips, sometimes more than one, to England, Canada, Mexico, and Japan, expressed interest in traveling to China, discussed arms talks and trade with visiting members of the Russian parliament and space technology with scientists from Russia, and had representatives on a trade delegation to Cuba. Jerry has also expressed himself more often on national issues, especially in the energy field. And his domestic traveling has increased—to places like regional and national meetings with other governors, to sessions with private financiers in New York City, and to political rallies as in New Jersey to support the incumbent Governor who had been friendly to his presidential candidacy in 1976.

Another important factor in the speculation over the likelihood of Brown running for President is that he has not definitely said he will not seek the office. In addition, he has done nothing to discourage the speculation. And remember what he said when asked about his possible presidential aspirations in the press conference concerned with his decision to seek a second term as Governor: "I am going to take one step at a time." A constant prod to Brown's presidential ambitions and contributor to Carter's insecurity must be the fact that Carter did not win one of the six presidential primaries that Brown entered in 1976, including Carter's humiliating defeat in California.

For Brown to have a chance to succeed in 1980 he would have to avoid his mistake of 1976—getting under way too late. Jerry would have to form a presidential campaign organization at an early date. He would have to enter the early primaries, do careful organizational work, and make extensive use of the media, which he does so well, to pull off the political miracle Carter attained in 1976. The Florida primary is one of the earliest and Brown might be able to win there in view of the state's heavy concentration of Jews and the animosity of many Jews toward Carter because of his statement about the "legitimate right of Palestinians." Even before Florida, Brown could pull a surprise in the New Hampshire primary which has a large Irish-Catholic population. The psychological stage could be set for the overthrow of an incumbent President if Carter at a low level of popularity lost some initial primaries.

If Brown wins the Governor's race in 1978 but Carter's popularity goes up sharply in the next year and Jerry decides against seeking the presidency in 1980, he will amost certainly enter the contest in 1984. By then he will still be only forty-six years of age. If completing a second term as Vice President, Walter Mondale would then try to make the move from Vice President to President, but as has been the case with most people in that post he is, and will likely continue to be, practically invisible despite promises to the contrary. The record of people moving from the vice presidency to the presidency through nomination has not been impressive in modern American political history. Even Nixon did not go directly from the one post to the other.

Jerry Brown was the first significant politician to come out of the post-World War II generation. He is a political leader for the 1970s and beyond, greatly affected by the civil rights movement, the struggles of the oppressed, and the Vietnam war. At the same time he was turned off by large-scale programs such as those of the Great Society which offered but did not produce prompt answers. Unlike President Jimmy Carter who made many programmatic promises to many groups (which he frequently has not kept), Brown makes few promises. And when he does make a commitment, such as not increasing any general tax, he has kept his pledge.

The prototype for a new realist breed of politician in the nation, Brown is well liked by the general public because of his use of the "tell it as it is" technique. Many people believe that what Brown says he honestly thinks, whether or not it is popular. His language is often blunt and sobering but in a time of continuing corruption and dishonesty (forty-seven indictments in one California county alone last year), many people like his candor. And they appreciate his turning away from special privilege of public office. For instance, of a total of 127 state legislators and constitutional officers, Brown was one of only twelve to accept no gifts in 1977. In contrast, one of his Republican opponents for the governorship took $5,096 in gifts, much of it in free meals but also including $800 in clothing, several rides in private planes, and complimentary tickets to university football games.

While some of Brown's critics feel that anyone who says he does not have the solutions should resign from the governorship, Brown knows there are no immediate and easy answers to complex problems. He thinks that quick "answers" tend to be delusions and end in public frustration and cynicism. We need to come to terms, he has said, with the ability of government, people, and institutions to measure up to the overblown rhetoric and expectation that those in charge have given the public.

Jerry Brown is both an avid learner and an effective teacher. He has learned a vast amount as Governor and has matured a great deal in the job. Simultaneously he has communicated much of what he has learned to the people in what has been a process of citizen education. Both his learning and his teaching have been accomplished by questioning the assumptions under which governmental programs operate. The dropping of the atomic bomb, the Bay of Pigs disaster, and the Vietnam war might all have been avoided by appropriate prior questioning, Brown has pointed out.

In an age when politics is less centered on party organization than before, Brown has demonstrated his mastery of the communication media whose power he recognized at an early time. Never does he look bad in pictures whether on television or in still photographs. He reveals a handsome directness and seriousness of purpose. On television and radio he speaks not in the style of an orator but of that of a conversationalist. In public speeches he displays more forcefulness. Jerry is charismatic; a crowd does not have to be warmed up for him as is necessary for many politicians. After the briefest and simplest introduction, Brown arouses and excites the crowd.

As is true of effective political leaders in general, Jerry uses symbolic words on occasion. But he is also a person of substance and attainment in office. He believes that people will continue to have faith in an officeholder only if he or she does not try to do too much. He dislikes being told that something is routine and simply needs his signature. This he regards as the sign of a favor or a grant. Highly important to his success is his uncanny ability to perceive the public mood.

A blend of political moderation, liberalism, and conservatism, Brown in his governmental objectives seems to be basically humanitarian and progressive. He would like to veer society at least somewhat away from its great emphasis on materialism. To a degree he is an economic leveler, as manifested in his flat or uniform percentage salary increases for public employees and the attempt to tie property taxes to both assessed valuation and personal income. And Brown believes that the long-run survival of American society requires its integration.

Will Jerry Brown become President of the United States in 1980, in 1984, or later? Even if not elected until the year 2000 he would then be sixty-two years old, which is several years younger than the present age of Ronald Reagan who stands in the wings awaiting the presidential call. Here are three statements about Jerry's presidential possibilities. Former Governor Edmund G. (Pat) Brown Sr., who aspired to be President, has said, "I think my son could be President. It's possible he could do what [John] Kennedy did. He's a great intellectual and he's not that wealthy but he has that mass appeal. . . ." Lieutenant Governor Mervyn Dymally feels that Brown may test the presidential waters in 1980 but will make his real challenge in 1984—and may be the victor. Likening Jerry to a "golden boy," Dymally has said, "Jerry is perceived as the kid down the block everybody liked, the kid who grew up to be successful. Everybody is proud of him. . . ." And Paul Ziffren, California's Democratic national committeeman from 1953 to 1960, who is said to have an eye for these things, has predicted that Jerry Brown will be President of the United States some day.

We shall see. We shall see.

Notes

We have used several kinds of sources in the development of this book. One consists of many personal observations by the authors of Jerry Brown, such as at sessions of the Los Angeles Community College Board, news conferences and public meetings as Secretary of State and Governor, campaigning in 1974 for Governor at various California locales and in 1976 for President of the United States in California, Oregon, Nevada, Maryland, New Jersey, and Rhode Island. We have also observed Jerry Brown at numerous speaking engagements during his governorship as well as many other persons—Cesar Chavez, Thomas Quinn, Richard Maullin, and Gray Davis, for instance—who have had important interactions with him.

A second source is made up of 186 personal interviews. Some of them involved contemporaries and teachers of Jerry Brown at elementary and high schools, University of Santa Clara, Sacred Heart Novitiate, University of California (Berkeley), and Yale Law School. Others concerned individuals associated with Brown in his periods of legal work, civil rights and farm worker activities, community college board member, Secretary of State, and Governor. Included were legislators, administrators, judges, activists, lobbyists, acquaintances, and a large number of newspaper, magazine, radio, and television personnel. Also interviewed were many people who supported or opposed him in his campaigns for Secretary of State, Governor, and President of the United States.

A third source is composed of the writings of other individuals. Most have been short descriptive reports, while others have been analytical, interpretive, or speculative. Only those writings on which we drew directly are cited in this Notes section.

Written records and radio and television presentations represent a final source. Voting positions, statements at public meetings, and news releases are examples of types of written records used. Jerry Brown's comments on radio and television talk shows (on which he has recently appeared with increased frequency), speeches on such media, news reports about him, and the remarks of commentators all illustrate the latter.

Some people who were interviewed and made remarks that deserved direct quotation did not want the statements attributed to them. In these instances we have usually characterized these individuals in a generalized way, for example, as a veteran state legislator. The principal sources of materials are indicated for each chapter. *Only quotations from written and media sources are cited; many not listed come from personal interviews.*

1—A Political Alternative

Personal interview with Jerry Brown. Quotations by Jerry Brown from Richard Reeves, "How does the Governor of California differ from a shoemaker?" *New York Times Magazine*, August 24, 1974, and Playboy interview with Brown in *Playboy*, April 1976. A quotation and a paraphrase by other people from *Los Angeles Times*, Jan. 6, 1975, and *Time*, April 26, 1976. For a fine political history of California see Royce D. Delmatier, Clarence F. McIntosh, and Earl G. Waters (eds.), *The Rumble of California Politics, 1848-1970* (New York: John Wiley & Sons, 1970).

2—In the Beginning

Personal interviews with Pat Brown, a boyhood friend of Jerry's, a fellow seminarian, Jesuit fathers at Sacred Heart Novitiate, and administrators and governing board members of the Los Angeles Community College District. Personal observations of Jerry Brown as a member of that board. Dick Nolan, "Governor Brown's Boy," *Esquire*, Nov. 1974; Peter Oppenheimer, "An Inside-the-Family Look at California's Controversial Leader," *San Gabriel (California) Tribune*, Family Weekly, Jan. 11, 1976; and Charles Fracchia, "My Life in the Seminary with Jerry Brown," *City of San Francisco Magazine*, Jan. 20, 1976. Further quotations by Brown from *Washington Post*, Feb. 20, 1974, and *Playboy*, April 1976. Quotations by others from *Los Angeles Times*, Jan. 6 and Feb. 2, 1975.

3—First Step Beyond Original Sin

Personal interviews with Secretary of State and Brown campaign personnel. Personal observations of Brown as candidate for Secretary of State. Tom Hayden, "The Mystic and the Machine," *Rolling Stone*, Dec. 19, 1974. Quotation by Brown from *Los Angeles Times*, Oct. 23, 1970. Quotation from *Sacramento Bee* editorial, Oct. 13, 1970. Quotations by others from *Los Angeles Times*, July 28, 1974 and Jan. 6, 1975; *Sacramento Bee*, August 28, 1970. Brown-Quinn relationship, *Los Angeles Magazine*,

Oct. 1974. The year 1970 was a time when California relatives of several celebrities ran for public office—Jerry Brown, Barry Goldwater Jr., Susan Marx, and Myrlie Evers.

4—The Anti-Politician Comes of Age

Personal interviews with newspaper and radio reporters. Personal observation of Jerry Brown's inauguration as Secretary of State. Press releases from Brown as Secretary of State. Quotations by Brown from *California Journal*, April 1972; *Los Angeles Times*, August 20, 1972 and May 24, 1974; and *Esquire*, Nov. 1974. Quotations by others in Hayden's article in *Rolling Stone*, Dec. 19, 1974; *Los Angeles Times*, Dec. 21, 1975.

5—The Anti-Politician Wins the Governorship

Personal interviews with Robert Moretti and campaign staff members of Brown, Joseph Alioto, and Houston Flournoy. Personal and television observations of campaigns of Brown, Moretti, Alioto, and Flournoy for Governor. Quotations by Brown from *Time*, Oct. 21, 1974; *San Gabriel (California) Tribune*, Feb. 15, 1976; *Los Angeles Times*, Feb. 22, 1974 and Nov. 4, 1974. Quotations by others from *California Journal*, Oct. 1974; Connie Chung, Television KNXT, Los Angeles, Nov. 8, 1977; *Los Angeles Times*, March 28, 1974. Mary Ellen Leary in *Phantom Politics: Campaigning in California* (Washington: Public Affairs Press, 1977), an excellent study of the 1974 campaign for Governor, agrees that the Brown forces sought to make the campaign as dull as possible. She also concludes that television gave viewers only superficial glances of the contest.

6—The Philosopher Governor

Personal interviews with teachers and practitioners of various philosophies. Personal observations of Reagan-Brown meeting and news conference after 1974 election. *Spiritual Exercises of St. Ignatius Loyola*. Kevin Starr, "The Reforming Conservatism of Jerry Brown," *City of San Francisco Magazine*, Jan. 20, 1976. Alan Watts, *The Way of Zen* (New York: Pantheon, 1967). E. F. Schumacher, *Small Is Beautiful: Economics as if People Mattered* (New York: Harper & Row, 1975). Theodore Roszak, *The Making of a Counter-Culture* (Garden City, N.Y.: Anchor Books, 1969). Quotations by Brown from *Playboy*, April 1976; *New York Times Magazine*, Nov. 25, 1974. Quotations by another from Radio KFWB, Los Angeles, Nov. 13, 1977.

7—Brown's Activities as Governor

Personal interviews with Governor's staff members, state legislators, state and academic administrators, state judges, lobbyists, activists, service recipients, and media reporters. Personal observations of Brown at various official and public meetings. Press releases from Governor's Office and those of various legislators, courts, and administrators. Governor's state of the state and veto messages. Newspaper articles since 1974 from *Sacramento Bee, Sacramento Union, Oakland Tribune, San Francisco Chronicle, San Francisco Examiner, Los Angeles Times,* and *San Diego Union.* Ed Salzman, *Jerry Brown: High Priest and Low Politician* (Sacramento: California Journal Press, 1976) and some of his articles in *New West* and *California Journal.* Brown's appearances on Phil Donahue Show, KHJ-TV, Los Angeles, May 3, 1977 and KNBC News Conference, Los Angeles, July 24, 1977. Joseph Lelyveld, "Jerry Brown's Space Program," *New York Times Magazine,* July 17, 1977. *Notice, A Publication of Academic Council, UCLA,* Jan. 1978. John C. Hoy, "Brown Schooled on Regents," *Daily Pilot,* Jan. 26, 1975. Three topics not included in this chapter on which Brown has spent considerable time are medical malpractice insurance, improvements in state mental hospitals, and consumer protection measures.

8—Brown and His Governmental World

Most of the same sources mentioned through the reference to the *California Journal* in the notes for chapter 7 have also been used in this chapter. Robert Pack, "Brown Rides California Toward Revolution," *Los Angeles Times,* August 21, 1977. J.D. Lorenz, "An Insider's View of Jerry Brown," *Esquire,* Feb. 1978. Ronald Blubaugh, "Brown's New Breed on the Bench," *California Journal,* Feb. 1976. Jack Wintz, "We Need More Saints—Governor Brown Launches New Volunteer Plan," *St. Anthony Messenger,* August 1977. Speech by Gray Davis, Southern California Political Science meeting, Los Angeles, Feb. 3, 1978. Quotations by others from Connie Chung, Television KNXT, Los Angeles, 11/7/77; *New York Times Magazine,* August 24, 1974; and Radio KJOI, Los Angeles, Jan. 25, 1978. For more details about state constitutional offices, see Winston W. Crouch, John C. Bollens, and Stanley Scott, *California Government and Politics,* 6th ed. (Englewood Cliffs, N.J.: Prentice-Hall, 1977).

9—Now He Belongs to the Nation

Personal observations and interviews in six states in which Brown campaigned for the presidency. Newspaper articles and media reports from these same states. Brown's telecast on NBC network, June 25, 1976. Personal interviews with television personnel. Jules Witcover, *Marathon: The Pursuit of the Presidency, 1972-1976* (New York: Viking Press, 1977) was useful with respect to Brown's thinking in 1975 about running for President, his decision in 1976 to enter the race in a number of states, his strategy immediately before the three primaries of June 8, and

Daley's pronouncement, after talking with Carter, about Ohio being the decisive primary. Brown interview in *Playboy*, April 1976. Brown interview on "60 Minutes" program, CBS television network, March 27, 1976. The maneuvering between Robert Strauss and Charles Kirbo, Carter's senior adviser, on the one hand and Brown and his staff on the other over whether Brown would be permitted to appear on the podium at the convention to announce the switch in the California vote to Carter is described in Richard Reeves, with additional reporting by others, *Convention* (New York: Harcourt Brace Jovanovich, 1977). In Appendix A of the Reeves book, the incorrect date is given for the California, New Jersey, and Ohio primaries; the correct date is June 8. The Reinhardt quotation is from the *Los Angeles Times*, June 6, 1976.

10—Today and Tomorrow

Jerry Brown's general popularity in the California polls outruns the latest public appraisal of his job performance. Nevertheless, as revealed in the California Poll released on March 18, 1978, his good job to poor job rating ratio is still three to one and his good rating is 29 percent (plus 46 percent fair) as compared to Reagan's lowest favorable rating of 28 percent. Field California polls of Oct. and Nov. 1977 and Feb. 1978. Governor's press releases of Feb. 21 and Feb. 22, 1978. Ed Salzman's "Brown's Plan to Become President in 1980," *New West*, Nov. 1977 and "The Improved GOP Climate—Except for One Party California," *California Journal*, Jan. 1978. Brown's remarks about how further questioning might have avoided certain national disasters were made on Newsmakers program, Television KNXT, Los Angeles, May 30, 1976.

Index

267